The Protestant Interest

THE PROTESTANT INTEREST

New England
after Puritanism

Thomas S. Kidd

Yale University Press
New Haven & London

Published with assistance from the Annie Burr Lewis Fund.

Set in Minion Roman type by Keystone Typesetting, Inc.
Printed in the United States of America by Sheridan Books,
Ann Arbor, Michigan.

Library of Congress Cataloging-in-Publication Data
Kidd, Thomas S.
The Protestant interest : New England after Puritanism / Thomas S.
Kidd.
p. cm.
Includes bibliographical references and index.
ISBN 0-300-10421-9 (alk. paper)
1. Protestantism—New England—History—18th century. 2. New
England—Church history—18th century. I. Title.
BR530.K53 2004
280′.4′097409033—dc22
2004049749

A catalogue record for this book is available from the British Library.

The paper in this book meets the guidelines for permanence and
durability of the Committee on Production Guidelines for Book
Longevity of the Council on Library Resources.

10 9 8 7 6 5 4 3 2 1

To Ruby

Contents

Acknowledgments

It is a satisfying and humbling task to acknowledge the many people who helped bring this book to completion. First, I want to acknowledge the community of scholars at the University of Notre Dame, where I wrote an earlier version of this project as my dissertation. George Marsden proved to be a model adviser, setting high expectations and offering much helpful advice on matters academic, professional, and personal. He is known for being a Christian scholar, and I have found that George takes the personal aspect of that calling even more seriously than the professional. His continuing counsel has proven invaluable to this book's development. I also thank David Waldstreicher, Greg Dowd, and Tom Kselman for reading the dissertation and raising hard questions about what direction to take the book, and Gail Bederman and John McGreevy for giving much help and counsel along the way. I further acknowledge the assistance of the University of Notre Dame libraries, especially the microtext unit, who generously acquired a screen scanner for those old microcard readers during my season of intensive research.

Thanks also goes to my colleagues and friends at Baylor University, which has proven a wonderfully supportive home to finish this book. In particular, Jim SoRelle provided wonderful leadership in the history department, and Mike Parrish gave timely publishing advice. My student assistant Logan Simmons read the whole manuscript and made many helpful corrections. Thanks to the many other friends and colleagues in and out of the department that make Baylor such a great place to teach and write. Thanks, too, to the Baylor University Libraries, and in particular to Interlibrary Services, who have not blinked at any request I have made for materials.

Thanks to the many scholars who have read all or portions of the manuscript and given helpful and encouraging advice. This particularly applies to Mark Noll and David Bebbington. I appreciated John Murrin and Skip Stout discussing the manuscript and its future with me. I also appreciate the work of the various anonymous readers who read part or all of the manuscript.

Thanks to Yale University Press, especially my editor, Lara Heimert, for her kindness and support, and my manuscript editor, Joyce Ippolito, for her painstaking efforts in helping me produce a better book.

From my time at Clemson University, I wish to acknowledge the particular encouragement I received from my master's adviser William Steirer, who got me interested in the Puritans. Also, thanks to Dave Woodard, who first helped me become seriously engaged in the life of the mind.

Many thanks to the staffs of the research libraries who helped make archival research for this project possible, especially at the American Antiquarian Society, the British Library, and the National Library of Scotland.

An earlier version of chapter two was published as " 'Let Hell and Rome Do Their Worst': World News, the Catholic Threat, and International Protestantism in Provincial Boston," *New England Quarterly* 76, no. 2 (June 2003): 265–90. An earlier version of chapter four was published as " 'The Devil and Father Rallee': The Narration of Father Rale's War in Provincial Massachusetts," *Historical Journal of*

Massachusetts 30, no. 2 (Summer 2002): 159–80. I gratefully acknowledge permission to publish from these journals.

Portions of the manuscript were presented before meetings of the American Society of Eighteenth-Century Studies, the Midwestern Association for Eighteenth-Century Studies, the American Society for Church History, and the Notre Dame Colloquium on Religion and History.

It is particularly gratifying to give thanks to friends and family. I owe many personal and professional debts to friends from Notre Dame days, including Bryan Bademan, Darren Dochuk, Patrick Mason, Mike DeGruccio, Kurt Peterson, and Michael Kamen. I also want to acknowledge the fellowship at Oak Creek Community Church, in Mishawaka, Indiana, for helping me to maintain perspective and sanity through my South Bend years. I especially appreciate the friendship and counsel of Pastor Darin Garton. Thanks to our new church home, Highland Baptist Church, for offering so much hope and encouragement.

I want to thank my longtime friend Soren McMillan for his continuing friendship, conversations, and interest in my work. Thanks to my parents, Mike and Nancy Kidd, for their love and support, and for teaching me to love books. Finally, I want to express my love for my wife, Ruby, and our son, Jonathan. Ruby understands what I do and why I do it. She is steady, reassuring, gracious, and beautiful. She deserves much more than the dedication of an academic book, but I am glad to show her my love in this small way. We were so glad to welcome Jonathan into the family in 2003, as well. I love you both very, very much.

Introduction

With news flooding the Boston presses of George Whitefield's awakenings, Thomas Prince preached one of the masterpieces of eighteenth-century evangelicalism, *The Endless Increase of Christ's Government* (May 25, 1740). In this sermon, Prince argued that the kingdom of God was advancing inexorably toward the conversion of millions across the nations, bringing people from all over the world into the fold of Christ before his final return. His vision was internationalist and utterly optimistic about God's ultimate triumph in the end of history. Perhaps Prince hoped that the victory of God was beginning at that moment:

> For as this gospel of the kingdom shall be preached in all the world, for a witness to all nations, before the end of this present state shall come. . . . I cannot expect, that not only all the southern, western, and north-western parts of this new world, and Calefornia, will, in their times, be full of pure and pious churches, rejoicing in the great Redeemer; but even all that further western continent, extending from America to Asia, and that the gospel will go round and conquer every nation in Japan and China, Tartary, India, Persia, Africa, and Egypt, until it return to Zion, where it rose. . . . And when this whole globe shall be thus successively enlightened, then comes on the end of the present earthly scene: but it is then suprizingly to change,

> and, it is highly likely, by the conflagration, open into a glorious state of universal and abundant light and grace, and peace and blessedness.[1]

Prince's vision of Protestantism expanding across the globe was one of the most articulate expressions of a distinct departure in identity for many leading New Englanders during the fifty years between the Glorious Revolution and the Great Awakening. During these years, many began to think of themselves as part of what they called the "Protestant interest."

Despite the realization that the religious character of Puritan New England changed dramatically after 1689, historians have done very little to explain what kind of identity began to supersede Puritanism and how the change occurred. This book seeks to fill that gap by explaining how many in New England came to see themselves as belonging to the international Protestant interest. The political and military necessities after 1689, the sense of participating in an ongoing war for the fate of Christianity with Catholic foes, and the ways that print allowed elite New Englanders to imagine themselves part of an international Protestant community all led to an identification with the Protestant interest, a beleaguered but faithful world community of Christians reformed from the corruptions of Catholicism.

On March 29, 1692, Increase Mather and the new provincial governor of Massachusetts, Sir William Phips, set out from Plymouth, England, for the long trip across the ocean to Boston. Because it was a time of international war, many of Mather's friends in England worried that French privateers would intercept the ship. But God's hand was on "the Convoy of the None-Such Frigat," and the one encounter with French ships resulted in a "notable Deliverance" from four French men-of-war returning to French port from Martinique. Six weeks after departing England, Phips, Mather, and their entourage sailed into Boston Harbor. It was a Saturday night, and the

Sabbath had already begun so the celebrations upon their return were rather muted. Nevertheless the Town House was shining with welcoming candlelights, and eight companies of Boston militia escorted the men to their homes. Increase Mather hoped that he had done his best in securing Massachusetts' new provincial charter, and that the old Puritan way would be preserved in large part if not in the whole.[2] But as English metropolitan power centralized and French Catholicism threatened, identities in New England shifted, just as during the same period the meaning of Britain shifted through the expansion of commerce and the print trade, the Williamite settlement following the Glorious Revolution, the wars with France and Spain, and the political union with Scotland in 1707.[3]

Although the initial reception of the settlement acquired by Increase Mather and brought back in 1692 was mixed, there can be no doubt that the Glorious Revolution and the subsequent revision of the charter marked an important turning point not only in Massachusetts politics but also in provincial New English cultural identity.[4] In general, the mood of elite New Englanders toward involvement in metropolitan affairs changed from a seventeenth-century model of deceit, hostility, and avoidance to an early eighteenth-century model of pragmatic and sometimes remarkably enthusiastic taste for imperial cooperation and things British. The strongest impulse toward allegiance to the new monarchs became preserving the Protestant succession against the Catholic and Jacobite (supporters of a return to the Catholic Stuart line in the British monarchy) threats, and a belief that toleration of religious dissent in the new charter provided the foundation upon which a post-Puritan New English dissenting establishment could be protected.

Previously, the Puritans of the seventeenth century had based their godly commonwealth on the maintenance of the special charter originally granted in 1629. Once Charles II returned to the English throne in 1660 and the cause of Puritanism had largely failed, the reformed Protestants of Massachusetts watched with increasing trepidation as the imperial policy of the crown began to emphasize "dependence, uniformity, centralization, and profit." None of this could bode well for Massachusetts' previously lucrative trading arrangements, nor could it allow its unique religious establishment to continue unfettered. In 1685, events brought all the negative potential of the imperial policies to fruition, as the Catholic James II assumed the throne, and processes began to put Massachusetts, Maine, New Hampshire, Plymouth, Rhode Island, Connecticut, New York, and New Jersey all under the single imperial control of the Dominion of New England. In 1686 the final blow came as James effectively dissolved Massachusetts' old charter and put a new imperial government in its place, the high point of the increasingly centralizing tendencies of Stuart colonial policy in the English Atlantic.[5]

Sir Edmund Andros assumed power of the new imperial government in December 1686 and quickly introduced a number of measures and practices that alienated many if not most leading Massachusetts figures, especially by commandeering Samuel Willard's Third Church meetinghouse for Anglican services. By 1688 many leading pastors and officials believed that Massachusetts needed to send an independent agent to London in order to plead for toleration of the Congregational system. Increase Mather seemed to many a good choice, and so, without the blessing of the suspicious Andros government, Mather and his son Samuel stole out of Boston in April 1688. Mather hoped to gain audience with James and high-ranking British officials and convince them that James's pro-Catholic Declaration of Indulgence, which had suspended the Test Act and penal laws against dissenting religious groups, should in Massachusetts mean a preservation of the rights of the Congregational system.[6]

In April 1689 news arrived in New England's ports of William's invasion, and many residents of Massachusetts began to agitate against the Andros regime, with troops mutinying against the government and assembling in a tumultuous Boston.[7] The cry of the crowd was against popery[8] and arbitrary government, and on April 18, Andros was deposed and he and many of his chief officials were imprisoned by a local committee meeting to manage this dangerous and important moment.

The agents of revolution quickly began constructing the act as driven by providence and as a key moment in redemptive history. Created in large part by Gilbert Burnet, the standard Whig interpretation of 1688 became that the conflict between James II and William of Orange reflected the larger conflict in history between the two mystical churches, one of Rome and Antichrist, and the other the true reformed church of Christ. Burnet, serving as the chaplain for William's invading forces, developed a narrative of William's successful assumption of the English throne as uniquely favored by God. The Boston presses produced propaganda asserting this narrative, too, including key sermons by Burnet himself.[9]

Massachusetts observers quickly embraced the Williamite narrative of the revolution as a providential deliverance from popery, and a great victory for Protestantism, taking a significant place in redemptive history. From the beginning New England rebels justified their revolt against Andros as a revolt against Roman Catholicism.[10] The *Declaration of the Gentlemen, Merchants, and Inhabitants of Boston* of April 18 made clear the connection between the revolution and the war against popery. The *Declaration* began by placing Massachusetts' rebellion in the context of the "Popish Plot," Titus Oates's 1679 "discovery" of a murderous plot by English Catholics against Protestantism: "We have seen more than a decade . . . since the English World had the Discovery of an horrid Popish Plot; wherein the bloody Devotees of Rome had in their Design and Prospect no less than the extinction of the Protestant Religion: which mighty Work they called the utter subduing of a Pestilent Heresy." The committee stated plainly that papists, "such as were intoxicated with a Bigotry inspired into them by the great Scarlet Whore," plotted against them too. The scheme began as the charter was revoked and the protection against French and Indian massacres taken away. The popish government of Andros systematically deprived the colonists of their rights as Englishmen, and perhaps most suspiciously, New Englanders had become engaged in a war against the Indians (the Second Indian War), but the imperial government seemed more concerned with raising a large standing army under "Popish Commanders" than actually killing Indians. Again, to the rebelling Bostonians this looked like "a branch of the Plot to bring us low." Perhaps the imperial governors were setting up New England, the preserve of true Protestantism, to be "attaqu'd by the French, who have lately . . . treated many of the English with worse then Turkish Cruelties." But God heard their cry for help, and now they learned that "Almighty God hath been pleased to prosper the noble undertaking of the Prince of Orange, to preserve the three Kingdoms from the horrible brinks of Popery and Slavery." It was a key moment in the course of the transcendent war between Christ and popery, and most in Boston believed they could do no other than stand with William and the Protestant monarchy.[11]

The revolt against James II and the Dominion of New England was not without its domestic opponents, however. The most articulate was Connecticut physician-politician Gershom Bulkeley. In Connecticut, Andros's opponents called for new elections in May to erase the Stuart taint from the government. Bulkeley considered this mobocracy, "Lawlesse Usurpation & Tyrannie." He called for continuing respect for the Dominion's laws and procedures, unless and until the king had directed otherwise. Bulkeley justified his call for submission to the king's authority by means of New England's Protestant identity. "Consider your Profession," he wrote, "we are all Protestants." He thought the clear counsel of Scripture was to obey those in authority, and Protestants were nothing if not respecters of the Word. Moreover, Bulkeley was as aware as James's opponents of the "strong engagement to root out the Protestant Religion" by European Catholics, but he believed, in stark contrast to most leading New Englanders after 1689, that continued support for the Stuart monarchy was England's and Protestantism's best hope to stand against the Catholic threat. Factionalism and rebellion could lead to their ruin, and Bulkeley even wondered if a Catholic plot had inspired the revolt against Andros. "I wish there be not some Jesuit that has foisted in this Project amongst them in the Bay and us here," but he believed that "that Diabolical sort" meant to use any means possible to divide Protestants against themselves. James's not-so-secret Catholicism seemed not to bother Bulkeley, for to him Britain was Protestant, even with a Catholic king. Despite his objections, the colony voted in May 1689 for a return to Connecticut's charter before the Dominion, and Bulkeley's brand of Toryism would become exceedingly rare in New England for the next generation.[12] However, one can see in his arguments against the Glorious Revolution that the question of what it meant to be a faithful Protestant could be hotly contested in British culture, and New England's dissenters would have constantly to face questions from London about their loyalty as British Protestants in the coming decades.

The imperial governors of Massachusetts after Andros might have disagreed with dissenting Bostonians on a whole host of points, but on the question of the Protestant succession and the war against popery there was no conflict, especially in public proclamations. For years after 1689, fast and thanksgiving proclamations from various governors and lieutenant governors asked for prayer to establish the Protestant succession against its popish and Jacobite enemies. For instance, the General Court declared a fast on February 12, 1690, recommending "to the earnest Supplications of all that fear God, the common Interest of the Protestant Religion in the World, which hath so many potent Adversaries [and] that King William and

Queen Mary may have their Throne Established, and be made great Blessings."[13] Such language would color Massachusetts' civil discourse for another fifty years and beyond. Elite New Englanders had suddenly become quite committed to the power of the British monarchy.

As the *Declaration* indicated, many in Boston feared that James II had planned on handing over control of New England to the French, and so the revolt against James and support for the Protestant succession became attacks directly against French Catholicism. Beginning with the revocation of the Edict of Nantes in 1685, the same year as James's accession, many English Protestants read of dragoons harassing the "poor persecuted" French Protestants (Huguenots) and heard of French atrocities as refugees poured into England and even a few into New England. In the combination of French Catholicism, English Catholicism, and Jacobitism, English Protestants (particularly low-church Anglicans and "dissenters," meaning those who would not attend or support the established Anglican church) perceived their greatest enemies and the greatest enemies of Christ. The dissenters of New England feared the French more than anyone in the Atlantic world, for few natural boundaries would prevent the French and their Indian allies from swooping out of Canada to destroy the Protestant bastions of New England.[14]

Increase Mather believed that the Andros regime was purposefully placing New Englanders in harm's way, setting them up for an invasion of French Canadian and Indian forces. Falling in line with Burnet's propaganda, Mather published *A Narrative of the Miseries of New England* in London in January 1689. In it, he lamented the forms of "arbitrary government" represented by Andros and his minions, and he particularly worried that Andros had plotted to give New England over to the French, who would undoubtedly treat New Englanders with the same barbarity as they had the Huguenots. Once the charters of Connecticut, Rhode Island, and Massachusetts had been "declared to be void and insignificant, it was an easie matter to erect a French Government." Mather believed that the process had begun "to deliver that Country into the hands of the French King," because the "French Indians are . . . beginning their cruel Butcheries amongst the English in those parts." In the final appeal of the *Narrative,* Mather asked for "speedy Relief" for New England, which he believed should be forthcoming from William, "whom a Divine Hand has raised up to deliver the Oppressed."[15]

If Mather hoped that God would preserve New England from war with the French, he would be sorely disappointed, for 1689 saw not only a great political shift in the British Atlantic world, but also the start of the Anglo-French contest for empire. Though the population of Massachusetts, New Hampshire, and Connecticut outnumbered French Canadians about eight to one, the French Catholic threat remained ever-ominous, especially because the French seemed adept at cooperating with the Wabanakis, who formed a buffer of sorts between the two imperial powers. The Wabanakis and others who survived the epidemics and wars of the earlier seventeenth century, ironically, were now in a stronger position militarily and economically than before, experienced in European diplomacy and warfare and also better armed. Once King William's War (1689–97) opened the door for renewed French and English hostilities, the Wabanakis seized their opportunity for defense against land encroachments and also the sometimes lucrative practice of taking and exchanging prisoners.[16]

Massachusetts' leaders watched as in 1690 Sir William Phips led an expedition against Port Royal in Nova Scotia. With seven hundred Massachusetts troops backing him, Phips quickly secured the surrender of the pitiful French fort manned by sixty troops. Phips allowed the desecration of the Catholic church there, and brought back two priests among his military prisoners. Buoyed by this meager success, Phips raised an armada of thirty-four ships and two thousand men for a grand expedition against the heart of French Catholicism in North America, the city of Quebec. Apparently the hand of God was not with the New Englanders this time, for a string of bad luck and disease among the troops brought to Quebec in October 1690 an armada that was cold, sick, and late. The invasion was beaten back easily by the French forces, and Phips and his remaining troops limped back to New England in the cold of winter storms, ultimately having lost a thousand of the men and forty thousand pounds sterling in materiel. In the future, New Englanders would think more carefully about large-scale invasions of Canada, and the Boston presses fell largely silent about the loss, unsure of what had gone wrong and why God had not destroyed the despised papists in the wake of the great Protestant triumphs of 1688–89. Andros's replacement, Simon Bradstreet, wondered, on behalf of many, why God had "Spit in our Face."[17]

With his reputation significantly tarnished, Phips left Massachusetts to join his pastor Increase Mather in London, and through Mather's negotiations, Phips returned in 1692 as Massachusetts' new imperial governor. The negotiations over the new charter in London and its controversial reception in Boston have been well documented.[18] The new political settlement in Massachusetts represented a middle way between the old charter, which granted near-total independence, and the Dominion of New England, which severely undercut local autonomy and even seemed to the colonists possibly designed to put high-church Anglicanism or even Catholicism in place as Massachusetts' official religion. The governor now would have a great deal more authority and would be appointed by the monarch, but the Massachusetts House of Representatives would also now become one of the most powerful of the provincial legislatures.

This settlement and the growing necessity to identify globally with a beleaguered world Protestant interest changed leading New

Englanders' religious interests even more dramatically. Now required to tolerate all Christians save Catholics, the Massachusetts establishment found itself forced legally into a more irenic and ecumenical stance both by the toleration required in the charter and by the knowledge that Anglicanism was in Massachusetts to stay, often in the form of Anglican imperial officials who seemed willing to threaten revocation of the charter should Massachusetts fail to appreciate the benevolence of the Protestant monarchs. In order to help win allies in England and to secure New England's churches' identity as loyal nonconformists, Increase Mather had also worked in 1691 with his London friend John Howe on the *Heads of Agreement* unifying in principle English Presbyterians and Congregationalists into one dissenting cohort.[19] The once-Puritan church establishment was now committed to formal toleration, it had accepted and even embraced a politico-religious alliance with low-church/Whig Anglicanism, it faced a common enemy with world Protestants in French and Spanish Catholicism, and had formally agreed to a dissenting alliance with Presbyterian brethren in England. Though the Mather family would fight to preserve vestiges of it for some years more, the old form of insulated and precisionist Massachusetts Puritanism, struggling for life since the 1660 Restoration, now seemed to be taking its last breaths. Much of the old Puritan identity now vanished before the concern for presenting themselves loyal nonconformists. As a 1699 address by Boston's ministers to the newly arrived governor, the Earl of Bellomont, put it, "What Hearty Friends, the vast Body of Non Conformists are to the English Liberties; and what Loyal Subjects to the High and Mighty Prince, unto whom (under God) We are all Indebted, for the Recovery of those Liberties; and how much an Union between all Good Men, whether Conformists or Non Conformists, will contribute unto the Strength of the Protestant Interest."[20] Whether conformists or nonconformists, all British

Protestants now owed their liberty and protection from Catholicism to the Protestant monarch of Britain.

In the years following the Glorious Revolution, then, New England's international Protestant movement began to emphasize distinctives that distinguished it from Puritanism. On many points the differences were subtle and entailed a change of emphasis, not a radical departure. Both movements certainly were biblicist, but their activism was directed toward different goals. Puritanism sought moral and ecclesiastical reform within the Church of England, and pursued political hegemony as best demonstrated in the Puritan/parliamentarian synthesis of the mid-seventeenth century in England. Puritanism proper was therefore reformist, magisterial, and specifically English. New England Puritanism, even more than its seventeenth-century English counterpart, was in its "orthodox" form usually isolationist and suspicious of transatlantic or cosmopolitan ventures, whether military, commercial, or missionary. While many Puritans emphasized personal conversions of nonbelievers, the New England Puritan movement in general focused much less on engaging the unregenerate than on establishing pure churches in a godly state. Even Puritan eschatology often seemed to encourage withdrawal over missions, suggesting that the judgment would be preceded by the saints' departure for the New Jerusalem instead of a great harvest of souls. The new, increasingly revivalist, decreasingly doctrinaire Protestant interest sought massive conversions across national and ethnic lines, and grew less interested in political or ecclesiastical reformation.[21] Its leading advocates became revivalist, more broadly internationalist, and British.

New England's leading cosmopolitans, finding themselves forced into war with Catholic powers and regularly hearing of the persecution of European Protestants, also began to emphasize gospel essentialism. This meant that churches that had embraced the essentials of reformed Christianity, whether Congregational, Presbyterian, Lutheran, or Calvinist, counted as part of the Protestant interest. This essentialism had limits, of course, set largely by reformed theological orthodoxy, and the Calvinists of New England remained staunchly opposed to suspected proponents of Arminianism or other innovators. But the more that the leaders of the Protestant interest understood the true church to be persecuted and threatened with extinction, the more willing they became to share common cause with Protestant groups across their known world. Their sense of the beleaguered state of true religion internationally turned their thoughts away from reform and toward the need for miraculous and massive revival. This theme became a common emphasis in New England by the 1720s, and by the 1730s the language of eschatological revival was to be heard from pulpits across not only New England but also Britain and Protestant Europe.[22]

Although this book will argue that New England's leading pastors, merchants, and officials were increasingly internationalist and ecumenically Protestant in the early eighteenth century, a few caveats should temper that claim. First, I do not mean to say that everyone in New England participated in these trends equally. One must not assume that the laity and clergy shared identical religious views.[23] The trend toward Protestant internationalism seems to have developed primarily among elites in the seaports and their immediate surroundings, and in the Connecticut River Valley. Lay and backcountry opinion are not well represented here. Certainly the transition toward international pan-Protestantism was led primarily by men who had substantial transatlantic connections in commerce, religion, and/or politics.

Second, to associate this cultural identity generally with international reformed Protestantism does not dismiss the more complicated view needed to understand the competing political and religious identifications among eighteenth-century New Englanders.

If religion in a cultural sense is a web of symbols, beliefs, and meanings that makes sense of the ultimate meaning of existence, then that web is also constantly changing shape.[24] Cultural identifications shift with changing circumstances, and particularly in the early modern period religious identity fluctuated in tandem with political and national identifications. Among leading New Englanders these combinations of allegiances took a bewildering variety of forms. To say that the Protestant interest emerged during this period is perhaps more convenient than precise when one realizes the lived complexity of elite New Englanders' cultural identity. The particular heritage of New England, or Massachusetts and Connecticut, still heavily shaped self-identity in certain cases. The idea of a chosen New England was becoming more rare and often was supplanted by a British chosenness, or a belief that God was working uniquely in British history. As leading New Englanders focused more on knowledge about their Protestant brethren in Europe, however, they could also imagine themselves allied with the international Protestant interest, further demonstrating the power of print to help create imagined communities.[25] So these New Englanders might identify with their province, their nation, or the international community of Protestantism depending on the rhetorical or political need of the moment.

They could also claim diverse religious identities. For instance, though the leaders of the Protestant interest no longer called themselves Puritans, they certainly borrowed heavily from the traditions of the Puritan way, even in revivalism. They now often called themselves either "nonconformists" or especially "dissenters." They also identified with "evangelical" churches, or spoke of an "evangelical" gospel, such as when Benjamin Colman of Boston described George Whitefield's preaching as based on the "right Evangelical Articles of Faith upon which the Church reform'd from Popery."[26] "Evangelical" could also refer more specifically to German *evangelisch* churches that the New Englanders counted among their most loved brethren. Many leaders of the Protestant interest in New England came to embrace the cause of evangelical revivalism, beginning in the 1720s with a new emphasis on the miraculous work of the Holy Spirit, and culminating in the Atlantic ministry of George Whitefield. Significant inheritances passed from Puritanism to the Protestant interest, and from the Protestant interest to evangelicalism.

W. R. Ward, David Bebbington, Mark Noll, Richard Lovelace, and others have shown how the evangelical movement of the eighteenth century was fundamentally internationalist in mentality, and that its leaders mastered communication technologies to promote the growth of the movement. The Protestant interest was not coterminous with the later evangelical movement, as the friends of the Protestant interest could become Old Lights or New Lights in the 1740s. Some prominent friends of the Protestant interest, such as New London's Eliphalet Adams, remained friendly to the moderate evangelicals in the 1740s, but became extremely hostile to radical itinerants. One can see in this study, however, that the internationalist mindset and public and personal correspondence networks, so characteristic of the evangelical revivals, began developing at least as early as the 1690s. Thus, the Protestant interest served as a bridge to connect Puritanism to evangelicalism. Much of the work on the "Great Awakening," led by Susan [Durden] O'Brien, Frank Lambert, and Michael Crawford, has suggested that Whitefield's media revolution was a significant break from the past, helping to "invent" the Awakening itself. This book significantly revises that notion, showing that Whitefield, Edwards, and others in the transatlantic network refined previously existing communication practices to serve the particular interests of the revivals.[27]

Despite the pan-Protestant sensibilities of the Protestant interest, some of its proponents could also become theologically particular when the occasion called for it. They regularly claimed to defend "reformed" theology: reformed from the corruptions of Catholicism and distinguished from the heresy of free-will Arminianism. Sometimes they might align with specific denominations within Protestantism, especially Congregationalism, Presbyterianism, or low-church Anglicanism. Though this mix of identifications is less conveniently packaged by the historian than a simpler static and homogenous view of cultural identity, one is also freed by this complexity to acknowledge the "multicultural realities" in which people usually live and their "everyday necessity of crosscutting identifications."[28]

While recognizing this wide variety of competing identifications, this study advances three primary elements as crucial to the development of the new cultural identity of the Protestant interest. First is the sense of a shared identity with *international Protestantism*. The English Reformers and Puritans featured transatlantic and international traits from their origins, from the Marian exile on the Continent to the great migration across the Atlantic, and from the continuing "congregational communion" of the English Puritan diaspora to the sprawling interconnectedness of Samuel Hartlib's circle. Many seventeenth-century New England Puritans shared internationalist sensibilities with their English and continental counterparts. But appeals to pan-Protestant unity among the Puritans usually failed to escape the pitfalls of precise ecclesiastical and doctrinal differences, and New England's orthodox elites rarely gave much latitude for transatlantic pursuits and interests before the Williamite Revolution. After the Glorious Revolution, however, two factors gave leading New Englanders a renewed identification with the international reformed community. First, the burgeoning print trade and more reliable transatlantic shipping made information about international Protestantism more generally and quickly accessible in Boston and its environs. Second, the mostly Catholic versus Protestant wars that raged or threatened across Europe and the world after the Glorious Revolution, culminating in the Seven Years' War, helped create a thoroughgoing internationalist sentiment in which these New Englanders identified with reformed Protestants across confessional, national, and ethnic lines. The newspapers carried accounts of "orthodox dissenters" with religious and political agendas strikingly similar to the New Englanders' own. The European brethren, moreover, often found themselves threatened by real or suspected agents of the Roman Catholic church. With the French (and later Spanish) Catholic threat periodically breaking out into hot war in New England, it is hardly surprising that leading dissenters in New England would imagine these groups as comrades in the fight against world Catholicism.[29]

The second positive identification that this study asserts as a primary building block of reformed pan-Protestantism is *British nationalism*.[30] This identification surged in importance with the coming of the Protestant succession in the British monarchy, and the toleration of the New England dissenting establishment that the succession seemed to guarantee. The public devotion of leading New Englanders to Britain became at once a political and religious duty, as such observers as Boston's Benjamin Colman equated "fidelity to Christ" with fidelity to the Protestant succession and the British throne. The Protestant interest endowed the monarchs, especially William, and later the Hanoverians, with the "divine right by Providence" that saw Britain, and particularly the monarchy, as the vanguard of international Protestantism, divinely chosen to lead the fight against Catholicism.

Anti-Catholicism provides the third and final building block in this study.[31] Again, Puritans certainly had seen Catholicism as a primary if not the ultimate enemy, but the wars of empire and the perceived and actual declining fortunes of the European Protestant community made the rising pan-Protestant cohort much less interested in combating other Protestants, especially if those Protestants defended the Protestant succession.[32] This became increasingly true as New France and its Jesuit missionaries made the Catholic threat very near and personal to the early eighteenth-century New Englanders. If leading New Englanders imagined themselves as British nationals helping lead the international Protestant community, it was largely with the end of defeating the evil "other" of international Catholicism, and especially their French Catholic neighbors. These New Englanders' hostility to Catholicism was apocalyptic, as most believed that before the return of Christ, the Catholic church and the papacy would be destroyed. They longed for a role in the eschatological destruction of Catholicism, and prayed and sometimes fought to see its fulfillment. There is no question that far above Native Americans or any other group, Catholics provided the most stark contrast against whom the Protestant interest defined itself.

This study examines the transatlantic public sphere and print domains in order to show how international Protestantism, British nationalism, and anti-Catholicism shaped a post-Puritan identity in New England society. From rhymes in almanacs to newspaper reports of persecuted Protestants, and from sermons on the apocalypse to balance sheets of the contest between world Catholicism and Protestantism, print facilitated leading New Englanders' move from Puritanism to the Protestant interest. Print allowed this growing religious identity to move out from the ministerial networks that had largely sustained Puritanism, and gave the Protestant interest a voice in the developing public sphere of print and the transatlantic trades. Public print and correspondence networks helped many New Englanders imagine not only a British nation, but also an international Protestant community and a mirror opposite international Catholic community.[33] The events that faced leading New Englanders after 1689 increasingly encouraged many pastors, officials, and merchants to identify with the cause of British and international Protestantism.

Following Increase Mather's return with the new charter, many in Massachusetts kept up a critical and sometimes hostile relationship with the imperial governor or the high-church Tory interest in England, but this did not prevent a cordial public relationship with the crown or a growing identification with the British nation as the bastion of Protestantism. Despite the distance in geography and in interests between New Englanders and the metropolis, many increasingly imagined themselves as having an interest in creating a powerful British nation, their best hope for the preservation of international reformed Protestantism. Jeremiah Shepard of Lynn spoke for leading New Englanders in the 1715 election sermon when he celebrated "the Mercy of God to our Nation! Wherein the Glorious Arm of Divine Conduct is remarkable in two famous Revolutions," the 1689 Glorious Revolution, and the 1714 accession of George I, which made all Britons "secure from a Despotick or Arbitrary Government, or having our Liberties Invaded by Papal Usurpations and Tyrannies." As Gauri Viswanathan has described it, the dissenting interest in New England "adopted a strategy of inflating cultural continuities" between them and the metropolis so that these mutual concerns overshadowed the obvious differences between the dissenting establishment of New England and the Anglican metropolitan establishment. Many high-church Anglicans continued to view all dissenters with disdain, and especially during Queen Anne's reign dissenters faced all manner of political and popular threats to their tolerated status and safety. Especially offensive to the high churchmen was the occasional conformity practiced by some English dissenters, taking the Anglican sacrament in order to qualify for the legal benefits under the Test and Corporation Acts. Many

Anglicans, moreover, questioned the validity of dissenting pastors' ordination. How, then, could the dissenting establishments in New England lay claim to legal legitimacy as British Protestants? New Englanders found themselves tenuously drawing protection and resources "from the parent state [in order] to set up a private domain of their own" that would in some measure still resist imperial or Anglican hegemony over their religious establishment.[34]

It is a matter of some debate whether expressions of loyalty to the English and then British nation like those in the Boston presses amounted to a thoroughgoing British nationalism or pragmatic propaganda. One imagines elite New Englanders' sentiments to have been a mixture of both. But it seems likely that the factors of a shared British Protestantism and a common enemy in France and Roman Catholicism, combined with a belief that the Protestant kingship was the key to the preservation of New England's liberties, generated an immature but powerful form of British nationalism among leading New Englanders. This only increased after the 1707 union with Scotland (to which some date the creation of "Britain" proper), the accession of George I in 1714, and the Jacobite revolt in 1715. The English dissenters were among the leaders in the creation of a biblical discourse of British nationalism in 1707, and New England dissenting ministers shared in the creation of that discourse on their side of the Atlantic.[35]

Even when those in Massachusetts attacked the imperial governor and his policies, their concern often involved fears either about preserving the rights of English dissenters, or about illicit trade and cooperation with French Canada. For instance, in an appeal to Lord Nottingham, Increase Mather, likely angry about aggressive Church of England missionaries, pleaded for a replacement for Governor Joseph Dudley in 1703, recommending the low-church Anglican Charles Hobby, "in Religion a Protestant of the Church of England as by Law established, but of great moderation, having a respect for dissenters who are good men & loyal subjects, as I know your Lord-ship also has."[36] Massachusetts' leaders became agitated when impe-rial officials seemed not to support the defense of all loyal Protes-tants against the Catholic menace, but they never wavered in their conviction that the true purpose of the British nation was defending the Protestant faith.

Massachusetts' leaders also became invested in promoting the Protestant succession, which by force of the Act of Settlement (1701) raised the prospect again of switching hereditary lines after Wil-liam's successor, Anne, who had no living children, died. Despite Jacobite pleas for a return to the Stuart line, England looked to Hanover for the next queen, Princess Sophia. To prepare Britons for the coming of a German monarch to the throne, propagandists began promoting the house of Hanover as godly and noble. In Mas-sachusetts, effigies of both Queen Anne and Princess Sophia were placed in the Council Chamber as early as 1705 in order to align Bostonians with the cause of the Protestant succession.[37] There would be no sympathy whatsoever among the dissenting interest for a return to the Stuart line, a fact referred to again and again in coming years by those in Massachusetts defending their peculiar rights as established dissenters.

The death of Anne, the accession of George I, and the suppres-sion of the 1715 Jacobite uprising by the Stuart Pretender brought the high point of British nationalism during this period, as New En-gland's coastal towns from Portsmouth to New London welcomed the Protestant succession of the recently dead Princess Sophia's son George to the British throne with celebrations "beyond what ever was known in the English America."[38] New England's clerical and political leaders met the news with the now-familiar sense of provi-dential design and placed the succession and the revolt within the ongoing world contest between the godly Protestant interest and the forces of evil.

Edward Holyoke's 1715 almanac memorialized September 22, 1714, the day in which "King GEORGE was Proclaimed at Boston." Holyoke did not think it coincidental that the same night of the celebrations for the new king, rain broke a long drought. "Night's Showers Crown the Pomp of Night & Day: King GEORGE, as Rain on Mown Grass, Come Away!"[39] After years of wondering whether Anne would have a Protestant successor, the British Protestant and New England dissenting interest received George's succession as a refreshing blessing from God.

Massachusetts' leading pastors also stepped forward to construct a narrative of George's succession as ordained by God, and part of the unfolding of God's agency in British history. By July 29, 1715, the dissenting churches of Massachusetts and New Hampshire had presented their formal address in tribute to George by way of New England's agent Jeremiah Dummer. The *Boston News-Letter* printed the document on its front page once news arrived that the new king had received the address. The address embraced George while it also nervously advanced the ministers' hope that their status as established nonconformists would not become a problem under Hanoverian reign. There was no doubt to the ministers that it was "the most High GOD our Saviour, who has placed your Majesty on the Throne over us; the refreshing Rays of your Government like those of the Sun, reach your most distant Dominions." They petitioned the king, however, to continue treating New England's dissenters with the same respect and toleration as the United Brethren in England. The ministers reminded George that they were his most loyal followers anywhere in the empire, that Anglicans received fair treatment despite their nonestablished circumstances in New England, and that they hoped that all parties involved could unite around "Conformity to the Doctrines and Maxims of the Religion which our Gracious Redeemer hath revealed to us."[40]

On September 23, 1714, Cotton Mather preached a sermon on Isaiah 6:1, soon recommended to Bostonians by the *News-Letter* as a model interpretation of the Hanoverian succession. Mather noted the fear and trepidation with which Bostonians and others through the "European and American World" waited for news of the succession, hoping that the plans of the papists and Jacobites would not foil the Hanoverians' safe arrival and assumption of power. Not that Mather and his cohort had not appreciated Anne; on the contrary, Mather commended her heartily, for "there could be nothing more Endearing to us, than the Expressions and Assurances, which Her MAJESTY often Uttered from the Throne, of Her Zeal, for a Protestant Succession." New Englanders had remained largely quiet, at least publicly, as they watched hostility to dissenters percolate during Anne's reign. At least she supported the Protestant succession, as Mather noted. But now, God had quickly and surprisingly brought the Hanoverian to the throne, extinguishing all hopes of the "Popish Pretender." Mather sang the praises of this new king given by the hand of God. "We see ascending to the British Throne, A KING whose Way to it is Prepared in the Hearts of His Joyful Subjects . . . A KING, in whose Dominions Lutherans and Calvinists Live Easily with One Another . . . A KING, of whom we have all Possible Reason to hope, that He will Discern and Pursue the True Interest of the Nations; and give the Best Friends of His House and of the Nations, cause to Rejoyce. . . . Among, whom it is incredible, that the DISSENTERS, who have been so Universally true to That, and His Interest, should not be regarded as a Body of People, too true Britons, and Christians, to be Excluded from a Share in the Common Joy of their Fellow Subjects."[41] Mather believed that God had brought George safely to the throne in part to defend the rights of members of the dissenting interest as loyal Britons.

The idea of Massachusetts' Protestants as faithful dissenters never was so important as during and immediately after the 1715 Jacobite uprising. In the tumult and uncertainty surrounding George's accession, Scottish and English Jacobites took the opportunity to proclaim James II's son King James III of Britain. While the rebellion and invasion were not without precedent, especially in Scotland, and despite the fact that the rising in northern England "went off like a damp squib," as one historian of Jacobitism has put it, the insurrection was nevertheless one of the most significant threats against the Protestant succession during the eighteenth century.[42] It took on highly symbolic importance across Europe and in the Atlantic world, not least in Massachusetts, as we shall see in chapter five.

Although 1715/16 was undoubtedly the high mark of British nationalism during this period in Massachusetts, sentiment for Britain as the defender of an ecumenical, international Protestant interest against Catholicism had become a staple of New Englanders' cultural identity. In some rhetorical moments Massachusetts pastors still held out a special place for New England in providential history, referencing the special circumstances of the founding as they approached the hundredth anniversary of the great migration out of England, or celebrating New England's unique and universal support for the Protestant succession. But certainly by the end of the Jacobite rising, the most vocal spokesmen of the new Protestant interest saw themselves as Britons and dissenters who united around the essentials of the reformed faith with churches throughout much of the known world.

As we shall see, in the early 1720s, the affinity for the Protestant monarchy was helped along by Father Rale's War (1722–1725), a direct threat against New England by the eastern Wabanakis and ultimately by French Catholic power. Leaders in eastern New England recognized that they needed continual support from the crown against the French threat, despite the formal peace between the two states. Joseph Sewall, for one, hoped that despite God's judgment against New England through the "Sword of the Wilderness, and other wasting Calamities," they could find hope under the protection of God and king.[43]

New Englanders' admiring sentiments toward George I soon transferred to George II upon his father's death in 1727, and Massachusetts' and Connecticut's leaders quickly rose to welcome the succession and the continued protection of the Protestant interest. Fears over Jacobite plots remained current in Britain and in New England, as only in May the *Boston News-Letter*'s front page reported an address to the king by London clergy denouncing the Jacobites and warning of the "unavoidable Misery and Ruin that a Protestant Church and Nation must always expect from a Popish Prince." But upon George II's accession there would be no similar great revolt as happened in 1715. Nevertheless, New England's public voices rose together as one to proclaim that George II was the king in their provinces. Most notably, on August 16, Massachusetts' leaders assembled at the courthouse in Boston to sign a pledge of fidelity to the succession.[44] By late year the presses in Boston were producing reassurances that George II, like his father, and also Queen Caroline were noted not only for their "Firmness to the Protestant Interest," but also for their sympathy to dissenters. Though as recently as 1725 Tories in Parliament had proposed a bill revoking Massachusetts' charter, upon the succession the New Englanders reassured themselves that they need not worry about their establishment of dissent being threatened as long as the Hanoverians were on their side.[45]

The leading dissenting pastors celebrated the providential design in George II's succession. Thomas Prince spoke before the General Assembly in late August with a sermon comparing the succession to the passage of Israel's throne from David to Solomon, and he hoped that George II would have "a Largeness of Heart, as the Sand on the

Shores of his extended Empire." He prayed that the Lord would give him such "Royal Majesty" as had not been seen before in the "British Israel." And of course he hoped that George II would continue his father's protection of Massachusetts, considering "Sacred our Precious CHARTER; which with the PROTESTANT SUCCESSION, the Two inestimable Legacies of King WILLIAM and Queen MARY, will render their Names most Blessed." Finally, Prince hoped that Massachusetts would remain faithful to the Hanoverian line, "That we who dwell in the Wilderness may be happy in Bowing before Him," and that his enemies the papists and Jacobites "may lick the Dust." Many pastors, including Joseph Sewall, Thomas Foxcroft, and the elderly Cotton Mather weighed in with similar sentiments.[46] Israel Loring of Sudbury, Massachusetts, was moved to meditate on George's death in his diary, mourning the loss of "a king Whose accession to the British throne was esteemed by the Wise discerner of the times, as life from the dead, to his Dominions and the protestant interest."[47] Even to clerics like Loring, living in Boston's hinterlands, the matter of the Protestant succession was critical.

By 1727 the friends of the Protestant interest in New England had become thoroughly committed to a broad British Protestant identity, finding common cause with the Hanoverian monarchy and Whig Anglicanism. Their enthusiasm for Britain was in some ways pragmatic, born out of the circumstances of war and the memory of the Dominion of New England. But more importantly, in a massive shift from the 1680s and previously, many New Englanders now placed their best hope in the house of Hanover. The public face of religious and civil society in Massachusetts could no longer afford pettiness or precisionism. Under the old charter there might have been occasion to dream of God's special covenant with New England. After 1689, however, New England's national chosenness became British, centered in the Protestant monarchy and the monarchs' support and protection even of dissenters. God chose Britain not for itself alone, but also for the highest purpose of defending the worldwide Protestant interest.

To tell the story of New England's Protestant interest, chapter one begins with a study of Benjamin Colman, who during this period became the most recognized pastor in Boston. Though his leadership was bitterly contested at the founding of his Brattle Street Church in 1699, by 1707 Colman had become Massachusetts' key spokesman in matters related to the British nation and the Protestant succession. Moreover, Colman worked feverishly to establish missions to the Native Americans that would compete with Jesuit missions. Not surprisingly, Colman became one of the key links in the evangelical movement of the 1730s and '40s. Chapters two and three examine the print domains of New England and their relationship to the Protestant interest. Chapter two considers how Boston newspapers' coverage of Catholic versus Protestant hostilities across the known world helped New Englanders imagine themselves part of a global Protestant interest. Chapter three details how New England almanacs served the interests of British nationalism through preserving the memory of key dates in the British monarchy, and singing the monarchs' praises in poetry.

Chapter four considers Father Rale's War (1722–25) in northern New England. The Jesuits were much more successful than the British colonists at proselytizing among the Wabanakis, and in the 1720s Father Sebastien Rale successfully encouraged them to rise up against British colonists' land incursions. New Englanders, however, narrated the war as the next stage of the global conflict between Catholicism and Protestantism. Chapter five considers the imagined threat of Jacobitism in New England, and analyzes the reasons for the common accusation of Jacobitism, despite there being almost no Jacobites in New England. The language of Jacobitism helped New Englanders construct a low-church Anglican/dissenter synthesis that stood against the perceived threat of British high-church Anglicanism and the Catholicism they thought the high churchmen masked. Finally, chapter six discusses the role of eschatology in building the Protestant interest. Many New Englanders assumed that before the return of Christ, the Catholic church would be destroyed, the Jews would return to the true Messiah, and massive global conversions would begin. These expectations created a ready theological framework for understanding the meaning of the revivals that began in the 1730s and culminated in Whitefield's tours. The sense of the Protestant interest's global crisis, then, fed directly into an expectation of eschatological revival that might finally bring the triumph of world Protestantism over Catholicism. Eschatological disappointment, of course, did not prevent the establishment of a global evangelical movement that continues to grow today, which is the subject of the epilogue.

CHAPTER ONE

"Fidelity to Christ and to the Protestant Succession"
Benjamin Colman and the Protestant Interest

As new converts flocked to the Brattle Street Church in October 1740, Benjamin Colman knew that something significant in redemptive history was happening through the ministry of the "singular servent and holy Youth," George Whitefield. For the evening lecture on October 21, Colman chose as his text the millennial passage Isaiah 60:8, telling the overflow audience that the nations would come to the Messiah in great numbers at the end of the age. Was this the promised time? He thought perhaps so, but he equivocated: "The Prophecy is daily fulfilling, and at Times in more remarkable Measure; but more especially it will be so in the latter and more happy Days of the Church when the Calling of the Jews and the Fulness of the Gentiles shall come on—The Lord hasten the promis'd Day."[1]

Here at the crowning moment of his career was the key leader of the Protestant interest in New England before 1740, Benjamin Colman. Colman was distinguished by his extensive British network of correspondents and friends, orthodox Calvinism, and latitudinarian ethos.[2] Through his publications, leadership, and connections he helped take New England's leadership in a direction friendly to Britain and the Protestant succession, and in the late 1730s he helped prime the cosmopolitan churches of New England for the arrival of

Whitefield. He also helped win support for missions among the Native American societies of North America as a means to counter the threat from French Jesuits, a threat that would become even more manifest in the 1720s with the coming of Father Rale's War. A consideration of Colman's work and thought will help demonstrate the means by which New England's cosmopolitan leaders became much more concerned for the world Protestant interest after 1689.

Colman's leadership in Boston was hotly contested at the outset, as he and his patrons established the Brattle church only after much controversy with Cotton Mather and his colleagues, who were suspicious that Colman was a theological innovator. Leading Boston merchant Thomas Brattle and a number of his business associates had become frustrated with what they saw as the provincialism of a Mather-dominated church establishment in eastern Massachusetts, and by 1698, Brattle and others began the process of building a new church in Boston. He sold a tract of land to the new church corporation, and by January 1699 twenty-two "undertakers" had agreed to help build the new church. Among the most prominent leaders of the founding group were the merchants John Mico, Thomas Cooper, and John Colman.[3]

These wealthy supporters, with the encouragement of Harvard tutors John Leverett and Thomas's brother William Brattle, took the necessary steps to plan and build the church. Actual construction began in April 1699, at which point the founders needed to find a pastor, one with appropriate education and previous pastoral work. The new pastor also had to support the church practices toward which the founders inclined, and had to accept the responsibility of standing up to the criticism that would inevitably come against the church from Boston's pastoral establishment. The Brattle group needed to secure a pastor that had orthodox beliefs and high social standing, but whose authority and ordination came from somewhere outside the spheres of New England clerical power. Naturally, they preferred someone with the stamp of metropolitan authority, bypassing the sanction of the Boston authorities with an appeal to the cultivation and power of London. Fortunately, John Colman knew someone who fit the requirements: his younger brother, Benjamin.

Benjamin Colman's father was a wealthy shopkeeper who had come to Boston from London in 1671, two years before Benjamin's birth. Choosing the ministry over shopkeeping or trading, Benjamin graduated from Harvard College in 1692. At Harvard, Colman and his classmates studied under the Anglophilic and latitudinarian tutors John Leverett and William Brattle, and Colman apparently became Leverett's favorite student. Colman polished his pastoral qualifications by establishing connections in England, learning about the Presbyterian polity, and imbibing the latitudinarian ethos of toleration, love, and gospel essentialism. Upon finishing his master's degree at Harvard in 1695, he left New England for London.[4]

After a tangle with French privateers in his Atlantic crossing, Colman arrived in London. Colman's experience in England further molded his intellectual and religious commitments toward a more English style. However, the experience (as recorded by his son-in-law) reads like a post-college fling in Europe as well, with much time devoted to romantic flirtations and partaking of his British friends' wine and food. Nevertheless, Colman eventually found pastoral work from the Presbyterian board in London, working in Cambridge, Ipswich, and eventually Bath. The pastors told Colman that the post at Bath represented "the best Stirrup in England, whereby to mount the best Pulpits that might be vacant." Apparently his colleagues assumed that Colman would eventually take a prominent pastoral position in London, perhaps never to return to New England.[5]

Two years after accepting the position at Bath, however, Colman received the offer that would lead him back across the Atlantic. In

July 1699, he got a letter from the "undertakers" of the Brattle church asking him to be their minister. The proposal to Colman made explicit two of the policies which the founders wanted to initiate: public reading of Scripture without comment during the services and not requiring a conversion experience for admission to the Lord's Supper. He received encouraging notes from Leverett, William Brattle, and Ebenezer Pemberton (soon an assistant pastor at the Old South Church, which along with the Brattle Street Church became the most cosmopolitan of Boston's congregations). Pemberton's words suggested that Colman could count on a secure living in Boston: "The Gentlemen who sollicit your Return are mostly known to you—Men of Repute and Figure, from whom you may expect generous Treatment."[6] Upon Colman's arrival in Boston, John Colman would see to it that Benjamin received a good salary and free lodging.

The letters also asked Colman to seek Presbyterian ordination before he left London. This request reflected the need to circumvent the clerical establishment by an appeal to an alternative and higher polity. The church knew that Boston's ministers would not ordain him, they liked his endorsement from reputable English Presbyterians, and they believed that pastors could receive ordination outside the endorsement of a particular church body. All this prompted the Brattle group's controversial request. Some historians have suggested that the merchants wanted the Brattle church to be an Anglican congregation, but the evidence does not support this idea because the founders encouraged Colman to receive Presbyterian ordination and because they placed so much control of their church polity in the Presbyterian pastor's hands. As Colman later wrote to Robert Wodrow of Glasgow, "we are entirely upon the Presbyterian foot so far as our Lott among Congregational Churches will admit of it."[7] Colman received his ordination in early August 1699, and then sailed for Boston, arriving November 1.

Before the church began holding services, the founders and Colman thought it best publicly to declare their intentions, which they did in *A Manifesto,* published November 19. While this brief document spelled out the new church's principles, it functioned mostly as a preemptive strike against the church's opponents. "We think it convenient," the *Manifesto* read, "for preventing all Misapprehensions and Jealousies, to publish our Aims and Designs herein." From the beginning, the Brattle church took the rhetorical position that opposition could come only from misunderstandings or jealousies: certainly no one could object to their church polity in good faith.

A Manifesto then laid out the sixteen basic principles of the church, beginning with the declaration that the founders "Approve and Subscribe" to the Westminster Confession, a broadly acceptable definition of reformed doctrine in the English Atlantic world. This statement sought to defuse the arguments crying heterodoxy, but it also expressed their honest intention to remain orthodox in the sense established by the Westminster divines. While the Brattle church changed the status quo in Boston, one can see from their commitment to Westminster that the new church was in no useful sense "liberal." They also declared their intention to worship according to the practice of the "UNITED BRETHREN in London, and throughout all England."[8] Here one can see at least two purposes: first, the church's continuing desire to associate itself with English practices, and second, a further undermining of the arguments they knew might come from the Mathers. The Mathers had been promoting ecumenical unity with Presbyterians in London for ten years, especially since the English Toleration Act of 1689. While Increase Mather was in London in 1691, Congregationalist and Presbyterian leaders produced the *Heads of Agreement,* an ecumenical document establishing their basic articles of faith and ostensibly abolishing the two groups' disagreements. As late as 1700, Cotton Mather still promoted the idea of Presbyterian/Congregationalist unity, writing that English nonconformists "have needlessly been sometimes Distinguished into Presbyterian and Congregational," but he hoped they would unite in essentials under "that more Christian Name of United Brethren." The Mathers and others would hold no such warm feelings for the new Presbyterian church in their own backyard, for they realized the threat this represented to their local authority. Cotton Mather in particular had been dabbling for years in transatlantic literary and reformed circles, but up until this point his feelings concerning the transatlantic ethos were conflicted at best, and when the cosmopolitans rose to question his power, Mather again became decidedly localist and precisionist.[9]

The new church admitted that it would make some changes from the usual policies of New England's Congregationalists, most notably by reading Scripture without pastoral exposition, admitting people to communion by the pastor's assent without a public profession of conversion, giving every baptized adult a vote in choosing a minister, and abandoning an explicit church covenant. However, the group argued that these minor changes did not make their church drastically different from the usual practices of the "Churches of CHRIST here in New-England." The Brattle church wanted to "hold Communion with the other Churches here, as true Churches; and we openly protest against all Suspicion and Jealousie to the contrary, as most Injurious to us."[10] The Brattle group had made their preemptive strike, but the *Manifesto*'s clever maneuvers did not prevent a harsh response from New England's pastoral leadership, or panic on the part of Cotton Mather.

The founding of the Brattle Street Church unleashed an exceedingly nasty pamphlet war.[11] By early 1701, however, it became evident that Colman and the Brattle Street Church were in Boston to stay: the Brattle church survived its factional challenge to the Matherian hegemony, and Colman would eventually emerge as the leader among Boston's pastors in the Protestant interest. Colman's cosmopolitan style and British connections helped turn the clerical establishment of Boston and Cambridge toward the ethos of the Protestant interest: outwardly focused, British, internationalist, and latitudinarian.

Colman and the Brattle church also eventually got along with the Mathers. The Mathers grudgingly accepted the new arrangements; they seemed to have no other options if they wanted to maintain their now-divided authority. By 1705 Colman and Cotton Mather even worked together on proposals to implement a more Presbyterian form for New England's clerical synods. Though the 1705 Proposals failed to unify Massachusetts' churches, Colman's British and interdenominational sensibilities continued to flourish among the friends of the Protestant interest in New England. This was perhaps nowhere better demonstrated than in Connecticut in 1708, where the adoption of the Saybrook Platform formally committed the province's churches to the Savoy Confession of Faith (1658) and the *Heads of Agreement*. This act was a clear step away from New England particularity and toward common cause with British dissenters. Even Cotton Mather had to accept the implications of British interdenominationalism in Boston, and his once-conflicted approach to transatlantic concerns now flowered into a full-fledged sympathy. Mather expanded his correspondence with such figures as Scotland's Robert Wodrow, England's John Edwards, Danish missionary Bartholomew Ziegenbalg, the Halle Pietist agent Anthony Boehm, and other key figures in the international Protestant interest.[12] Colman, backed by such figures as Ebenezer Pemberton, Joseph Sewall, and Thomas Prince Sr. of the Old South Church, articulated a new vision for Boston and New England's churches to become ardent defenders of the Protestant succession in Britain and the cause of Protestants everywhere. Colman eventually became the key spokesman for Boston's churches on matters related to Massachusetts' place within the British empire, and also its role in the ongoing wars between Catholicism and Protestantism.

Eight years after the founding of the Brattle church, for instance, on the occasion of the Treaty of Union between England and Scotland, Colman preached a celebratory sermon before Governor Joseph Dudley, affirming as never before Massachusetts' allegiance to Britain and the Protestant succession. This sermon would help cement Colman's place as the leading promoter of the Protestant succession among New Englanders. Colman was both explicitly nationalist and also broadly internationalist in his vision of a worldwide Protestant interest led by a unified, transatlantic British cohort. He reminded pious New Englanders to pray for the world church and for its leader, Britain: "we ought affectionately to Pray for & Rejoice in the Prosperity of the CHURCH OF CHRIST in the World, & especially in the Peace & Flourishing thereof in that particular NATION or KINGDOM whereof we are." Colman's vision was broadly ecumenical, at least compared to the old Puritan vision, but there was no doubt in his mind who stood in the vanguard of the Protestant cause. "We must needs consider GREAT BRITAIN as the Illustrious Head among the Protestant Nations & Churches. The Religion of Christ is no where more purely Professed, and (alas! for the Reformed World) no where more of it in its Power. . . . Therefore as Members of the Catholick Church . . . we must needs Pray for its Prosperity, Temporal and Spiritual."[13]

Colman reminded his listeners and readers of this dual cultural identity as Britons and members of the true catholic church. Though the reformed tradition and Puritanism had always held to the doctrine of a true world church, the threat of Catholicism and increasing availability of news concerning persecuted Protestants in Europe, combined with the irenic sensibility of English latitudinarianism, made Colman promote the doctrine of the mystical body of Christ more vehemently than New Englanders had previously heard. But the mystical body had a national head. "Nor does the Flourishing of Religion only within its own Spacious Empire depend [on prayer], but also the Security of the Reformed Churches in Europe. So has God honour'd our Nation, and taken it Nigh unto Himself, making it the Potent Bulwark of His Church; against which we trust the Gates of Hell shall never prevail."

Colman likened Britain to Jerusalem in the Old Testament, the centerpiece of God's earthly kingdom, and a prelude to the true kingdom to come when Christ returned. Colman urged the people to pray for the "Ruine of the Papal Interests" through the Union of Great Britain. He reminded dissenting New Englanders of their duty to promote the Protestant succession without hesitation, hoping they would send an unmistakable message to Westminster across the wide ocean: "May [Queen Anne] Long Reign, with Additions to Her Graces and Her Fame! And from true Hearts let us breathe over the Atlantick the humble Assurances of an Inviolate Allegiance."[14]

Colman also took the lead in New England's public response to the 1715 Jacobite uprising in Britain. He was quick to condemn the actions of his traitorous countrymen and lift New England up as the model of loyalty to the Protestant succession. On the day of prayer and fasting in March 1716, Colman wondered at the madness of the rebellion, but remained encouraged that "In this day time of public Treacheries, Perjuries, Rebellion, & Treason, not a dog can wag his tongue to charge us with Disloyalty, Undutifulness or Disrespect to Government, or want of Zeal and Fidelity to the PROTESTANT SUCCESSION, the peaceful Reign of the KING, & the true Interests of the Nation as to their Civil and Religious Rights." Colman was astounded at the Jacobites' treachery, thinking it "an Amazing Thing . . . that any Protestant or Member of the Church of England should be in the late Rebellions against his present MAJESTY, to set up a popish Pretender whom they have so often and justly Abjured."

These traitors could certainly be no true Protestants or even Christians; it was the "Atheistical and Immoral part of the Nation" that had done this. Colman was optimistic because the rebellion had been put down, and he hoped that soon "the Day may come when We may no longer hate to be reformed, and that the KING may live to be the Glorious Instrument in the Hand of GOD of our Reformation in every Respect."[15] Colman typically equated faithfulness to the Protestant succession with God's continuing project of reforming state and society.

Similarly, at a public day of thanksgiving following the defeat of the uprising, Colman rose to help pious New Englanders understand the divine agency within the succession of George and defeat of the Jacobites. He particularly emphasized the divine favor shown toward Britain historically, noting the early arrival of Christianity while "the Greatest part of the Continent continued Pagan and in gross Darkness." Likewise, the Reformation took hold easily in Britain, notwithstanding the Marian persecutions. Since the reign of Elizabeth, despite numerous efforts by Rome to reestablish its authority, Britain had defeated popish plots against Protestant liberty time and time again. "So has a peculiar Care of Providence from time to time guarded the Liberties and fill'd the Throne of Britain."[16]

Colman celebrated the coming of the Solomon-like George I, exulting, "O what a GIFT of God, not only to us, but to Europe and to the Reformed Churches, must a Wise and Just King upon the Throne of Britain be." It was a sign of God's great love and mercy for his chosen people, both in the empire and among the reformed churches of Europe. These truths made the Jacobite rebellion all the more intolerable to Colman. "O the Ingratitude to Heaven, the Profaness and Contempt of Providence, in the Vile and Traiterous Rebellions lately carried on in Great Britain," he cried. Moreover, "How have a base and stupid Faction, mindless of God's Wonders and Mercies to the Nation, been murmuring first and then mutiny-

ing, and then rising in Arms against God and his Anointed! Quarel-
ling with their Happiness, weary of their Religion, Liberties and
Laws, courting Popery and Slavery, rejecting not the King so much
as God that He should reign over them, and this by the blackest
Treacheries, Perjuries, Hypocrisies and Mockery of God." Colman
commended his loyal countrymen who put down the rebellion and
who prayed for the Protestant succession, especially those among
the dissenting interest in the British Isles and North America.
Among the "United Brethren" of dissenters there could be found not
one man disloyal to the succession or who gave a thought to supporting the despicable rebellion. "Let us continue stedfast," Colman
urged the dissenting fellowship, "to our Religion and Allegiance, and
wait upon God for his further Mercies to our King and our Nation
and the Protestant Interest."[17] The dissenting ministers of New England, including Colman, echoed similar sentiments in their address
to George on the uprising, delivered by their agent Jeremiah Dummer on November 21, 1716. They knew that fidelity to Hanover was
the best hope for continued liberty in religion and state, so they
emphasized that "We cannot hear of so much as one single Person
among either Ministers or People of our Denomination, that has
been found in the late Unnatural and Cursed Rebellion."[18] The Jacobite threat provided one more sign to dissenting New Englanders
that their best interest lay in unity with other dissenting and reformed churches, but also in aligning clearly with the Hanoverian
succession, for on these allegiances the preservation of the world
Protestant interest depended.

The Jacobite revolt helped maintain good relations between Colman and low-church Anglicans in England with whom he might
have otherwise clashed, such as White Kennett of London, later the
Bishop of Peterborough. Colman wrote in 1712 to Kennett complain-
ing about the Society for the Propagation of the Gospel's (SPG)
missions to dissenting New England churchgoers, as if they were fit

targets for evangelization. Colman thought it a much better strategy for the SPG to target the "Heathen" and "Heathenish Places" where there was no settled ministry. Kennett responded well to the criticisms and assured Colman that the SPG did not mean to intrude on the New England churches' rightful ministries. Colman and Kennett were both latitudinarians who dreamt of eventual union between all true friends of the Protestant interest, but their broad-mindedness ceased with regard to Jacobitism. Kennett wrote Colman in 1716 about the ongoing Jacobite threat in Britain. He regretted the high-church influence among the common people of London, where he thought disloyal Anglicans had for years cultivated an intense hostility toward dissenters, thinking that this would "smooth the Way for a Popish Pretender." The high churchmen and secret papists' influence encouraged the "Herd of People" toward Rome, and to "this Madness of the People was the Rebellion owing."[19] In light of the Jacobite/Catholic threat, Colman and Kennett could hardly afford to be enemies.

Colman, usually irenic in temperament when compared to Cotton Mather and the older generations of Boston pastors, by the late 1710s was using the harshest language to contrast faithful Britons to the despicable and traitorous Jacobites. In his 1718 election sermon, Colman raged against the Jacobites and celebrated the preservation of the charter and the reign of George I. Reminding the audience and his readers from II Timothy 3:1–4 that "in the last days perilous times shall come" when men would turn away from God, he suggested that this prophecy had come to pass with the advent of Jacobitism: "These are the viprous brood of a base, private Selfish Spirit, and into the woful time of the reign of this wretched lust our days is cast. For with our own eyes we have lately seen the Apostles words fulfilled in the Character of a restless party in our own Nation (a parcel of proud, fierce, false, perjur'd traitors; ungrateful, unnatural, haughty, heady, boasting, sensual men) who in the most perfidious & shameless manner have attempted, by secret Conspiracies and by open rebellions, to sacrifice the Civil and Religious Interests of the Nation to their own private Interests." Fortunately, their cause had found no adherents in New England, and in fact in most of England they had found no sympathy either. Colman rejoiced that the election sermon coincided with George's birthday (increasingly a significant holiday in New England ports celebrated with fireworks and "illuminations"). He thought it only right that New Englanders "Pray the more fervently for the long life and happy Reign of the King," and for the succession, so that Protestant kings could continue to reign "in the hearts of all that have at heart the Interests of Justice and Piety, the Protestant Religion and the Liberties of Britain."[20]

After the Jacobite crisis of 1715, Colman continued to play his role of helping New Englanders transition through momentous occasions in the history of the Protestant succession, as in 1727 when he equated support for the new king, George II, with attachment to the cause of Christ. In *Fidelity to Christ and to the Protestant Succession in the Illustrious House of Hannover,* Colman framed the succession of George II as the next step in the providential history of the monarchy beginning with William in 1688. He again distinguished New Englanders as those "which know not of one single person in their Communion that is not loyally affected to [George II] and his House." He prayed that George II might "shine long at the head of the Protestant Interest, its powerful Friend and Protector; and reign always in the hearts of all his protestant Subjects, being ever to them as the light of the Morning." Colman then stated baldly that "Our faithful zeal for and adherence to the Protestant Succession in the House of Hannover, is our fidelity to CHRIST and his holy Religion." Preaching on I Chronicles 12:18, Colman established as clearly as one can imagine Massachusetts' hierarchy of religious and national commitments: "And if it may be pleasant to us as Britons and Protestants to make before God our solemn protestations, thro' Grace, of an inviolate Loyalty to the House of our King, and to pour out our prayers to God for his long and peaceful Reign over us; How much more ought it to please and delight us as Christians to have an higher Application . . . ? I mean a cordial and fervent profession of our duty to Christ." For dissenters, Hanover was "the present bulwark against Popery; and for the security of the true knowledge and worship of God among us." Colman implored his audience to glorify God for his hand in establishing a Protestant succession and defeating all the "conspiracies and enterprizes" of the Jacobites. Finally, in this moment of testing for the succession, Colman asked for prayers for "tender Providence over the Person and Family of our King; beseeching God to establish his throne, and to build him a sure house; to bless all his helpers and blast all his enemies." Reflecting nearly identical assertions by English Whigs of the Hanoverian "divine right by Providence," Colman and his colleagues created a public narrative of providential design in the Protestant monarchy that apparently demanded near-total obedience, similar in kind to the devotion owed to Christ.[21] The irony of this claim given the recent memory of James II, Andros, and the Dominion of New England seemed lost on Massachusetts' dissenters.

Colman and the Protestant interest continued to worry about a return of the Stuart line even as the coming of Whitefield drew near. In 1739, Colman noted the threat of the Pretender in a letter to Isaac Watts. Colman recognized that war was again imminent, this time against the Spanish, allied with the French. He feared two developments the most: "their privateers swarming like our Merchandize, & they transport Popery over ye narrow channel, in ye Person of ye Pretender." He hoped that God would still fight for them against the Catholic powers, however.[22]

Colman feared that Britain and New England might be overwhelmed by Catholicism, either through the internal threat of Jacobitism, or through the external threat of attack from France or Spain. This concern led directly into what he considered a counterstrike against Catholic influence: missions among the Native Americans of northern New England. Colman and his associates saw this as a long-standing responsibility of British Protestants, who had ostensibly colonized New England with the purpose of evangelizing the "heathen" tribes. Colman's advocacy of Native American missions took on a larger purpose as he and his colleagues associated with the Protestant interest became convinced that the French Jesuits operating out of Quebec were co-opting northern Indians in order to destabilize the Protestant colonies of New England. With this threat in mind, Colman worked with missions organizations like the dissenter-friendly New England Company of London, and the Society in Scotland for Propagating Christian Knowledge (SSPCK) to compete for the souls of Indians, bringing the native societies into the contest between world Protestantism and Catholicism.[23]

Colman and his colleagues viewed the Society for the Propagation of the Gospel in Foreign Parts with disdain, however, despite the Society's missions work among Native Americans. The Anglican SPG missionaries questioned the legitimacy of the New England dissenters' status as faithful British Protestants. They sometimes successfully proselytized among New Englanders, too, as we shall see in the case of the "Yale apostasy" of 1722, and they denied the legitimacy of dissenting pastors' ordinations. The SPG had the particularly galling habit of arguing that New England's dissenting churches had no ministers (meaning none with proper ordination), thus necessitating evangelization among them. The governor of the New England Company, Sir William Ashurst, a dissenter himself, expressed disdain to Bostonians about these practices.[24] Colman's cooperation with the SSPCK and the New England Company helped magnify his and Boston's dissenting churches' association with the British Protestant interest and its growing missionary agenda, and continued to obfuscate potential problems with their established status in New England that some Anglican authorities found objectionable.

Colman became increasingly concerned in the 1710s and '20s for Indian missions as he became aware of the ongoing successes of Catholic missions. Unity against the Catholic threat was key to a cohesive Protestant interest. Colman expressed his thoughts on the need for evangelization to Samuel Wiswall, a missionary on Martha's Vineyard, one of the few places where New Englanders had maintained successful missions. Wiswall, a recent Harvard graduate, had hesitated to embrace the call to become a missionary among the Indians, and Colman encouraged him with a vision of what might come of the work. He hoped that Wiswall would see "Providence clearly call you to carry the Gospel to a People perishing in pagan & Romish Darkness blended together; to recover them if God pleases from their Barbarity & Idolatry, to Humanity & Christianity."[25] The clerical leaders of New England had not entirely given up on Native American missions after King Philip's War, though it took the threat of Catholic evangelism to spur them on toward substantive action.

In the 1720s Colman and his fellow Commissioners of the New England Company, including Cotton Mather, Benjamin Wadsworth, and Joseph Sewall, worked to promote Experience Mayhew's efforts on Martha's Vineyard. They eventually arranged for Mayhew's *Indian Converts* to be published in London in 1727. Mayhew's successes on Martha's Vineyard proved of singular value in deflecting the sense that New Englanders were doing almost nothing with regard to missions, a particularly embarrassing deficiency given ongoing Jesuit missions and the recent sensation created by Danish missionaries associated with the Halle Pietists working in the East Indies.[26] Mayhew's successes contrasted sharply with the disastrous consequences of Father Rale's War of 1722–25, which effectively halted progress in missions among Wabanakis whom Jesuits had successfully proselytized for years. Colman and his colleagues decided to make a serious effort at missions in the years after Father Rale's War, sensing the urgency of doing something to counter the Catholic threat.

Colman also renewed his motivation for Indian missions with his appointment in 1730 as commissioner for the SSPCK based in Edinburgh. This post gave him access to more financial resources, and put him in the critical position of appointing missionaries to go into Maine, precisely the region that had spawned the Jesuit-backed Wabanaki resistance in Father Rale's War. In 1731 Colman appointed Joseph Seccombe as one of the first three SSPCK missionaries to Maine. The New England Company had sponsored missions among Maine's Wabanakis for a number of years, but lackluster tenures by Joseph Baxter and James Woodside had done little more than embarrass the company and give the Jesuits a firmer hold.[27] Now Colman appointed Seccombe to go to Maine in the aftermath of war, hopefully to reap a new harvest among the Wabanakis.

Immediately upon sending Seccombe and others to the northeastern frontier, Colman took on the additional duty of combating French Jesuit adversaries who mocked the young missionaries. Colman addressed Father Stephen Lauverjat in at least two letters written in Latin. In the first, dated August 16, 1732, Colman attacked Lauverjat and the Jesuits for their rumored permission, even encouragement, of Wabanaki drunkenness. Colman acknowledged the Jesuits' zeal for the missions, but thought that their zeal was not so godly, because it appeared that they intended to control, deceive, and exploit the "Barbaros." Colman threatened Lauverjat with the judgment of God for their actions. "Væ illis qui inebriant hos stupidos Barbaros, ut super nuditates eorum aspiciant" (Woe to those who intoxicate stupid barbarians, so that they may gaze upon their nakedness). Colman was, predictably, willing to believe the worst about the Jesuit missionaries' motives.

In the second letter, dated 1733, Colman attacked the Jesuits' theology more directly, and showed a remarkable familiarity with

Catholic doctrine and practice, though his knowledge was refracted through Protestant lenses. He identified a litany of heretical doctrines and practices in the Roman Catholic church, most notably earned grace, papal indulgences, transubstantiation, the primacy of the pope, and the infallibility of the church. Moreover, they honored, worshipped, and prayed to things other than God, such as the blessed virgin, angels, saints, and relics. Colman thought it madness to continue in communion with "illius Ecclesiæ, cujus caput est Papa Iniquits ille quem Dominus in suo Tempore destruet Spiritu Oris Sui. Mysterium est Iniquitatis" (that church whose head is the Pope of Iniquity which God in time will pull down by the breath of his mouth. His rite is iniquity). The spirit of Antichrist was resident in that church's corruptions, he argued.[28]

Despite his contempt for the Jesuits' motivations and doctrine, Colman continued to have only limited hope for the success of the Protestant missions among the Wabanakis. Writing to the SSPCK in 1732, Colman warned not to have too high expectations of the missionaries, because they faced unusual challenges among the "popefied Indians, (for ye Friars have been before us among them)." Similarly, Colman wrote in 1733 that "Clouds & Darkness" encompassed the missions "from ye Prejudices of Popery sown in ye Minds of ye Salvages by ye French Jesuits & Friars." Seccombe was also frustrated with the lack of success and the continued verbal assaults of Lauverjat. He wrote to Colman in 1734 that Lauverjat was harassing him: "Mr. Lauverjat follows me with continual essays to make a Pervert of me."[29]

Despite these difficulties, Seccombe and his fellow missionaries were honored with ordination in a 1733 public ceremony at Boston in which Colman gave the charge, and his colleague Joseph Sewall of the Old South Church gave the sermon, *Christ Victorious over the Powers of Darkness, by the Light of His Preached Gospel*. The proceedings were prepared for publication and addressed to the SSPCK in

Edinburgh, and in the dedication Colman and Sewall made clear
their vision for the successes of the gospel as promoted by a thriving
British empire. They knew that the work against barbarism and
Catholicism was difficult both in Scotland and in North America,
and that particularly in northern New England "the Prejudices of
Popery sown in the Minds of the Salvages by the Jesuits and Friars
who sojourn among them" made the prospects for immediate success very dim. However, they were confident that God could break
through the darkness, and he seemed to be doing so in earnest as
the last days approached. Sewall and Colman proposed that improved communication and seagoing transportation technology
heralded those last times: "Our Days are happily fallen in those
Times whereof the DIVINE SPIRIT spake to the Prophet Daniel, when
many shall run to and fro, and knowledge shall be increased." Improved communications and shipping meant that "Knowledge of
the True GOD, and of the Only SAVIOUR," could be transported rapidly from one end of the earth to the other. The SSPCK missionaries
played only a small role in this ongoing work of evangelizing the
world.[30]

Colman charged the missionaries to go and "instruct the Heathen People . . . in the Principles of the Christian, Reformed, Protestant Religion." Prayers were given for "the Enlargement of the Kingdom of Christ thro' the whole Earth," and they thanked God for
what their "Fathers" had done in their time toward "Gospelizing the
Heathen, and Shame was taken to our selves that no more had been
done in ours."[31] Despite their theoretical commitment to missions
across the world, the friends of the Protestant interest at the Brattle
Street Church and Old South Church knew that they had done little
to evangelize the Native Americans, and even worse, had left them to
be proselytized by the Jesuits. Colman and his associates hoped that
the SSPCK missions would break the cycle of complacency and
violence, and turn the Indians toward the true faith.

Colman also kept up a regular correspondence with figures in Britain interested in missions in the colonies, and in Seccombe's work in particular. The most consistent of these was Captain Thomas Coram of London. Coram was one of Dr. Thomas Bray's "Associates" who worked toward opening new colonies in North America for the settlement of persecuted Protestants and further evangelization of Native American and African American populations. Coram had lived for ten years in Massachusetts and considered Colman his chief contact with regard to matters of Protestant expansion and evangelization in New England. During the 1730s, Coram sent Colman a series of letters addressing his hopes for Protestant missions and colonies in North America. Since the end of Queen Anne's war in 1714, Coram had been working to promote new colonies in North America, with the hope of settling Protestants in areas threatened by French or Spanish hostilities. This included the possibility of a new colony north of the Kennebec River in Maine.[32] Coram wrote in a 1734 letter to Colman that Thomas Bray had in 1729 discouraged the new colony in Maine because of the inclement weather there, but Bray (now deceased), Coram, and James Oglethorpe all agreed that establishing new colonies in North America could provide relief for poor British families, as well as for "such who were persecuted for their professing the protestant Religion abroad." Thus Oglethorpe and the Associates secured a charter for Georgia in 1732, which had the added advantage of opening possibilities for evangelizing slaves. Coram had not lost interest in the New England missions, however.

Coram supported Colman's SSPCK missionaries in northern New England by offering for the Associates to send them a parcel of books. He heard of their work through an account of their ordination in the *Boston News-Letter*, which his sister sent to him, and Coram was so impressed that he had it published in a London newspaper. He hoped that news of the Maine missions would inspire philanthropists in Britain to support "Missionarys in the Protestant

Intrest" in North America. He noted that the need for Protestant missionaries was much greater because of the zeal of the Catholic missionaries, who "spare no pains to Instruct those Indians in their Way to Consider English men as the Posterity of Jews that murthered our Saviour and the Virgin Mary, and I know not What." Colman warmly received the offer of books in letters back to Coram and Lord Egmont, another Associate.[33]

Joseph Seccombe communicated his thanks for the books directly to Coram, and Coram wrote back to Colman in 1735 recognizing how difficult Seccombe's work was, particularly with the antagonistic Lauverjat shadowing him. "I think Mr. Seccombe has much the Harder Taske in Grapling w'th the Jesuit and the Jesuited Indians I wish he had a fellow Labourer with him to Carry on that Glorious Worke." Coram was not sure whether he would be able to secure more help for the missions, but he continued to recruit philanthropists who could supply "books or other assistants against those Jesuitcal Men and ther Disciples." He also noted that he had asked his sister in Massachusetts to send "one of the 3 volumes of sermons against popery" to Colman, who could then forward it to one of the missionaries.[34]

Seccombe continued to promote his work to the Associates in 1735, as Coram wrote to Colman in September that he had received another packet from Seccombe "with some further accounts of the Indians and the Behaviour of the French Jesuit [Lauverjat] in that Quarter." Coram continued to work hard at raising financial and material support for the Maine missions, hoping that it would better enable "those Young Davids on y'r Borders to Beat down the Old Goliah's French Jesuits." Coram thought that many in England would welcome the opportunity to "do somthing for the better preventing the Growth of Popery on yo'r Borders," but warned that some suspected that the missionaries were only ministering to the English garrisons, not Wabanakis. By 1736, however, Colman was reporting to Coram that the missions were not doing well, and Coram wrote back that the Associates were "Sorry to find you are discouraged from hoping for any Success among the popish Clanns or Tribes it is a great pity if the best of the Missionaries were not sent where the greatest parts and Services were most Necessary." Colman had apparently expressed frustration to Coram about Seccombe and/or the other missionaries, and in 1737 Coram wrote back to Colman agreeing that "Mr. Seccombe is as you say not so learned as one or both of the other Missioners." Apparently, the attacks of Lauverjat and the demands of the mission proved too much for Seccombe, who withdrew from Maine in 1737. Coram hoped that the missions effort would not be "Droped," but for the time being the missions work among the Wabanakis languished.[35]

Colman knew that New England and the Protestant interest faced dire threats from Jacobitism and Catholicism, and from Spain, France, and their allied Native American societies. Like many of his colleagues, Colman began to hope for more than just moral reform to buttress the hopes of the Protestant interest, but instead, as we shall see in chapter six, he began to seek a great eschatological revival of the Protestant churches, that in turn would help secure their safety from the Catholic threat. When Colman received news that the young pastor of Northampton, Jonathan Edwards, had begun in 1735 to see great new concern for religion in his church, Colman requested from Edwards a "Particular account of the Present Extraordinary circumstances . . . with Respect to Religion" in western New England. When Edwards responded to Colman with an eight-page narrative of the revival, a chain of events was set into motion that would eventually lead to Colman's awestruck account of the massive awakenings in Boston in October 1740 that began this chapter.[36] Perhaps God had plans yet to deliver the Protestant interest from its enemies.

CHAPTER TWO

"Let Hell and Rome Do Their Worst"
World News, the Catholic Threat, and International Protestantism

The *Boston News-Letter*'s editors worried in 1722 that the time might have come for the long-expected resumption of war between Europe's Protestant and Catholic powers. The Treaty of Utrecht in 1713 brought a tenuous peace, but world war still looked possible if not imminent. The newspaper evaluated the balance sheet of Protestant versus Catholic Christianity in the known world, and was concerned, but optimistic. Reprinting an analysis from London's *Post-Man*, the *News-Letter* offered reasons for hope. The report acknowledged that some readers were "Phlegmatick" about Protestant prospects in a world war and thought that "Popery is in a formidable flourishing Condition," and that if the Roman Church and her allies should take up arms against the "Dissenters," they would "Convert the World" by military might. Not to fear, the article assured its readers, for if a war began that day "the Protestants would beat the Papists out of the Field, and out of the World." The *Post-Man* outlined eleven powers on each side of the contest for world Christianity, and argued that though the Catholic states might have a slight edge in manpower, the Protestant interest had the edge on the sea and in the trades. "Whilst then the Protestants have the Trade and the Money, let Hell and Rome do their worst: They will always be beaten."[1]

This kind of report reminds us that eighteenth-century New Englanders—especially friends of the Protestant interest like the *News-Letter*'s publishers—were waiting along with Europe's faithful Protestants and Catholics for that which seemed inevitable: a war to decide the fate of Christendom. As the availability of print increased, British Protestants on both sides of the Atlantic read and imagined the Catholic threat as a fundamental building block of their changing identity. Due in part to this steady supply of international news, many provincial New Englanders' imaginary residence spanned the whole known world.[2]

This chapter will explain some of what New Englanders knew about events in the transatlantic European world, and suggest that the knowledge of news helped New Englanders imagine for themselves new identities both cosmopolitan and apocalyptic. For those who kept up with the available news, the world seemed increasingly troubled and complicated, but also familiar, torn by conflicts over liberty and religion in which leading New Englanders saw themselves playing a significant if distant role. From their western outpost, many New Englanders watched and waited for news across the world, passing through sites of religious contest, as it were, in their own mental and spiritual landscape.[3] The news they received led them to believe that the world Catholic and Protestant communities were destined to clash in an apocalyptic war to decide the fate of Christianity. In light of this threat, New England's pastors asked their churches to pray for the revival of the world's Protestant churches, including their own.

During the post–Glorious Revolution period in Boston, printed sermons and newspapers commonly drew their readers' attention to the known world's religious balance sheet and weighed the Catholic menace against the Protestant churches. This scorekeeping helped

New Englanders increasingly imagine themselves part of the Protestant interest. As Benedict Anderson has argued, print culture provided an essential means for constructing imagined national communities, as via print and newspapers thousands of previously separated people "became capable of comprehending one another." Anderson portrayed these imagined communities as fundamentally secular, but he missed how in the eighteenth-century Atlantic world, such communities of print could also imagine themselves centered around a reformed Protestant church.[4]

The late seventeenth century saw an enormous rise in the amount of print in circulation, and Boston was no different: in many ways it was just one more provincial town on the outer limits of a small but growing British empire.[5] Boston saw a spike in print marketing immediately after the Glorious Revolution, and though the numbers of pamphlets, sermons, and books went down briefly again during the mid-1690s, they began a steady upward trend that would continue generally through the American Revolution and beyond. Leading New Englanders proved increasingly interested in news from England and the Continent, including news of religious matters. A variety of means, often abortive, were used in the 1690s to bring European news to Boston. The first proper newspaper published by Benjamin Harris, an anti-Catholic refugee from Jacobean London, was limited to one issue in 1690, mostly because of its impolitic commentary on domestic affairs.[6] Pamphlets from such sources as the radical Whig Londoner John Partridge dotted the print records of these years, reporting on among other items Jacobite plots to return the Stuarts to the throne. Through 1704, the most common sources of news were the London newspapers available through the incoming posts, and the most common sources printed domestically that reported European news continued to be ministers' sermons and pamphlets.[7]

Nicholas Noyes, the teaching pastor at Salem and former

prosecutor of witches, set a standard for New England's view of world news and the state of world Christianity when he preached *New-England's Duty and Interest* at the General Court on election day, May 1698. Bartholomew Green later published this sermon as a book, and it provides insight into the value of international news to New Englanders. Noyes wanted to consider "the RESTAURATIONS, REFORMATIONS, and BENEDICTIONS, Promised to the Church and the World in the latter dayes," and New England's part in those developments.[8] He told his audience to expect that God would bring about a final reformation of the true church before the second coming of Christ and the destruction of God's enemies. Noyes encouraged New Englanders to turn their eyes to events across the Atlantic to understand their eschatological solidarity with the true church that God at that moment might be preparing for the second coming.

Noyes advocated an informed prayer life through watching and reading about European news. Just as Elijah watched, waited, and prayed for rain to come in I Kings 18, so also New Englanders should "look out seven times, and pray, and pray again . . . believing on and praying to the Lord, till he send Rain on the earth, till he come & rain down righteousness on Asia, Africa, Europe and America." Though Noyes admitted that many of the signs might not suggest an imminent reformation of the church and destruction of God's enemies, he cautioned that friends of world Protestantism should maintain confidence in the prophecies that required these things to come eventually. "Though we know not the time just when; yet there are signals given whereby the Church of God may know that their Redemption draws nigh." Noyes reminded his listeners and readers that they should even expect the Jews, the long-rejected people of God, to come back to Christ in the last days. And so he told New Englanders to watch and wait for God to bring about the long-awaited changes: "The good words . . . which God hath spoken, give us ground to believe that the Mahometan Imposture and Tyranny will not always last; and that the Remnants and Fragments of the Grecian and African Churches will be gathered up, and restored. . . . It were Infidelity to conclude that God hath done with the Protestant People, and his Witnesses in Germany, Bohemia, Hungarra, France, the Valleys of the Piedmont; and many other places in Europe: where for his Name and Gospel sake they have been Killed all the day long." Despite persecutions of Protestants by the Turks and the Roman church, Noyes insisted that God would restore and reform the Protestant interest, and that soon the forces of Antichrist (the Roman Catholic church) would be destroyed, and that "the Kingdoms of this World shall become the Kingdoms of our Lord and of his Christ." And though Noyes worried about the declensions he and his pastoral colleagues discerned among many New England churches, he nevertheless hoped that God would include New England in the latter-day revival of the church.[9]

Noyes's speculations make clearer the reasons why Boston became ready for a newspaper of its own in 1704. Networks of personal correspondence and the circulation of London newspapers worked to some extent to supply the interest in international news in Boston, but the market there was certainly ready for a domestically produced newspaper. Despite a number of marketing problems, complaints about delays in updating the news, and poor editorial decisions, John Campbell's *Boston News-Letter* must be viewed as an important departure in provincial New England's print culture and a new means of helping readers imagine simultaneously a British and an international Protestant community. Religious news, motivated by an eschatological anticipation of an impending battle for Christendom, directed much of the content of the *News-Letter* and later Boston papers. Religious concerns, both overt and subtle, suffused the Boston newspapers through the mid-1730s. New England's early news in print had religious and teleological origins, reporting episodes that were often referential to God's agency and timetable in history. But the provincial Boston papers, which bridged the gap between seventeenth-century "teleological" news and the specifically revivalist news of the transatlantic evangelical connection's magazines, such as Thomas Prince Sr. and Jr.'s *Christian History*, deliberately included politico-religious world news to supply the eschatological interest in the contest between Protestant and Catholic powers. Thus Boston's early newspapers provide another example of how print in the Atlantic world grew out of the inheritance of reformed Christianity while simultaneously becoming a fixed commodity of mercantile capitalism and helping far-flung residents imagine developing nation-states, in this case Britain. Early modern European political thought often entertained overlapping ideas of a "medieval" Christian universal world order and "modern" sovereign states, and in provincial New England one can see these ambiguities of imagined political order, as the newspapers helped facilitate the conception of both a persecuted but eschatologically ascendant Protestant world church and an imperial British state.[10]

Campbell's regular inclusion of religious news also helps nuance our typical impression of Anglican/Congregational hostility in provincial Boston, as the Anglican Campbell, supported originally by the Anglican governor Joseph Dudley, for fifteen years provided a source of world religious news to figures like Boston's Samuel Sewall, who regularly possessed and distributed copies of the *News-Letter*, and ministers in outlying towns, such as Sudbury, Massachusetts' Israel Loring. Ebenezer Parkman of Westborough, Massachusetts, likewise reported in 1727 paying Bartholomew Green for a year's subscription.[11] World religious news became even more important as in the early years of the contest between the British and French empires, concerns about the Protestant succession, the ongoing threat of Jacobite revolts and Catholic persecutions, and the interminable wars and threats of war between Catholic and Protestant states gave Congregationalists and Anglicans more common ground than they had in the post-Restoration years. In view of the world Catholic threat, dissenters and Anglicans found common reasons to monitor news of the Protestant interest in the world.

Although the direct evidence for how readers interpreted the news is predictably thin, the evidence that exists indicates that New Englanders sympathetic to the Protestant interest did use the news as a guide to prayer and saw in the news signs of the potential fulfillment of biblical prophecies and the expansion of the kingdom of God. Few would be as explicit as Jonathan Edwards, who remembered that in his post-Yale years "I had great longings for the advancement of Christ's kingdom in the world. . . . If I heard the least hint of anything that happened in any part of the world, that appeared to me, in some respect or other, to have a favorable aspect on the interest of Christ's kingdom, my soul eagerly catched at it. . . . I used to be earnest to read public news-letters, mainly for that end; to see if I could not find some news favorable to the interest of religion in the world." Though he remembered this longing for news from his brief sojourn in New York City in 1722–23, such interest continued to characterize Edwards and other New Englanders like him. For instance, when the Reverend John Williams of Deerfield, Massachusetts, died in 1729, he was celebrated for "how careful was he to inform himself of the Transactions and Affairs of Europe, and to understand the State and Circumstances of this Province, that he might Calculate his Prayers accordingly."[12]

As we shall see more fully in chapter three, even the ubiquitous almanacs sometimes directed readers' attention to the news and its implications for the fulfillment of astrological prognostications or biblical prophecies. Samuel Clough's 1707 *Kalendarium Nov-Anglicanum* excitedly noted that "those that have read or heard the News we have had . . . from Foreign parts" would see that his earlier predictions of the downfall of some great person, derived from an eclipse on October 25, 1706, had been largely accomplished in Louis

XIV's losses in Queen Anne's War. Clough hopefully suggested that the eclipse of April 5, 1707, might foreshadow "great Controversies about Religion, which perhaps may make way for the downfall of Popery, and liberty of the Protestant Religion throughout Europe."[13]

The following analysis of Boston newspapers from 1704 through the early 1730s necessarily focuses heavily on the *News-Letter* because it was the only paper in Boston until the coming of the *Boston Gazette* in 1719.[14] Even after the coming of the *Gazette,* the *New-England Weekly Journal* (1727), and the *Boston Weekly Rehearsal* (1731), however, the *News-Letter* remained the most focused of all the papers on the foreign news items that primarily concern us here. Nevertheless, the other newspapers maintained the implicit teleological function as well to greater or lesser degrees. Perhaps predictably, the Franklins' *New-England Courant* (1721–26) served these religious functions the least directly of any Boston paper, making fun of the *News-Letter* at times for its excruciatingly detailed accounts of matters such as "the Secrets of the Popes Gutts." But even the *Courant,* the long-purported herald of secularism, was not entirely devoid of politico-religious world news; the Franklins at times provided their readers intricate details of matters such as the pope's coronation ceremony.[15]

Bartholomew Green, a Congregationalist who took over for Campbell (apparently in 1721, though Campbell did not legally transfer ownership until 1723) and who if anything led the paper more toward Protestant internationalism, explained his paper's particular interest in religious matters directly in January 1723, as he was now faced with the competition of the *Gazette* and the *Courant.* Green stated that it was his wish "to make this Paper, as profitable and entertaining to the good People of this Country as I can," and thus he promised to sustain and even increase news of religious matters. He offered this news specifically as a guide to prayer, so that those with a concern for "the State of Religion in the World" would know "how to Order their Prayers and Praises to the Great GOD thereupon." Green then included an excerpt from Anthony Boehm's *Propagation of the Gospel in the East*. Boehm, the key link between New England's developing evangelical cohort and the Pietist Halle school, was the model broker of the international Protestant interest, and his work's presence demonstrated the marketability of news concerning persecutions, missions, and world evangelism.[16]

Without this assumption of concern for world Protestantism and the Catholic threat, one might be hard pressed to conceive why there would be any interest in some of the content in the *News-Letter* and subsequent newspapers. The increasingly cosmopolitan Protestant interest, however, eagerly received accounts of persecuted Protestants and Jansenist controversies in France, troubles with the Jesuits in China, and all manner of incidents and crises between Catholics and Protestants. These stories mentally connected provincial Bostonians to religious controversies across the ocean that they could only visualize through print.[17]

As treatments of British newspapers during the period have generally agreed, one of the most important types of news concerned the activities of the Roman Catholic church and the machinations of Catholic states and princes, most notably France and Spain.[18] But the sheer variety and types of news concerning Roman Catholicism might surprise some. If a New Englander read or heard the news regularly, then he would have had access to detailed news reports about the activities and policies of the pope, persecutions of Protestants in a host of European states by Catholic princes, dragoons, mobs, and even renegade priests, as well as news of Jesuit missions and such problems as the Chinese rites controversy. Boston's newspapers also took every opportunity to present rank-and-file priests, especially Jesuits, in the worst possible light by reporting stories of priestly treachery, scandals, or laughable idiocy.

The papers included regular reports of duplicitous activities by priests, such as the 1706 report from Spain that told of the Franciscans there "exorcising" one of their members who pretended to be possessed by Satan. The priests "fully instructed him in all the Tricks he was to play," and then before a large crowd the priest was delivered from the demonic oppression and testified that he had been possessed to help the Devil get the people to revolt against the Duke of Anjou and promote the introduction of the Protestant heresy. A similar deception in Warsaw had the faithful believing that a statue of Christ had begun to issue blood, but upon investigation the blood turned out to be the "Juice of Cherries."[19]

Another report from France surely had New England readers laughing at the news that a "Gardener's Ass" had wandered into a parish and took a "hearty Draught" from the basin of holy water, and that the inquisitorial committee immediately seized, tried, and executed the donkey in a church court proceeding. This type of reported buffoonery helped New Englanders define priests not only as evil and predatory but also in some cases simply laughable.[20]

Many reports reaffirmed the impression that when Catholics ruled, Protestants could expect the harshest penalties for protesting against the authority of the church. One from Vienna told of the execution of two women, nineteen and twenty years old, who had dared to desecrate a crucifix. The women threw the crucifix on the ground, and though they seemed not to have considered themselves Protestant, they made the good Protestant defense of their action that true religion expressly forbade idolatry. The priests, chagrined by similar actions by laypeople in recent days, made an example of the young women by having their heads and right hands cut off.[21]

These sorts of stories provided a backdrop to New England's local problems with French Jesuits and their Indian allies, which reached their height during Father Rale's War of 1722–25. For readers and audiences of the *Boston Gazette*, it could be no coincidence that the same 1724 issue reporting that Father Sebastien Rale—the fomenter of the Wabanakis' war against New England—had been executed by Massachusetts forces also reported that the Jesuits were taking over the court of France, summarily executing French Protestant preachers, sending men to the galleys, jailing women and shaving their heads, and taking children from their families and giving them a Roman Catholic upbringing and education. To those familiar with the news the threat of French Catholicism looked ominously similar on both sides of the Atlantic.[22]

In these cases and many more one can see the sheer variety of stories the papers supplied concerning Catholics and their activities. However, one can also tease out several ongoing storylines that appeared again and again in the *Boston News-Letter* and later papers. Perhaps the most important during the early and mid-eighteenth century was the status of religion in France. The Boston newspapers regularly included material on two French storylines in particular. One was the ongoing persecution of French Protestants in the wake of the revocation of the Edict of Nantes in 1685, and the other was the Jansenist controversy. Both these episodes helped complicate New Englanders' imagined relationship with the French. While the French government was viewed as the greatest threat to British Protestantism, especially through the reign of Louis XIV, the "French" in general were never seen as unequivocally "papist" or Antichristian, and in fact the cause of French Protestants and reformed sympathizers among the Catholics elicited sympathy from British readers.

British Protestants watched with horror and fascination as starting in the 1680s Catholic France cracked down on its Protestant enclaves, quartering dragoons in Protestant homes and trying to force conversions to Catholicism. Eventually Louis XIV's anti-Protestant crusade culminated in the revocation of the Edict of Nantes. French Protestantism, already desperately weakened by persecution, almost completely collapsed after 1685 save for the Camisards of Languedoc and the Cévennes. There, beginning in 1695, war began between the

Camisards and the French government forces trying to stamp out Protestant resistance once and for all, and this resistance movement proved highly interesting to New Englanders. The prospect of a French Protestant remnant held considerable attraction, representing persecuted martyrs of the world Protestant cause.[23]

Reports from France concerning the Camisard revolt and the Huguenot persecutions were regular fare in Campbell's *News-Letter*. In 1704 Campbell printed a letter from a Camisard leader, detailing a battle against the royal army and demanding that "the Protestant Religion should be re-established in Languedoc, and that those who are in the Galleys or in Prison for that Religion, should be set at Liberty." The letter adopted a providentialist tone toward the Camisards' fight against the French Royalists, noting that they did not lose many men in the latest battle because "God fought for us; He overthrew our Enemies with all their Devilish Devices."[24]

A year later the news was not so positive as the Camisard revolt began to collapse under the weight of French royal arms. Campbell reported that a cowardly Camisard had betrayed some of the revolt's leaders to the French authorities, and also that the Camisards had been framed as having plotted to massacre the "Catholicks of Nismes." Nevertheless, the report maintained that the "French are very uneasie and full of Apprehensions of Danger from the poor Camisars, who retir'd to Switzerland, tho' they have no Arms." As prospects for French Protestants looked increasingly bleak, friends of the Protestant interest also followed accounts of their movements in London and America, including New England, and appreciated the beneficence of Huguenots in Massachusetts like Andrew and Peter Faneuil.[25] Pastors regularly called for prayer and sympathy for the Huguenots, warning the people that they easily could be next should the French succeed in their North American ambitions. John Danforth, pastor at Dorchester, told his congregation to thank God they had not yet met the fate of the French Protestants, that "Our ministers are not Banished, nor our Children (excepting a few in Captivity) forced from us, and brought up in Soul-Destroying Popery; Nor our Assemblies broken up, nor Dragoons let in upon us, to Torture us a thousand ways, to Compel us to Blaspheme & Abjure our Holy Religion. . . . Do we Escape the Woful Day, because of our Godliness and Righteousness, that is greater than theirs? No verily."[26] Up to that point, they had largely avoided the kinds of attacks that the French Protestant brethren had faced, but it might be only a matter of time before God allowed New England to be scourged too.

Although Boston's newspapers were concerned for the Huguenots' fate, they demonstrated an equal or greater interest in another issue within French Catholicism itself: the Jansenist controversy. Jansenism was born in the mid-seventeenth century out of the cooperative efforts of the devout at the Port-Royal convent in Paris and the Flemish theologian Cornelius Jansen, and the devotees of Jansen tended to be Augustinian and enthusiastic in theology and practice. Under his reign Louis XIV made a number of efforts to stamp out the Jansenists, and in 1713 he secured a papal bull *Unigenitus* against the propositions of the Jansenist *Moral Reflections on the New Testament* (1695), written by Pasquier Quesnel. Not least among the objectionable doctrines promoted by Quesnel were irresistible grace and predestination, drawing the sympathy of the international reformed community.[27]

From the beginning Campbell's *News-Letter* served as a distributor of information concerning the ongoing Jansenist controversy. In January 1706 Campbell included a report from the Low Countries that there was trouble brewing between the Jesuits and Jansenists. "The Roman Catholicks, who Idolize Jesuits . . . have assaulted and wounded one of their Priests suspected of Jansenism." Beginning in 1712 and continuing for many years after, the Boston newspapers closely followed the controversy over *Unigenitus*. Campbell's report on the matter in June 1714 mocked the French clergy who had initially affirmed the orthodoxy of Father Quesnel's *Moral Reflections,* only later to label him as heretical and ultimately securing the *Unigenitus* constitution against him. The report wondered how the bishops could have missed the one hundred one "Capital Errors and Heresies" contained therein for a number of years after its publication. "This will give a very ill Opinion to the World of the Capacity of the French Bishops, who must needs be guilty of Ignorance, or neglect in their discharge of their Episcopal Functions."[28]

After 1713 France saw years of conflict between the "appellants" against *Unigenitus* and the "constitutionalists" who supported it, and at times it seemed that the controversy would shatter the French church and state. The controversy commanded the entire front page of one *News-Letter* issue in 1718, which reprinted a letter denouncing the opponents of *Unigenitus* as schismatics and inheritors of the Lutheran tradition of heresy and resistance of papal authority. Readers in the British Atlantic world would have seen this accusation as a badge of honor. The *News-Letter* also reported in January 1719 that Louis XV and his advisers had ordered absolute censorship and silence concerning *Unigenitus,* and especially forbade anyone to "speak, write, print or distribute any thing against the Respect due to the Holy See & to the Pope." And yet, the *News-Letter* noted in 1721, despite the French government and the papacy's attempts to stifle criticism, a print had surfaced in Paris depicting the recently deceased Clement XI and Father Quesnel, the former being dragged to hell by the Devil and the latter being carried by the angels to heaven.[29]

Boston's newspapers also reported with some bewilderment a number of accounts of Jansenist miracles that began to happen with great regularity starting in about 1725. The Jansenist miracles and the Jesuits' opposition to them created a backlash against the order among the French people, as the *Weekly Rehearsal* noted in 1733 that two Jesuits had been tossed into the Seine by a mob, and that an arsonist had burned Grenoble's College of Jesuits. Perhaps the key to the continuing interest and selection of stories about the Jansenist controversy, in fact, lay in the threat it posed to the Jesuits. As the *Weekly Rehearsal* noted in an edition full of reports of Jesuit plots and support for *Unigenitus,* "all the World knows that the Drift of these Sons of Ignatius are not [sic] easily discovered."[30]

New England's newspapers also followed the "Drift of these Sons of Ignatius" to China, where the Jesuits had maintained missions since 1580 but enjoyed their greatest successes between about 1670 and 1720. During this period the missions witnessed the "Chinese rites controversy," in which many Jesuits argued that Christianity was not contrary to ancestral and Confucian devotions. This policy garnered the favor of the Chinese emperor Kangxi, but reports of such tolerance angered papal officials and led Rome to begin sending inspectors to China to monitor the Jesuits' activities. The *News-Letter* made note in 1707 that Charles de Tournon, the pope's inspector of Chinese missions, had been declared a cardinal.[31] Similarly, the paper reported in late 1708 that the bishop Charles Maigrot, ally of de Tournon, had arrived in Rome and accused the Jesuits of agreeing to worship "Confucius, the great Chinese Saint." Reports in 1711 suggested that the Jesuits were content to allow their "converts" to continue in specifically non-Christian practices, just so long as they remained obedient to the Jesuit order. One report told that de Tournon was so badly "abused" there that he would soon return to Rome, and it was heard that Emperor Kangxi was prepared to banish all Catholics but the Jesuits from China. The story asserted that the pope was deeply troubled by these and similar reports that had the Jesuits using "the same Methods to convert the Turks as they do to convert the Chineze, that is, that they allow them to practice, publickly, the Worship and Ceremonies, of the Mahometans."[32] Increase Mather, using unknown sources, noted in 1708 that "the Emperor of

China, has caused the Pope's Legat to be put to Death," one of a number of "Remarkable Providences" in world news that led him to believe that the downfall of Antichrist might happen in 1716.[33] Never mind that Mather's information was false; such news stories helped New Englanders imagine that their great enemy the Catholic church could be entering its biblically foretold time of destruction.

In 1712 the *News-Letter* correctly reported the death of the pope's legate de Tournon, and speculated that it would be difficult to find a replacement for him "after the cruel Treatment he has received there." After the death of de Tournon news of the Chinese rites controversy became less frequent and less dependable, though for many years it remained a periodic item of interest in the *News-Letter*. Because of Rome's intransigence the Catholic missions in China went into decline and the emperor Kangxi and his son Yongzheng became less and less friendly to all but a few Jesuit missionaries. The Boston newspaper accounts of course blamed these problems on the Jesuits, speculating that "if they would conform with the Pope's Orders about Divine Worship, all would be quiet." In 1719 a report surfaced, erroneously, that the Chinese had "Massacred all the Jesuits and their Proselytes," but the sense was correct that the missions were deeply troubled. Nevertheless, a report in 1720 held up the Jesuits as the chief missionary competition in Asia for the Halle school's missionaries, from whom Campbell published another letter.[34]

Beyond news from France and China, the papers also regularly reported news of Catholic persecutions of Protestants across Europe. Among the beleaguered Protestants were those of the Palatinate, a state in southwestern Germany that was a classic example of the war-torn and religiously divided societies of central Europe in the late seventeenth and early eighteenth centuries. The chief political office of the Palatinate, the Elector Palatine, passed from a Protestant to a Catholic line in 1685, resulting in troubling consequences for Protestant subjects. Following the Peace at Utrecht, correspondents regularly reported on the dismal conditions of the Palatinate's Protestants, especially in the Calvinist churches, and hoped that the cooperation of Protestant princes, led by the British and Prussian monarchs, could alleviate their suffering. An account in 1714 had Calvinist (almost always referred to as "Protestant" in the accounts) churches at "Nieusteyn" and "Schwasburg" being attacked by a Roman Catholic mob. In one episode, Catholics besieged a Protestant church while it was conducting services, forcing open the barred doors, wounding several parishioners, and driving the Protestants out of their church. These Protestants for their part took up arms, "retook their Church, and drove away the Papists." The article speculated that more civil unrest might follow and hoped that Queen Anne might protect Protestants' rights and persons.[35]

In 1720 the *News-Letter* began reporting regularly on happenings at the Church of the Holy Ghost in Heidelberg, one of the hottest grounds of Protestant/Catholic hostilities in the early eighteenth century. Since the Catholic succession in 1685, the burial vault of the church had been used by the Catholic princes, but the Protestant believers maintained use of the rest of the church. In 1719 the separating wall between the two areas was pulled down and the Reformed church was turned out of the building. The Elector Palatine did not help the tensions when he began seizing copies of the overtly anti-Catholic Heidelberg Catechism. Though the Elector would eventually relent, this local problem had international ramifications, and as W. R. Ward has noted, among the Protestant and Catholic faithful the controversies at Heidelberg raised again the "spectre of the ultimate Armageddon between Catholic and Protestant," a fear that would obtain through the 1760s.[36]

In mid-1720 the *News-Letter* was full of news from the Palatinate, often focusing on the Church of the Holy Ghost. One report had the Reformed church back in services there, with the pastor supposedly preaching on the text "The Dogs shall lick up the Blood of your Enemies." The same report told of a bizarre incident in Heidelberg in which a young Protestant woman was attacked outside a "Popish Church" by a Catholic mob. The crowd carried the woman inside the church and tried to force her to take the Eucharist. When she refused, the host "was cramm'd down her Throat," she was badly beaten, and soon thereafter she died.[37] Similar reports from Heidelberg and the Palatinate reminded New England readers of the plight of their "poor persecuted" brethren in 1720 and beyond.

Easily the most notorious and newsworthy episode of Catholic violence against Protestants during the period, however, was what the papers called the "Massacre at Thorn" [Torún]. Before 1724/25, there had been reports in the papers warning of the dangerous situation of the "Oppressed Protestants" in Poland and Lithuania, such as a reprinted letter from Frederick William of Prussia to George I that complained that the "Evangelical Churches" there "have from some time past been persecuted and oppressed by the Roman Catholick Clergy." The Prussian government worried that "the total Suppression of the Evangelical Churches will be accomplish'd . . . unless God Almighty sends some extraordinary Assistance to preserve his People from those great Persecutions." Frederick William appealed to the Hanoverian King George to take pity on these persecuted brethren of "our Communion" and to step in on behalf of the "Evangelical Inhabitants, or Dissenters" persecuted in northeastern Europe.[38]

Then in 1724 these tensions burst into extraordinary violence in Thorn. News came to Boston in April 1725 that in response to a Protestant disturbance against a devotional procession in summer 1724, the Jesuits had brought a tribunal in from Warsaw to prosecute the Protestants of the city for fomenting insurrection, and in a show-trial seething with anti-Protestant hatred, fourteen burghers were sentenced to death.[39] The executions began in early December, beginning with the mayor, who was tempted by the Jesuits to give up Protestantism, but who reportedly told them, "Content your selves with having my Body: As for my Soul that is my Saviour's." The mayor was beheaded and placed on public display "to glut the Revenge of the Nobility and Clergy." The Jesuits executed nine other prominent citizens, with a variety of tortures preceding and indignities following their deaths. In response, the international Protestant prints painted this as the latest and perhaps worst instance of Jesuit treachery and Catholic fanaticism. "The Jesuits had conformed to the Protestant stereotype" in this episode, and so from Prussia to Boston the presses seized upon the news as good copy.[40] In Boston it became the single most important news story of 1725.

The Boston papers reported on the incident for months in exhaustive detail. Follow-up reports discussed the lone pardon issued to one of the Protestant convicts who converted to Catholicism, which proved that "all the Crime of those poor People . . . was of their being of the Protestant Religion," and that if they had renounced the true faith they would have been spared. The *Boston Gazette* reported with disgust that the Jesuits "are far from thinking that they shall be called to account for their late Barbarities at Thorn" and to show their contempt they put on a comedy in which they displayed a number of "Calves-Heads" equal to the number of beheaded Protestants. Other editions reported the efforts of Frederick William of Prussia and George of England to redress the grievances of the Polish Protestants, who according to one report "were Non-conformist of this Kingdom," again indicating a sense of solidarity with British dissenters.[41]

Given such news as was coming out of Poland and the Palatinate, it was no wonder that during the 1720s and 1730s New Englanders were deeply concerned about the worldwide Protestant interest, which seemed harassed and persecuted on many fronts. Cotton Mather asserted in *Suspiria Vinctorum: Some Account of the*

Condition to which the Protestant Interest in the World is at This Day Reduced (a direct response to Thorn) that the persecuted brethren badly needed New Englanders' prayers, and in fact prayer was the "MARK and WORK of all Sincere CHRISTIANS, That are not actually under the Romish Oppressions." The editors of the *New-England Weekly Journal,* friends of Mather including Samuel Kneeland and Thomas Prince, agreed with him and excerpted *Suspiria Vinctorum* in the paper's first issues in 1727.[42] The plight of the persecuted brethren in Europe should revive and awaken New England's churches, Mather insisted, for "The Church of Rome, with the Man of Sin at the Head of it, entirely possessed by Satan, is resolved upon the Extermination of all the Christians upon Earth, who come not into a Combination with her, in her Detestable Idolatries." He specifically singled out France, the Palatinate, the Holy Roman Empire, Hungary, and most importantly Poland as the places where Protestant brethren needed New Englanders' prayers. But the result of knowing and praying for these beleaguered churches would be not only relief from their hardships. Mather and others also believed that God would use the world Protestant interest's pity for their persecuted brethren and their opposition to Antichrist as a means to revive Protestants across the world, even among the churches not immediately under the persecution of Rome. The churches should pray "That the Glorious GOD of our Life, would Revive Decay'd PIETY among them; and that His Quickning Spirit would not withdraw any further from them. Lord, Revive thy Work in the midst of the Nations. They are called . . . CHRISTIANS; Oh! Leave them not; and let not their Adversaries tread down thy Sanctuary among them."[43] We must, then, understand the awakenings of the 1730s and '40s as born partially out of a sense of crisis in the world church of Protestantism, which seemed threatened with extinction should God not deliver and revive them.

By the 1730s, many British Protestants agreed with Mather's sense that revival seemed increasingly the only hope for world Protestant-ism. The English Bishop of Bangor, Benjamin Hoadly, worried in a message printed in Boston that "the whole Protestant Power in Europe . . . is little better than a Creature with Pain and Difficulty struggling for Life." Hearkening back to Green's balance sheet of Catholic versus Protestant power ten years earlier, a similar chart in the *Boston Weekly Rehearsal* took an even broader view of world religion, revealing grim statistics for the Protestant church. Based on Patrick Gordon's hugely successful *Geography Anatomiz'd, or, The Geographical Grammar,* the chart noted that if one broke up the world's population into thirty parts, nineteen would be "Blind and gross Idolaters," six would be "Jews, Turks, and Saracens," two would be "of the Greek Church," and three would be left to the Catholic and Protestant communions. Reflecting on the fact that "the Chris-tian Religion is of a very small extent" in the world, the *Weekly Rehearsal* insisted that the time had come for British Protestants to become active in missions, especially with the Indians and Africans among whom they dwelt.[44]

In light of such continuing news and numbers, treatises on the subject of the world's religious condition in the 1730s became increasingly desperate and bleak concerning the fate of true reli-gion, but they maintained an optimistic view of what could happen should the Protestant interest pray, and should God in response send a great outpouring of the Holy Spirit. As John Reynolds's popular book *A Compassionate Address to the Christian World* (published both in London and Boston) asserted, the Roman church seemed to be winning the day, demanding a prayerful response: "How many Kingdoms are enslaved to the Pope, and to the Errors and Abomina-tions of Popery! . . . and so are sadly led by the Blind into the Ditch of Death, and Destruction. . . . And do not your Souls pity them? And do you not seriously pray, that God's Kingdom may come among them? If not, why do you pretend to be Protestants?" Paul Dudley's anti-Catholic treatise *An Essay on the Merchandize of Slaves & Souls of Men* went so far as to suggest that the successes of the Roman church were perhaps a sign of the Great Tribulation of God's church immediately preceding the destruction of Antichrist and the second coming. He pointed to the desolation of the churches in Asia, Bohemia, Hungary, and the Piedmont, as well as Jacobite plots that he associated with the Jesuits, all as evidence that the church might perhaps be in that time "immediately before the final Ruine of Antichrist" in which the "Tribulation to the Church of GOD" would be worse than any previous time.[45]

Israel Loring, pastor at Sudbury, similarly lamented the state of the world church in his 1737 election sermon. He pointed to the destruction of the churches of Africa, the apostasy of the Roman, Polish, and Transylvanian churches, and especially persecutions against Bohemian, Hungarian, and French Protestants as woeful signs of how "the Shadow of Death stretches it self over those once Happy Regions of Light." But Loring did not believe that the Protestant interest was without hope. He pointed to the Northampton revivals of recent years as signs of the outpouring of the Spirit, and encouraged his audience and readers to pray for more of the same. In view of the threats against the true faith in the world, and in view of the glimmerings of revival, it was time to set aside petty differences among Protestants and "lay out ourselves in promoting the common Interest of Christ's Kingdom, and the common Salvation of precious and immortal Souls . . . let us be one with every one, that is one with Jesus Christ."[46]

In view of the persecution of the world church, the need of the hour was international evangelical unity, not theological precisionism and bickering. From their far distant outpost, many New Englanders believed that just as they played a role in succoring the imagined Protestant community through prayer, so also they soon might participate in bringing in a great evangelical revival to that community through prayer. Much of the recent work on the "Great Awakening," particularly that which focuses on George Whitefield, has examined the religious periodicals' publicization and even "invention" of the revivals.[47] But it seems that before Whitefield's emergence, world news also helped New Englanders imagine themselves part of a beleaguered world Protestant community that, in light of the Catholic threat, was badly in need of revival. As Cotton Mather had advised new ministerial candidates in 1726, if you will "inform yourself about, The State of Religion, in the World . . . , it may bring you to form those Projections, by which, as little as you are in your own Eyes, whole Nations may anon come to fare the better for you."[48] Distant as they might be from the centers of power in the contest between the European Protestant and Catholic nations, New Englanders who were friendly to the Protestant interest increasingly imagined for themselves a crucial role in the battle for Christianity and the coming world revival, episodes that they could fully comprehend only through printed world news.

CHAPTER THREE

Protestants, Popery, and Prognostications
New England Almanacs

During the early years of the eighteenth century, Samuel Clough annually brought his new almanac to his printers, Nick Boone and Benjamin Eliot, hoping that its charts and ruminations would instruct, illuminate, and edify his readers and hearers. Borrowing from the famous London almanacker John Partridge, Clough's 1706 *Kalendarium Nov-Anglicanum* reflected on the future of Christianity in the Atlantic world and continental Europe. For 1702, the "Conjunction of Saturn and Jupiter in Aries that year" meant that war would come: "I judge it will be Universal, and will spread . . . all over Europe, and also in some parts of America." Clough explained that Partridge's almanac indicated "that the dawning of that Sabbath of Rest Promised to the People of God in this world begun in the year 1703 (but so darkly that it cannot be perceived at the first) and will not come to perfect Day until 1778." Clough was not so sure about the timing of the millennial Sabbath rest, but he thought that the war spoken of had happened with the coming of Queen Anne's War. Clough's next yearly almanac opined that the eclipse of April 5, 1707, "foreshews great Contentions, Strifes, and Debates in the World . . . which perhaps may make way for the downfall of Popery, and liberty of the Protestant Religion throughout Europe."[1] In almanacs like

Clough's, the religious culture of New England's early eighteenth century appeared to be thriving, but changing, in a new historical context. Almanacs, like the newspapers, often helped promote themes sympathetic to the Protestant interest, and showed that the new cosmopolitanism and "enlightened" thought about science did not necessarily lead to theological liberalism.

Almanac-makers commanded a unique position in early eighteenth-century print trades and serviced New England's interests in British identity and international Protestantism. Though after 1630 either Cambridge or Boston usually published at least one almanac per year, in the years following the Glorious Revolution almanac publishing became much more competitive, demanding that the almanac-maker keep his finger on the pulse of the market as well as an ear to imperial and scientific news. Almanac-makers usually published nothing else besides their almanacs and usually were not pastors. They assumed roles in the early stages of a British Atlantic public sphere as extra-governmental and extra-clerical brokers of scientific and religious knowledge. The almanac-makers reflected interests in a developing British Protestant identity not only in the calendars themselves but also in their ornamental poetry and often-plagiarized essays on politics, religion, astrology, and astronomy. Because of the almanacs' astrological/meteorological basis, writers like Clough also demonstrated changes happening in popular cosmology, and allow consideration of the popular effects of the British "Enlightenment" and Newtonian science. New England's almanacs provide a look at how developments in national identity, international Protestantism, and popular scientific belief played out in one very widely selling source.

Early eighteenth-century New England almanacs kept to the standard form established by English forerunners and contemporaries: they included a calendar, descriptions of planetary motions, conjunctions, and eclipses, and an "Anatomy" or "zodiacal man" with a basic description of the parts of the body and their relation to the signs of the zodiac.[2] The almanac also usually included an introduction with various editorial comments from the writer and/or printer, and ornamental verses on nature, the weather, the human condition, and the like. Because the almanacs usually came in sixteen-page folios, the printer had four extra pages to fill beyond the calendar, and these pages, particularly at the end, might contain any sort of information such as lists of roads and travel times, church and court meeting times, and weights and measures. Perhaps most interestingly, the almanacs often included brief essays that might predict the future based on astronomical events, interpret recent scientific innovations, particularly in the Newtonian strain, or reflect on religious/cosmological questions.

Some have suggested that the almanacs were essentially "secular" publications, standing out among the great wash of religious writings published particularly in colonial Boston.[3] This was not the case in any useful sense, for the almanacs tied together religious, scientific, and political concerns. While the enormous opportunities brought on by Enlightenment-style thinking may have opened up the possibility of considering politics, religion, and science as discrete categories by 1700, the almanacs and surely most of their readers and hearers did not think of these separately.

The almanacs presumed such religious views as popular millennialism and anti-Catholicism, and in the eighteenth century they increasingly brought those views to the service of British nationalism.[4] Jon Butler has incorporated the almanacs' religious assumptions into his wide-ranging claims about the persistence of heterodox religion and the occult in colonial America. He is correct in the sense that the almanacs rested on a foundation of astrology that lay in sometimes uncomfortable tension with strict reformed Christian doctrine. More commonly, though, the almanacs' astrology joined in unquestioned syncretism with orthodox Christian belief, whose adherents felt much more comfortable with providentialism and the agency of heavenly bodies than most later Christians would. The tension between astrology and biblical Christianity in the almanacs reflected a market and culture that demanded both, to the chagrin of some leading pastors.[5] Even Cotton Mather seems to have been quite conversant with the systems of astrology, as he completed a "spiritual" horoscope in his biography of the Reverend Jonathan Mitchel. The legitimacy of prognosticating according to heavenly signs came under question by pastors and some of the almanacs themselves during this period.[6] In general, however, the almanacs and their writers in New England were clearly committed to Christian orthodoxy, and among the chief purposes of their writings were Christian instruction and reconciling the new science with traditional Christian belief.[7] Like many of the great scientists and astronomers whom they admired, the almanac writers often celebrated the glory of God revealed in the heavens, and were a source of neither secularism nor heterodoxy.

The almanacs also give clues as to how New Englanders perceived their role in the British community. The clearest manifestation of the New England almanacs' "Britishness" was their celebration of the British monarchy, and especially their interest in the monarchy as the world's great bulwark against Catholicism, Jacobitism, and the French/Spanish menace. The almanacs embraced a historical consciousness that centered around the kings and queens of Britain. No doubt some of the adoring poetry and prose may have been motivated by colonists' desire to prove themselves loyal Britons, but more than that the almanacs' writers and publishers attached enormous historical significance to the monarchs and the Protestant succession, and they placed key moments in the monarchs' lives within the great events of Christian history. While the almanacs' borrowed sources are often obscure, some sources like London's John Partridge came from a radical Whig perspective, giving their concept of the British monarchy since 1688 a distinctly providential edge.[8]

The almanacs' calendars tell a good deal about their sense of religious and historical time, and the writers made deliberate decisions about what to include and what not to include. While until later in this period almanacs almost never included such Anglican church holidays as Easter or Christmas, they commonly included significant dates in the life of the current monarch. They also regularly included charts listing the known queens and kings of England as well as chronologies interspersing important dates in the monarchy's history with such events as the birth of Christ and the founding of New England. Finally, some authors either composed or plagiarized ornamental poetry singing the monarch's praises and praying for the defense of true Christianity.[9]

Samuel Clough's 1703 *New-England Almanack*, on the occasion of Anne's succession, included a list of England's monarchs beginning, impressively, with King Egbert, who came to the throne in A.D. 818. After the chart Clough listed this verse:

> Thou great Preserver of all mortal things,
> Who Rules the Hearts of Queens as well as Kings!
> By whom all Kingdoms stand and Princes Reign,
> Preserve Queen ANNE, Now our Dread Sovereign.
> Let treacherous Plots ne'r come to perfect birth,
> And Justice bring the Plotters unto Death.
> Oh! Be thou Her defence, Her safety tender,
> And be thou Hers, as She's true Faith's defender!

Clough saw Queen Anne as God's agent for defending the true faith. He also prayed that suspected Jacobite and French plots to kill Anne and bring back the Stuart Pretender would fail, suggesting Clough's attachments to English Whig politics and ideology. In Clough's understanding, history chiefly recorded the unfolding of God's plan for "those Happy Times promised to the People of God, and . . . the Destruction of their Enemies." Similarly, Nathaniel Whittemore hoped that Anne would be the "true Protestants Great Defender," and admonished readers to be thankful for continued deliverance from "Foreign Enemies" and "Heathen & Pagan Salvages." He also hoped that in God's providential design "the Pope that Man of Sin may [soon] come down wonderfully."[10] If in the classic Puritan mission God intended to use New England to bring about universal reformation, Clough, Whittemore, and other writers seemed more convinced of a British chosenness, led by the monarch.

The Hanoverian succession of 1714 and the failed Jacobite invasion of 1715 represented a high point of tension between the British Protestant interest and their perceived and actual Catholic foes, and for New Englanders these events only heightened their identification with the great struggle between Britain and its enemies for the fate of Christianity. Especially during this period the almanac writer Nathaniel Whittemore and his publisher, Thomas Fleet, began regularly including fulsome praises to the monarchs as successors to the Protestant defenders of the faith. Whittemore's 1717 *An Almanack* included an unusually brief chronology that revealed his strong correlation of British and Christian history: he listed "the Year of our Lord, 1717," the creation of the world (5,666 years previously), Noah's flood, the building of London, "our Deliverance by King William from Popery and Arbitrary Government," and the beginning of King George's reign. Out of only six items listed, the last three were distinctly tied to British history and identity, and the last two represented the grandest victories in securing the Protestant succession.[11]

Whittemore also included some of the most colorful and nearly worshipful praise of the monarchs in the form of yearly verses. For the 1718 edition, Whittemore sang "The Splendid Vertues of King GEORGE":

> He is the Mighty Christian King,
> And Emperour of Europe's Land,
> And a Great Part of America
> He has at his Command.[12]

Similarly, in the 1720 edition, Whittemore's almanac rhymed

> Behold in these our later Days
> there doth appear in Might,
> That Bright & Orient Star King GEORGE,
> whose Rays shine Clear and Light.
> Which makes the British Isles Rejoyce,
> and many Kingdoms more;
> And strikes a Damp to Popish Crews,
> and shakes the Turkish shoar.
> We Pray to GOD to bless King GEORGE,
> and add unto his Days;
> And that God's Church may still Rejoice,
> in their bright splendid Rays.[13]

One can see in Whittemore's verses a conflation of King George and Britain as the leaders in the defense of true Christianity, and a broader identification with God's providential plans for the world church. In "our later Days" George appeared as a semi-messianic king, come not only to lead the reformed church and state of the British Isles but also to serve as an example and leader for "many Kingdoms more." George was king by the intervening hand of God, providing him divine right by Providence. Whittemore's verse indicated a strain in New England's culture that understood the monarchy and Britain's imperial project as intended ultimately to defeat the forces of Antichrist and to liberate the church universal. As Clough's earlier almanacs had done, Whittemore anticipated the downfall of the "Popish Crews," meaning the insidious Jacobites and their French backers, as well as the Muslim Turks. As King George led Britain toward these ends, "God's Church," not only in Britain but also presumably through the known world, would rejoice in the extension of reformed Christianity. It was an eschatological drama in which New Englanders played a part because they were Britons and Christians: in other times and in other rhetorical settings New England had a more special place in redemptive history, but not in the almanacs. In these years of increasing commerce, knowledge, and contact within the Atlantic world and early British empire, the idea of a specially chosen and inwardly focused New English Israel was losing theological utility.

Into the 1730s and '40s, Whittemore led the way among almanac-makers in celebrating the "vertues" of the British monarchy, but many New England almanacs also included occasional verses celebrating Britain and its monarch, or at least they listed the birthday and date of succession for the current monarch. In fact, in almanacs that often included few notable dates or holidays on their calendars, the monarchs' dates appeared with distinct regularity. Almanacs helped create a heightened sense of British national identity by marking days both in the monarch's life and those signifying Britain's deliverance from popery and "arbitrary government."

No other notable day appeared with more regularity on the almanacs' calendars than the Gunpowder Plot, November 5. This date became doubly important in the memory of British Protestantism because it marked the foiling of Guy Fawkes's attempt to blow up Parliament in 1605 as well as King William's invasion in 1688 to oust the Catholic King James II. In New England, where almanac makers and many of their readers felt uncomfortable with any holidays associated with the Anglican church calendar, November 5 seemed a holiday that nearly everyone could enjoy, for it signified crushing defeats for Catholicism. Even such unconventional almanacs as "Poor Robin's" *The Rhode-Island Almanack* regularly included the Gunpowder Plot along with satiric verses and the Anglican calendar. As time wore on and the Gunpowder Plot became a more distant symbol, almanacs maintained its memory in the service of British nationalism, insisting that the "Gunpowder Plot is not forgot."[14]

The Anglican church calendar was a source of tension in the almanacs, and though it is difficult to perceive the writers' specific religious commitments, the evidence suggests that one could stake out a clear theological position by which church holidays one included in the almanacs' calendars. Such positions were subject to change, as demonstrated by John Tulley's early switch from Anglican to more traditional dissenting New England style immediately after the Bostonians ejected the Massachusetts government in 1689.[15] Just as New England saw increasing missionary competition during the early eighteenth century, particularly in such port towns as Boston and Newport, so also the almanacs' decisions about holidays could indicate a preference for "high-flying" Anglicanism or the more traditional Congregational system. Particularly in the Rhode Island almanacs, one also found increasing recognition of the Quakers and Baptists through listings of their meeting places. But it was questions of whether to include church holidays that revealed some of the most significant cultural tensions in New England.

In the early years of the eighteenth century, most almanac-makers were so set against acknowledging the Anglican church holidays that they usually preferred leaving dates like December 25 blank instead of listing the appropriate holiday. Surely everyone knew that the twenty-fifth marked Christ's birth on the Anglican and Roman church calendars, but that was precisely the point: Christmas was considered a popish invention disdained by primitivist New Englanders. As Samuel Sewall once noted in his diary, the Puritans "came hither to avoid anniversary days . . . , such as the 25th of December." But as New Englanders grew more used to the presence of Anglicans, and as more and more of the leading merchants and even church leaders converted to Anglicanism, some almanacs began listing church holidays. However, the Boston/Cambridge–based almanacs rarely embraced the church calendar as a regular listing. Edward Holyoke's brief series in the 1710s rather contentiously insisted on listing Anglican holidays, and Holyoke made it clear that on this and other points he was at odds with his more conservative colleagues. In his diary, Samuel Sewall noted his disapproval of the Anglican bias of Holyoke's almanacs, apparently "blotting" out the church holidays in his copy. Later Holyoke would become president at Harvard, chosen in part because of his moderate but still orthodox views.[16] Nathan Bowen was a longer-lasting exception to the rule of excluding church holidays; he began writing his *New England-Diary* in the 1720s, and from Marblehead he increasingly produced almanacs that listed church holidays, including some saints' days such as Valentine's Day.

The Rhode Island almanacs, including the Franklins' and Samuel Maxwell's, were typically much more comfortable with acknowledging the Anglican calendar, as was Robert Treat's brief series from New London, Connecticut, in the 1720s. Joseph Stafford's *Rhode Island Almanack* also regularly included Anglican holidays, though Stafford's own religious influences appear to have been varied, with family members connected to the Quakers and Baptists. Stafford himself worked as a physician, fortune-teller, and treasure-seeker, implying connections between his astrological interests and the occult.[17] None of the almanacs were as unabashedly Anglican in tone, however, as Benjamin Franklin's and Titan Leeds's, both based in Philadelphia but which were available at least to a limited extent in Boston and the other New England ports. With Boston's reluctance to acknowledge the Anglican calendar, one sees evidence of a continued preference for the English dissenting tradition. By the 1720s, however, the need to separate oneself from Anglicanism seemed to have faded significantly in the increasingly pluralistic ports.

Whatever specific confessional perspective the almanacs came from, however, they almost unanimously defended a broadly orthodox form of Protestantism. The widely popular almanacs carried on the "Protestant vernacular tradition" that supplied a biblical paradigm for understanding everyday life for so many British elites and commoners.[18] This tradition was dynamic, and the almanacs' version of the Protestant vernacular tradition seemed quite earnest in defending Christianity in the face of the possible heretical implications of the new science and discoveries with which the writers tried to remain current. The increasing availability of print and information from Europe, as well as increasing commercial competition in print in the colonies, required the almanac makers to do their best as brokers of scientific learning, popular educators, and apologists for Christianity.

One of the chief issues contested in the almanacs was the possibility of divining future events based on astronomical observation. Early in the period, Samuel Clough in particular tended to make Delphic pronouncements about eclipses foreshadowing great disasters, wars, and the like, but even he admitted that some orthodox teachers disdained such forecasts. Predicting the future based on eclipses and similar events "has not been usual in this Country, and the lawfulness of it doubted by many Divines," he warned in his 1705 edition. However, Clough and others such as John Tulley managed to find chastened means of making predictions. Consider Clough's 1703 essay in which he submitted to orthodoxy while suggesting that astrological prognostications confirm biblical prophecy: "Therefore these things being only Astrological Judgment, 'tis best for every man not to depend too much upon them, but take more heed to that sure word of Prophesie, (as the Apostle Peter says) 2 Pet. 1:19 to which we ought all to take heed . . . for alas! 'tis to be feared, there are terrible troubles and calamities hastening upon the World, and now

already begun, which may be a means to those Happy Times promised to the People of God."[19]

Almanacs eventually tended not to predict the future so much as
they declared the glory of God as revealed in the heavens. In *Tulley's
Farewell* of 1702, the almanac finished with a typical verse:

> When I, pure Heaven, Thy Fabrick see,
> The Moon and Stars, produc'd by thee,
> LORD, What is Man, or his frail Race,
> That Thou shouldst such a Shadow grace?[20]

Despite Tulley's apparent roots in Connecticut sectarianism, and
rumored suspicions about his orthodoxy, in most cases his almanacs
nevertheless supported traditional Christian theology.[21]

Other almanacs discussed the implications of new scientific discoveries and theories, particularly Newtonian ideas, and seemed at
least generally aware that the new discoveries had heretical potential.
The almanacs also revealed a comfort with certain speculations that
later traditional British and American Christians were likely to reject
out of hand.

One such line of speculation was the possibility of extraterrestrial life. For example, Thomas Fleet's 1719 almanac, "to fill up the
vacant Pages," entered an essay (also in Thomas Robie's from 1720)
on Copernican astronomy and its implications. The essay discussed
the heliocentric system and the relative sizes and rotation times of
the planets, "Calculated from the latest Observations by Sir Isaac
Newton's Rules." The essay marveled at the vastness of the uni-
verse, and posited that no one could "suppose that God made all
those Glorious & innumerable Lights purely for such poor Crea-
tures as we to stare & gaze on." The essay predicted that astronomers
would soon find other inhabited "earths" by people with whom God
shared the glory of creation. Nathaniel Ames weighed in similarly in
1735, arguing that the best astronomical observations had proven

such other planets as Jupiter and even the earth's moon inhabitable, so why would God not make people to live there? "What Reason or what Religion obliges us to think that our Earth (so much Inferiour to some of the rest for Magnitude) is the only Planet in the Solar System that is Inhabited?" he wondered.[22] Note that these speculations fit, albeit uncomfortably, into an orthodox understanding of creation, and did not suggest that the inhabitants of other earths might not be human, as post–World War II Westerners have usually imagined concerning extraterrestrials.

Most of the essays on science covered more mundane subjects, but almost all fit into the elite and popular scientific strain that held that God was glorified in creation; there seemed little interest in deistic notions of nature's laws suggesting less involvement by God in sustaining the created order. The almanacs also made little distinction between astrological learning and what modern academics would call "scientific" learning. In his 1721 edition Whittemore included an essay on the characteristics of the heavenly bodies and their significations on earth. For example, he described Venus as "making men fair spoken, pleasant, fair, given to pleasures. . . . But being ill affected, she is effeminate . . . a lover of Maids, lustful, and given to idleness." This list suggested certain conventions about the gendered nature of the passions. Similarly, "Luna maketh Men unconstant, fearful, prodigal, studious of Histories, and given to Navigation & Planting." While this description of the moon making people "studious of Histories" may pique our interest, it remains unclear how Whittemore and the other writers understood the actual effects of the planets and their characteristics.[23]

The almanacs easily combined ideas about redemptive history and science, much in the same manner as did their contemporaries Cotton Mather, Jonathan Edwards, and others. In fact, some of the writers surely knew Mather and respected his work, such as Daniel Travis, whose 1723 edition included an excerpt from Mather's

Christian Philosopher on the weather and planetary motion. Similarly, Whittemore's 1726 edition, following his customary verse to King George in which he prayed that "Christ's Kingdom be inlarg'd throughout the World," discussed the four elements (fire, air, water, earth) and the effects of the fall of man on the balance of the elements. Sin disrupted the perfect balance of the elements, the essay explained, and the longer the time since Adam and Eve were driven out of Eden, the more imbalanced the elements become. "The Earth grows more corrupt since that time by the evil Aspects of the Planets; and by the grievous Sins of men, and so shorten mens Lives."[24]

The leading critic of prognostication among the New England scientists and almanac-makers was Harvard tutor Thomas Robie. Robie's 1719 *Letter to a Certain Gentleman* was a significant departure in the evaluation of cosmic phenomena, as he discussed the natural causes of a recent comet. He contemptuously dismissed prognostication based on its appearance: "As to Prognostications from it, I utterly abhor and detest 'em all, and look upon these to be but the Effect of Ignorance and Fancy." He thought it silly to imagine that any dramatic world events might follow in the wake of a natural event. However, even Robie conceded that "fearful sights in the Heavens" would signal the arrival of the Day of the Lord, and he cited Isaac Watts's poetic description of Judgment Day as a passage that came to mind as he observed the comet.[25] While suspicious of the "science" of prognostication, Robie still held to a traditional view of cosmic disturbances heralding the Day of the Lord. Others in the almanac trade remained more confident about reconciling the new science with old beliefs, including the practice of prognostication.

No other almanac-maker during the later years of the period was so concerned with reconciling scientific discovery and orthodox Protestantism as Nathaniel Ames of Dedham, Massachusetts, who printed his *Astronomical Diary* in both Boston and Portsmouth, New Hampshire. Marion Stowell has suggested that Ames's along with the Franklins' almanacs were deistic, but in Ames's case this characterization is not accurate. Historians have often too eagerly looked for the effects of the Enlightenment in America in the form of theological liberalism, and though one can see the seeds of deism or even an Emersonian pantheism in Ames's almanacs, we should understand Ames in the context of his time. He was by the almanacs' appearances a pious and inquisitive person concerned with demonstrating how new understandings of science should augment God's glory.[26]

Ames often included extensive verses reflecting on creation and its theological and cosmological implications. He returned to the subject again and again, seemingly fascinated by the created order. Ames often scolded his readers for not worshipping God properly for his goodness and majesty. He explicitly rejected the idea of chance in creation and nature, calling the principle "Stupendous Atheistical Nonsense!" in 1731. Despite his regular emphasis on the beauty of creation, Ames did not hesitate to discuss other traditional features of reformed Christianity, including sin, redemption, and the end times. For instance, Ames's 1732 verses revealed him as a moderate Calvinist, rhyming that "GOD's Decree, Don't inconsist with Humane Liberty, We freely have our choice in every way. Yet all the while GOD's firm Decrees obey." In 1735 Ames borrowed from Cotton Mather to make a point about the nature of animals' physiology, and the monthly verses in Ames's 1736 edition were an extended reflection on the apocalypse.[27]

Ames also stood as one of the last writers who remained optimistic about the ability to prognosticate according to astronomical events. By the 1730s this traditional function of almanacs had come under attack from both religious leaders and other almanac writers, most notably Benjamin Franklin. Franklin of course was a master of mockery and satire, and used his talents to make fun of prognosticating almanacs in Poor Robin's and Poor Richard's almanacs.[28]

Meanwhile, Ames remained doggedly confident that prognostication could have a place in almanacs and astrological studies. In fact, Ames took a similar approach to his predecessor Samuel Clough's, and the two sometimes cited the same English authorities on the effects of eclipses in the world. In 1738 Ames wrote, "By what follows I would not have you think that I am a superstitious Bigot to Judicial Astrology. But so far as Astrology is built on the Effects and Influences of the heavenly Bodies on our earthly Bodies . . . so far (I think) Astrology has a rational and phylosophical Foundation." Ames went on to argue that astronomical events had a mathematical correlation to events on the earth, though the correlation may be much easier to perceive in hindsight than with foresight.[29]

As Ames demonstrated, perhaps the most common feature of the early eighteenth-century almanacs was the attempt to reconcile new developments in politics or science with traditional understandings of redemptive history and God's agency in the world. These almanac-makers understood such varied issues as rising British nationalism, fading New England Puritan identity, and new science as progress in the unfolding of God's redemptive history. Scholars from Weber and Durkheim to more recent theorists such as Benedict Anderson and Marcel Gauchet have with varying degrees of eagerness anticipated the detachment of state, society, and science from religion in history, but often much too early. As Gauchet's *The Disenchantment of the World* would have it, sometime "around 1700 . . . specifically Christian history comes to a halt. . . . The enormous shift from a religious organization based on a hierarchically organized overlapping of the visible and the invisible to one based on separation had been essentially completed."[30] Perhaps this "separation" was true for some intellectual elites, particularly on the Continent, but in New England's almanacs, evidence suggesting secularization that separated religion from other social and academic categories did not exist.

Even in our supposed era of postmodernism, historians still often use secularization or some form of it as a master narrative, and most have seen the period after 1700 as a time of significant secularization in elite New England culture, the transition "from Puritan to Yankee."[31] However, a close look at the almanacs suggests that this was in many ways a time of religious change, not decline. Instead of simply losing their cultural identity as Puritans, friends of the international Protestant interest co-opted wide-ranging developments in national identity and science, and placed them in the context of traditional Christian history. If the almanacs comfortably embraced such "modern" developments as nationalism and the new science, then perhaps in this and other cases orthodox Christianity rode the tide of rising modernism instead of being swamped by it.

CHAPTER FOUR

"The Devil and Father Rallee"
Narrating Father Rale's War

Cotton Mather's calendar had just rolled over to January 1, 1723, and with the turn he wrote his friend Robert Wodrow of Scotland concerning frightening though unsurprising news: "The Indians of the East, under the Fascinations of a French Priest, and Instigations of our French Neighbours, have begun a New War upon us."[1] Though they had enjoyed a respite from actual war since the Peace of Utrecht postponed hostilities between the French and British in 1713, New Englanders always knew that it was only a matter of time before the aggressive interests, uncertain borders, and conflicting visions of the religious contest between them and the French Canadians would lead to more bloodshed. Especially uncertain was the status of the "eastern settlements," above Salem and beyond the mouth of the Piscataqua River, where French missions and British settlements came uncomfortably close, and where in times of peace native land holdings became more and more valuable to the colonists. Some New Englanders worried that movement into the northeastern borderlands brought settlers closer to physically and spiritually miscegenated French and Indian Catholics, such as the "half Indianized French" and "half Frenchified Indians" that Cotton Mather described as decimating Salmon Falls in 1690. After 1714, British farmers began again to advance their settlement into the eastern regions, literally putting the borderland Wabanakis in the middle between French and British imperial claims.[2] In 1722, the Wabanakis' lands would erupt again into a conflict to which the combatants would assign very different meanings.

The period after the Treaty of Utrecht, the death of Louis XIV, the failed Jacobite insurrection of 1715, and ultimately the Triple Alliance between Britain, France, and the United Provinces (1716) has usually been seen, rightly, as a time of politically expedient rapprochement between France and Britain that never appeared likely to last. Yet however great the tension remained between France and Britain in the European theater, the tension was even greater between the French and British settlements of North America, and the settlements of Canada and New England in particular. This heightened tension resulted from several factors. First, the colonies had less clear boundaries, political and physical, separating them. In Europe, aggressors would always have to brave the waters of the Channel. In New England and Canada, the frontier was more fluid despite the presence of the White Mountains and other barriers. Also, the Wabanakis injected a volatile element into the economic and military relations between the competing empires. Though decimated by disease and increasingly by rum, the Wabanakis still proved important trading partners and capable fighters, both factors that the French and British wished to have on their side. Finally, the religious sensibilities of the clerical, political, and mercantile leadership made relations with the French take on a tone that could suggest the apocalyptic. In England, the marginalized dissenters viewed the French with a particular hatred, but in New England those same dissenters held sway over much of the trades, churches, and government.[3] Though at the periphery of empire, the leaders of the French Canadian and New English provinces were the worst sort of enemies.

By the 1720s, New Englanders had long experience with Native American warfare and the failure of English missions, leading to a psychological rawness concerning the threat of attack from Jesuit-backed Wabanakis. King Philip's War of 1675–76 was unsurpassed in mortality rates and brutal tactics, and in narrator William Hubbard's words, too awful to "deserve the Name of a War." This war only began a series of conflicts between New England and its Native American neighbors, however. The so-called Second Indian War of the 1680s and '90s heavily influenced the Salem witchcraft crisis, as fears concerning the war with Wabanakis helped turn what might have been a locally contained minor episode into a massive outbreak of accusations and nineteen executions.[4] Moreover, no experience was more frightening for New Englanders than the infamous raid on Deerfield in 1704 in which the Reverend John Williams's family was taken captive, and from which his young daughter Eunice never returned, marrying a Kahnawake man and converting to Catholicism. In 1706, Israel Loring of Sudbury confided in his diary that God's controversy with New England had been expressed in "Characters of blood," as New Englanders were "destroyed by the heathen both in the Eastern and Western parts of the Country."[5] All these and countless other attacks, worries, and rumors helped brew a particular hatred among New Englanders for the Wabanakis and their French Catholic allies.

Leading New Englanders and their metropolitan correspondents still envisioned successful English missions among the Indians of northern New England, however. The commissioners of the New England Company, such as Cotton Mather and Samuel Sewall, entertained a number of schemes and efforts before 1722, all designed to compete with the French Jesuits for the souls of the Wabanakis and others. In a 1692 letter, the New England Company's Robert Thompson of London proposed to the New England commissioners that they should arrange for French Huguenot ministers to "instruct

some ingenious converted Indians in ye French tongue" in order
that Indians who already spoke French might be convinced "of the
deceits of the Popish and nobility of heart Religion." In 1699, William Ashurst likewise proposed to the New Englanders that they
send missionaries out who "may be able to Cope with ye jesuites
who are subtill Enemies & very insinuating & prevailing amongst
simple ignorant People." These grand designs seemed to go nowhere, and in 1703 William Ashurst complained to the Mathers that
he suspected some of the Company's money was being used to pay
English ministers preaching to English congregations.[6]

With these past experiences of violence and failed missions in
mind, in August 1717 Governor Samuel Shute and a diplomatic party
made their way to Arrowsick Island at the mouth of the Kennebec
River, where at the tiny settlement of George Town they met with
representatives of the Wabanakis, including, most significantly, dele-
gates from Norridgewock, where the French had maintained a successful Jesuit mission for more than fifty years.[7] Shute wanted to
convince the assembled Indians that King George was the authority
over them now, not the young French King Louis XV. With trans-
lated and liberally interpreted dialogues as the chief records of such
meetings one can hardly be certain of how things went, but if nothing else Shute's nervous condescension comes through clearly.

In the negotiations the British demanded deference and the
proper use of symbols to indicate good faith and a submissive spirit,
all of which the Indians practiced haltingly. Shute ordered that before the Indians come to meet they fly a "British Flagg" in their
"headmost Canoo." In his speech he told the Indians that he had
come to introduce them to their new king, George I, the great defender of British liberty and the Protestant interest, and that they
should remember that "they are KING GEORGE's Subjects, under His
Allegiance and Protection, and they must by no means hearken to
any contrary Insinuations, that they will always find themselves saf-

est under the Government of Great Britain." He needed not specify who might insinuate otherwise. Shute told them that since "KING GEORGE, and the British Nation" were "Christians of the Reformed Protestant Religion" they would for the Indians' benefit send among them a proper missionary (not like the deceitful Jesuits), and he asked that this missionary be treated with gratefulness and respect.[8]

The Wabanakis were not quite as deferential to the governor as he had hoped. When the conference resumed the next day, the spokesmen for the assembled bands said they were pleased to have such a high representative of the great king with them, but that they would obey "KING GEORGE" only "if we like the Offers made us." Shute said that they had the order wrong: their obedience would be rewarded with "just Offers." The Indians would not concede on land or religion, however, insisting that the British not encroach on their land, and perhaps more ominously, telling Shute that as far as his missionary, "GOD has given us Teaching already, and if we should go from that, we should displease GOD." The Jesuits had their hold among them, as the New Englanders had suspected. On the second night of the conference the Indians, "in a hasty abrupt manner," left behind their British flag. That night the Indians sent over a letter brought to the Jesuit mission from Quebec's governor, the Marquis de Vaudreuil, who said that Louis XV had instructed him that the French had not given any Indian lands away to the British and that if necessary the French would defend Indian land rights. The letter came by way of "their Jesuit," Sebastien Rale.[9]

Sebastien Rale was reared in the Counter-Reformation zeal of French Catholicism that sent Jesuits and other missionaries on journeys across the known and unknown world. He came to North America in 1689, and after several brief stints among various tribes he settled at Norridgewock on the Kennebec River. Zealous and hardly averse to controversy with French or English authorities, Rale found himself at one of the most hotly disputed grounds of the early imperial contests. Rale exhibited an unusually high personal sympathy toward Wabanaki culture, as he memorably wrote to his brother that after many years among them "I assure you that I see, that I hear, that I speak, only as a savage." For Rale, the conversion process seems to have been at least culturally mutual.[10]

Although it is not clear to what extent Rale's influence catalyzed the Wabanakis' resistance against the British, there is no question that Rale viewed the contest as a matter of British incursions against Wabanaki land rights, and also as a matter of religious principle. As Rale noted in a 1720 letter widely circulated among the British authorities (Samuel Sewall would call this "Friar Ralle's railing Letter"), "The English say it's the Fryer or Mr. Vaudreuil that stirs up war, but . . . 'tis you English, you seize our Lands against our will and thereby take away our prayers, more valuable to us than our Lands or bodies . . . Shall they be Cheated, driven from their Lands & prayers, & shall not I counsel & defend them? They shall sooner take away my Life than hinder me." By July 1720 the Massachusetts government had become sufficiently alarmed by Rale to put a one-hundred-pound bounty out for his apprehension.[11]

Seeming to relish the role of advocate for the Wabanakis' rights, Rale became an irritant and then a major threat to New England's security, and the perfect image of evil: a conniving and deceitful French Jesuit inciting the Indians to resist British encroachments and eventually rise up and attack British settlements. As the superior-general of the Jesuits in New France later reported, Rale eventually became "very odious to the English." The British had long entertained images of the evil French Catholic "other," and New Englanders had regularly heard about the lies and agitations of the Jesuits among the Indians of New France, most notably in Cotton Mather's relation of Bomaseen's "confession" in 1699. Bomaseen was a captured Indian chieftain who reportedly told a minister in Boston in 1692 that "The French taught 'em, That the Lord JESUS CHRIST, was of the French Nation; That His Mother, the Virgin Mary, was a French Lady; That they were the English who had Murdered him; and, That . . . all that would Recommend themselves unto his Favour, must Revenge His Quarrel upon the English, as far as they can."[12]

French Jesuits had previously been imagined primarily through secondhand accounts and rumors, but now the evil other had been made flesh in the form of Sebastien Rale. The conflict that Rale fomented manifested in political terms "the theological myth of the war between good and evil," as David Shields has put it, and this "war between civility and barbarism" represented by the British and the French/Indians respectively "preserved the theological interdiction of 'the other.'"[13] The symbolic power of Rale in many New Englanders' minds therefore should not be underestimated. While peace lasted in Europe for twenty-three years after the Triple Alliance, in New England the French threat was exacerbated and finally shifted to the hot war that New Englanders imagined was born out of the literally hellish mixing of Jesuit lies and Wabanaki savagery.

Governor Shute eventually elicited signatures to an agreement of submission, but the George Town treaty solved little in the ongoing tensions between the British, the French, and the Indian gobetweens. Shute and the commissioners of the New England Company did leave a missionary, Joseph Baxter of Medfield, among the Wabanakis, but Baxter quickly realized that Sebastien Rale's sharp intellect and the Wabanakis' resistance would make his job nearly impossible. He proved easy pickings for the learned veteran Rale, who wrote to Baxter in Latin a hundred-page defense of Catholicism to which Baxter was hardly prepared to reply.[14] The difficulties of missionizing the Wabanakis, especially in light of Rale's winsome appeal to them, served only to increase the growing sense of desperation to do something about these eastern Indians and their Jesuit backers.

Also heightening the tensions was the sense that the French meant to encircle and destroy the English colonies. Among the sources reflecting this fear was a pamphlet published in London called *Some Considerations on the Consequences of the French Settling Colonies on the Mississippi,* written by an anonymous author, likely a New Englander, perhaps in summer 1718.[15] The pamphlet expressed hope that the political situation in France had improved with the death of Louis XIV, but cautioned that French plans to develop the North American backcountry with "their most vigorous Efforts for establishing Commerce, and planting Colonies in this promising Country" should give the British settlements and governments grave concern. This author was certainly more interested in trade and land issues than religion (since we do not know his identity we cannot connect this with his religious persuasion), but he knew that part of the French effort toward commercial hegemony in the backcountry was converting the Indians.

Some Considerations made it clear that French peacetime expansion was going forward, and France's ties to the Indians were becoming ever stronger. Britain, and New England specifically, had to respond in kind. The pamphlet argued that the British should focus particularly on the fortification of Nova Scotia in order "to make Head against the French." Otherwise, from "Canada to Louisiana" the French would surround the British colonies with their own colonists and allied Indians, forming a backcountry noose ready to hang the defenseless Britons. Besides the enticements of trade, the author suspected that the French controlled the Indian populations through miscegenation and conversion. The French territory was burgeoning with a "prodigious Increase . . . chiefly ascribed to their inter-marrying with the Indians, whom by this means they firmly engage in their Interest." As for the Jesuits, in "every Tribe there are some Missionary Priests, and tho' few or none of the Savages have ever been made thorough Converts to the Truths of the Christian

Religion, yet in all other Matters they look upon these good Fathers as Teutelar Gods, and give themselves up entirely to be directed by their Councils." This was the worst case imaginable: the Jesuits controlled the Indians for French purposes but gave them no saving religion. It was no wonder that the French used the Jesuits to control the backcountry Indians, this author concluded: "he ought to be a cunning Man that treats with the Indians, and therefore the French leave that Business to the Jesuits."[16]

The New England Company commissioners worried about the threat posed by the French as well. The company's governor, Robert Ashurst, wrote from London to Samuel Sewall in 1720 that the English Protestant missions would of course save Indians' souls, but just as importantly they would help buffer the French threat. Perhaps he had read *Some Considerations,* as he noted that "the French by their former and late Settlements" have "quite Surrounded all our Colonys." Though the French and British were at peace, Ashurst knew that any "Incidents" could bring them to war again. Thus, "the gaining of those Easterne Indians to our side may afford us good Security against the attempts of the French."[17]

Ashurst also made a remarkable request of the New England commissioners: in order to win over the Wabanakis, the Massachusetts government should strive to respect the Indians' land rights. In several frank and insistent letters, Ashurst stated that much of the trouble between the two sides was caused by English disrespect for the Wabanakis' lands and that the commissioners should lobby the government to secure clearer borders between the two sides. The Londoners desired that "some measures maybe taken to remove the Jealousys of those poor people, which we believe are really owing to the Incroachments the English made upon their Lands." Ashurst urged the New England commissioners to persuade the government to settle boundaries and stop all encroachments so that the missions could go forward without unnecessary obstacles. Again in 1722

Ashurst wrote to Samuel Sewall that the encroachments could cause "Revolts, and enmity to our Religion," and that if the government could be convinced to stop the abuses then it would contribute to the Indians' "conversion from Heathenisme and Popery to a pure Religion." Finally, Ashurst insisted to Sewall that the Indians "cannot thinke those Persons in earnest to Direct them to heaven, who take away that Portion of Earth that by the Law of Nature & Common Justice belongs to them."[18]

Samuel Sewall made an honest but futile attempt to fulfill Ashurst's wishes by writing *A Memorial Relating to the Kennebeck Indians* in 1721. In this pamphlet, he wondered whether the government had done all it could to stop the war, and noted that the Wabanakis had requested but not received fixed boundaries between their lands and the British line of settlement. Sewall reminded Shute's government that the charter obligated Massachusetts to do what it could to "Recover the Aboriginal Natives from their Heathenisme, and Antichristianisme." He thought the war would be costly and unprofitable, and believed that it would make better sense to "perswade the Kennebeck Indians to be our Dependents and Friends." Sewall attached a letter from Northampton's Solomon Stoddard that speculated that New England was provoking God by threatening war against the Wabanakis instead of evangelizing them.[19] Few among New England's leaders besides Sewall and Stoddard, however, even among the New England Company commissioners, took Ashurst's requests seriously. Ashurst would die in 1726, by which point the question of respecting land rights was moot, and the New England Company's work among the Wabanakis was in disarray.

At George Town in November 1720, agents of the Massachusetts government again conferred with the eastern Indians, attempting to convince them that the Jesuits were wrong to question British land claims in Maine. New England's commissioners pleaded with the

Indians not to listen to "Ralle": "we must further Observe to you how wickedly the Jesuit has Imposed on you," especially given the peace between France and Britain. They insisted that Rale was full of "falsness and Deceit," and they warned that aggressive cooperation with the French would only lead to their "utter Ruin and Destruction." Ominously, the Wabanakis "made no Reply."[20]

By 1721 these suspected threats by the French and their Jesuit-influenced tribes became terrifyingly real to the New Englanders of the eastern settlements. In August, Governor Shute warned the General Court and New Englanders that "the Indians to the number of 200 have marched in a hostile manner under French Colours, accompanied by two Jesuits into the town of Arrowsick . . . and afterwards delivered an insolent and menacing Letter directed to me your Governour." According to Shute, it was time to prepare for war.[21]

By March of the next year Shute was warning the colony against "Monsieur Rallee, the French Jesuit" specifically. Shute reported that a detachment of New Englanders stationed in the eastern settlements had been sent to capture the Jesuit, but that Rale had escaped, leaving behind incriminating letters that made plain that Rale, as the agent of the French Canadian government, was inciting the Indians "against His Majesty's Liege Subjects," promising the Indians ammunition enough to "drive the English from their just Settlements."[22] This confirmed what the Massachusetts' leadership and the eastern settlers believed all along, that the French Canadian government and ultimately the French crown was using Jesuit deceptions to co-opt the Wabanakis into murdering Englishmen, capturing their families, and burning their towns, all part of a hellish plot to annihilate their religious and mercantile liberties.

Shute had his own troubles with the Massachusetts General Court concerning his power to act against Rale, part of a general contest common to the period between governor and assembly's powers. After the failed attempt to seize Rale, the Wabanakis

responded with revenge raids on Brunswick and other British settlements, and in July 1722 Shute declared war against the eastern Indians, proclaiming them, "with their confederates, to be robbers,
traitors, and enemies to his Majesty King George." The assembly did
not seem opposed to prosecuting the war against Rale and the Indians; they just wanted to control the purse strings to finance the
campaign. Shute, in a remarkable display of the unpredictability of
British imperial agents, became furious with the assembly's intransigence, and in January 1723 he boarded a merchant ship for London
and left New England, apparently without notifying anyone but
personal servants.[23] With this, Lieutenant-Governor William Dummer took over the management of the conflict that in British memory would become known as Dummer's War.

While Shute's efforts at prosecuting the war had almost ground
to a halt because of arguments with the assembly, Dummer enjoyed
more success both because of his political tact and because as fac-
tions in the government squabbled over power, Indian attacks pro-
ceeded apace. Most notably, at the easternmost British settlement at
St. George River, Penobscots under the guidance of the French Jesuit
Father Étienne (Stephen) Lauverjat made several raids and in winter
1723 laid siege to the garrison there. For their part, New Englanders
also made raids against Lauverjat and the Penobscots, burning the
village of Panawamske and the mission chapel there in February.[24]
The Jesuits and the Indians proved elusive, though, and through 1724
New Englanders seemed to be able only to destroy their property,
instead of taking their lives.

With New England's worries about a Jesuit/Indian alliance in
war having come true, the pastors quickly constructed this as a
godly, noble war, a narrative that the Wabanakis had no printed
means to counter. Benjamin Colman, like Mather, thought to send a
report to his Scottish Presbyterian correspondent Robert Wodrow,
the author of *The History of the Sufferings of the Church of Scotland*,

and someone well familiar with the travails of the Protestant interest. Similar to the Halle Pietists and Samuel Hartlib, Wodrow had worked to cultivate an international network of Protestant correspondents, which included the leading New Englanders.[25] Colman wrote to him that the war was a great burden on New Englanders: "We need your prayers. . . . These Salvages are also papists, and entirely frenchifyed." Likewise, Cotton Mather wrote to another English correspondent, couching the war in terms of the French Catholic and Jacobite threat to Britons generally: "A French priest, with Countenance from the Governor of Canada, has instigated our Eastern Indians, to begin a war upon us; animated with an Expectation, that France and the pretender were bringing things to pass, that would allow all Canada, openly to back them."[26] Colman, Mather, and others helped narrate and publicize the war as a new episode in the European and North American battle between Catholicism and Protestantism, news of which had filled the Boston presses for years.

For his Boston audience, Benjamin Wadsworth of the First Church gave what would become the dominant narrative of the war when he preached *True Piety the Best Policy for Times of War* in August 1722. It was normal to expect that God's enemies will sometimes come to attack God's people, Wadsworth argued, and in those times "when GOD's People are assaulted, molested, threatened with ruin by their enemies; they're oblig'd to stand on their own defence, and to indeavour the conquering of those, who unjustly strive to conquer and destroy them." But Wadsworth was equivocal, for he also hinted that New England's sin may have brought this attack from the north. "We are a professing but a very degenerate People, GOD is angry with us." God had sent smallpox the previous year, "yet we're not at all Reform'd by it." Increasingly pressing the New Englanders, God had sent a drought, increased the activity of pirates, and now war had come. Wadsworth used the threat of defeat as a rallying point for holiness, and he insisted that if New England would trust in God for victory it would surely come, for "GOD never fails those, who sincerely Pray to Him and Trust in Him." If this was a jeremiad in the classic sense, then it struck a rather optimistic chord: it was a relatively simple matter for New Englanders to win the war, they needed only to trust in God, stay away from provoking sins, and God would destroy their wicked enemies. Especially in the face of Catholic and heathen oppressors, many New Englanders remained concerned but confident that God would intervene on their behalf.[27]

Other pastors had sterner warnings for New Englanders, though, that they might possibly lose to their Catholic and heathen foes. Thomas Foxcroft warned that this latest episode might reflect a hardening of God's judgment against the "incorrigible" people of New England. This "day of Battel & War, wherein we are frequently made to bleed by the Sword of the Wilderness" was the latest in a series of severe physical judgments. But Foxcroft was more concerned, as New England's leaders seemed increasingly to discuss, that "the too sensible Withdraw of the Spirit of GOD from among us, affords the most awful Symptom, that GOD is setting his face against us."[28]

Solomon Stoddard emerged to issue the sternest indictment of all, however, and traced New England's judgment to failures in evangelism. His relatively well-known *Question Whether* GOD *is not Angry* (1723) is best understood in the context of Father Rale's War (Stoddard was also responding to Grey Lock's War, a separate but closely related conflict between western Wabanakis and English settlers north of Stoddard's Northampton beginning in 1723, though Stoddard made no distinction between the two conflicts). Stoddard argued that ever since the Jews rejected the gospel, it had become incumbent upon the people of God to preach the gospel to the Gentiles, many of whom like New England's natives waited in darkness for the light of God's truth. Everyone knows, even in England, that "we have little care of the Heathen," and God in judgment has sent "Epidemical Diseases and Devourers." Not only have the Indians remained ungospellized, but "God has made them a terrible scourge to us, in Philips War and since that by their joyning with the French; and in this present War." Because New England would not obey God and bring the gospel to them, New England's natives became "instruments to punish us."[29]

The charters of Massachusetts and Connecticut had expressly intended to evangelize the colonies' Indians, "but we have done very little to Answer our Profession." Stoddard, lamenting that their English brethren knew all about their neglect of the gospel, held up an international model to shame his readers further. "There is at this day a great deal done in the East-Indies, by the Germans and Danes for the Propagation of the Gospel. Worthy Men are sent over; many are brought to the Profession of the Faith; the Bible is Printed in their own Language; great Contributions are sent over to advance that Work; and the Name of Christ is renowned among them; and the People that have been in Darkness have seen great Light. And it is a matter of Shame, that when others are carrying the Gospel many thousands of Miles, from their own Country; We suffer them that dwell among us, and that are Borderers to us; to lie in Darkness, and Afford them very littile Help for their Deliverance."[30]

Stoddard saw great advances in world evangelization happening through the agency of the Halle Pietists, and in light of their work New England looked sinfully complacent.[31] Making them look even worse, however, was the example of the Catholics. Consider Stoddard's pan-American perspective on the state of religion: "The Spaniards, have done a great deal to bring the Indians in Peru and Mexico to their Religion: And the Portuguese to bring the Indians in Brazil, and the Indies, to theirs. And the French, are diligent in Canada, and elsewhere, to gospellize them." New Englanders, who have access to the "true Religion" and yet with few exceptions will not share it even with their heathen neighbors, should be ashamed in light of the Catholic works.

If only New England's Christians would share the truth with the Indians, then the Indians would certainly become less hostile to New England's settlements. But if they remain complacent, Stoddard warned, some believe that "the Christians in America will Indianize and become that Gog and Magog spoken of, Rev. 20."[32] What a terrible irony if New England was to become so apostate that they became like the Indians instead of the Indians becoming like them. This fear seems to have had a subtle currency among New Englanders who cringed at settlers founding towns with no established churches too close to the Indians. Such developments might lead in the end to a special place in eschatology for New England, but shockingly as Satan's Gog and Magog instead of as the New Jerusalem.

If only New Englanders would obey the command to evangelize, the provinces would be far better off in temporal affairs, Stoddard predicted. "If they continue Heathens they will be apt to fall in with the Papists; if they continue Heathens they will carry it Provokingly . . . But if they be brought to Religion, then there will be Hopes of a Durable Peace." In a bleak close to the tract, Stoddard proposed that converting the Indians would be "much better, than to Destroy them." Some, Stoddard conceded, wanted nothing more than to annihilate the native populations. "These men shew a Bloody Spirit: 'Tis much better to convert them," Stoddard offered.[33] Some might wonder at the magnanimity of even Stoddard's proposal, but the question was really moot: with few exceptions the record of New England since King Philip's War was meager in benevolence and brutal in violence, especially once the conditions of international war, both hot and cold, placed many of the Wabanakis in league with the Britons' inveterate enemies.

Regardless of Stoddard's reservations, by summer 1724 the colonies had become sufficiently alarmed to try to bring the war to a bloody end. Reports of Indian aggressions became more numerous: in August 1723 the Reverend Joseph Willard, a Yale alumnus, was killed near Rutland, and in April 1724 the Indians' "greatest stroke" came when they managed to ambush the patrolling company led by Captain Josiah Winslow, a promising recent Harvard graduate. Winslow was killed along with many of his company, including a number of "friend" Indians. Reverend Ebenezer Parkman of Westborough, Massachusetts, recorded personal discussions of Winslow's death more than two years later, and in the 1740s John Adams of Newport and Mather Byles of Boston would both publish poems devoted to Winslow.[34] An increasing number of reports were coming from the eastern settlements of attacks on church members and elders, women, and children, some of whom were carried to Canada. With frightening news coming in weekly from the frontier, Dummer secured support from the Assembly to cut off the serpent's head, as they saw it.

In August, an expedition was commissioned to go the heart of Rale's mission, destroy the town of Norridgewock, and hopefully kill the Jesuit, which would likely end the war.[35] A group of two hundred eight men sailed in whaleboats up the coast of Maine, got off at Teuconick (Taconic Falls), and marched toward Norridgewock. On August 12 they entered Norridgewock, and from the beginning the fight was a rout: the colonists killed and drove out scores of Indian men, women, and children, while the poorly trained and overmatched Indians apparently killed none of the British. Norridgewock and French memory had Rale dying submissively under a large crucifix, while the British reported that upon returning to the village they found "Monsieur Ralle the Jesuit, their chief Commander," in one of the houses firing on them. The soldiers reported that they burst in and discovered Rale loading his gun to fire again. Rale supposedly declared that "he would give no quarter, nor take any," upon which one of the lieutenants shot Rale through the head. The soldiers plundered the village, destroyed the icons and sacred vessels of the mission, scalped Rale and the dead Indian men, and marched back to Teuconick. After noting his execution, the *Boston News-Letter*'s *nota bene* remarked in its report, "Ralle the Jesuit, has generally appeared at the Head of the Indians in their Rebellions and was the Chief Fondater of this War."[36] Ebenezer Parkman recorded the good news in his diary: the Massachusetts troops had "slain 5 or 6 score Indians at Norridgewock with Sebastian Ralle the Old Jesuit and brought in his and 26 or 27 Scalps besides. . . . Capt. Harmon (it is storied) found an Iron Chest with the Jesuit which had many Letters in it, Some from Gentlemen at Boston (O Horrids) Betraying our Country." Parkman had apparently heard rumors of letters revealing that some Bostonians had collaborated with the Jesuits—the ultimate treachery. Hugh Adams, pastor at Durham, New Hampshire, rejoiced that God had brought final judgment on Rale, a "man appointed to utter destruction" who had "so subjugated The Savages (as he named them) under his Arbitrary Power as to influence them into all their so barbarous Hostilities."[37]

Cotton Mather, for his part, provided this reading of the war and Rale's death: "The Barbarous and Perfidous Indians in our Eastern Country, being Moved by the Instigation of the Devil and Father Rallee; have begun Hostilities upon us. They did it, when the French Hopes of a Fatal Revolution on the British Empire, deceived them. And it was not long before the Hairy Scalp of that Head in the House of the Wicked, paid for what Hand he had in the Rebellion, into which he Infuriated his Proselytes." In Mather's mind, there was no doubt that the French Jesuit and Satan were in league against New England. For his dalliance with the devil and the Indians, Rale was not only killed but his "hairy scalp" taken, finalizing his descent into savagery and degradation in many New Englanders' imaginations. Mather also traced Rale's plot to Jacobite threats, including the Atterbury plot, "discovered" in England in 1722, that would have supposedly murdered King George and his family.[38] Mather viewed both the Jacobite threat to return the exiled Stuart kings to the throne, and the present war with the Wabanakis, as motivated by a general French conspiracy against the British empire, the bulwark of the Protestant interest.

The presumed connections between the French Catholic, Jacobite, and Wabanaki threats made sense to those remembering New England's recent past and reading the newspapers. For readers of the *Boston Gazette,* it could be no coincidence that the same issue that reported Rale's death also reported that the Jesuits seemed to be taking over the court of France, and that the Jesuits were summarily executing French Protestant preachers, sending Protestant men to the galleys, jailing women and shaving their heads, and taking Protestant children from their families and giving them a Roman Catholic upbringing and education.[39] Such stories were nothing new. From news of the revocation of the Edict of Nantes in 1685 to reports of the massacre of Polish Protestants at Thorn in 1725, newspapers' and sermons' constant refrain of Catholic persecution of Protestants in Europe warned New Englanders that they could be next, should they fail to be vigilant and pious.

French authorities saw matters differently, and for about a year after Rale's death the French and their Wabanaki allies remained motivated to seek revenge for Rale, whom they saw as a political and religious martyr. Governor Vaudreuil wrote an inflammatory letter to Dummer soon after Rale's death. He assumed that Dummer would have to answer to George I for "the late Murther Committed by your order on the person of that french Missionary whose head I know you set a price on." Rale had not been a political agent of the French, Vaudreuil insisted, but had only done his religious duty, and the Norridgewocks among whom he ministered had a sincere commitment to the "Catholick Religion." Vaudreuil did not completely rule out a moderated peace (assuming, of course, that it could only be moderated by him), but he chastised Dummer, saying that "you must blame no Body but your selves for all the Violence and Hostilities those Indians have Committed against your Nation." These Indians are truly Catholic and true friends of the French, Vaudreuil insisted, and therefore when the English invaded their lands and tried to steal their allegiance, it was no wonder that they violently resisted. Likewise, Vaudreuil warned, it will be no wonder if they respond with violence to the "last Cruelty and unjust Attempts Committed of late against them and their Missionary."[40]

Regardless of the French desire to gain vengeance for Rale, the war slowed during late 1724 and through 1725, becoming more focused on periodic raids and the ventures of New England's bounty hunters. New Englanders were tired of the war but also seemed to agree with Cotton Mather, who again reported to Wodrow that Rale's "wretched Scalp" had paid for his stirring up the "Eastern Indian proselytes," and that now "we are in a hopeful way of utterly destroying them." Toward this end, Dunstable's John Lovewell raised up parties of border-dwelling men to range about northern New England seeking to exterminate as many Wabanakis as possible, with the promise of government bounties according to how many scalps they could bring home. New England's prosecution of the war had sunk to a grisly low.[41]

In May 1725 Lovewell and his party went deep into the borderlands, toward Lake Winnepesaukee (in present-day central New Hampshire), seeking to take more Indian scalps and to push Wabanaki settlements as far back toward the White Mountains as possible. There Lovewell and many of his men would lose their lives in the immediately celebrated "Fight at Piggwacket" on the Saco River, after which Lovewell would be immortalized as a martyr to the Protestant cause. When Lovewell and his party came upon a lone Indian shooting ducks, they advanced but were met by another Indian, whom they swiftly killed. Their chaplain, Jonathan Frye, reportedly peeled off the man's scalp.[42] Suddenly the company was overwhelmed by a heated Indian attack, and Lovewell, Frye, and many others were mortally wounded. The bounty hunters limped back south with only one-third of their men left alive.

Lovewell and his men fit well into the growing literature on Christian adventurer-heroes coming out of the Boston presses. Samuel Penhallow argued that the Lovewell expedition showed that "though our actions . . . can bear no comparison with those of our British forces (which have caused the world to wonder) yet not to mention the bravery of these worthies, who died in the bed of honor, and for the interest of their country, would be a denying them the honor that is due unto their memory." Perhaps these were not as great as the British forces at Blenheim (which Penhallow surely had in mind), but these provincials were due an honored memory.[43]

Thomas Symmes, pastor at Bradford, agreed and immediately delivered the sermon "Historical Memoirs of the Late Fight at Piggwacket," and sent it off to Boston for publication. Symmes argued that just as it was appropriate for Israel to memorialize Joshua's defeat of the Amalekites and the "Aborigines of Canaan," so New England rightly should remember Lovewell's men. Symmes recounted the battles and Lovewell's death, and then reflected in his sermon on II Samuel 1:27, part of David's funeral poem for Saul and Jonathan. Symmes said that David's poem was not effete or overly passionate, but instead was "sufficiently Brave and Manly," fit to commemorate the masculine and pious man of God dead in battle. The sermon warned not to take Lovewell's death as a punishment specifically against the men, for "the most Skilful, Dextrous, Couragious and Successful Soldiers, had need be truly Religious and well prepared for Death; seeing they'r not Invulnerable, but as liable to Die as others." True religion does not teach that death in a holy war will bring heavenly rewards, in contrast to "the wretched Jesuites or Friers," who promise "their deluded Proselytes, the barbarous Indians" that they will bypass Purgatory and go straight to heaven if they die in battle. However, Symmes did speculate that God's providence intervened both to raise the men up and to strike them down. "They were Men form'd and rais'd up by Providence to serve us in pursuing an Enemy," and yet, "the Hand of the LORD appears in all this, that so many brave Men should descend into Battle and perish."[44]

What could Symmes say to explain the death of these "magnanimous Soldiers," these ones who had supposedly gone out as the Israelites against the Amalekites? At this difficult point Symmes retreated to the harshest kind of jeremiad, asking whether New England's sins had not actually killed the brave Lovewell? The pastors had repeatedly asked the people of New England to reform their ways, to "Repent and do our first Works!" But the people had not listened, and now "by the sore Judgment of War, and particularly by the Fall of our Brethren we are now weeping over, GOD is loudly calling upon us to amend our Ways." Symmes therefore attributed this particular failure to the sins, not of Lovewell and his men, nor of the pastors, but of the "people" generally. But he did not despair, and sounded the typical optimistic note, because in the end God could do no other than destroy his enemies on the borders: "Let us return to the Almighty and he will build us up. He will soon subdue our Enemies, and give us Peace in our Borders. . . . Is the brave Lovewell and other brave Men dead! Who made them what they were? . . . It was the Lord of Hosts, who . . . can easily raise up others."[45]

In the end it seemed that the death of Rale and the fatigue of the Wabanakis led to the war's end. With Rale's death, the apparent leader of the French/Wabanaki menace was gone, and despite the patriotic value of Lovewell's martyrdom, the British soon lost interest in taking more Indian scalps, particularly if it meant searching deep in the New Hampshire and Maine borderlands for the enemy. In November 1725 representatives from the leading tribes met with Massachusetts officials to put a rather anticlimactic end to the conflict. The proposed treaty had a hollow ring of expedience and fatigue. The tribal representatives agreed to submit to British rule, especially agreeing to maintain "a firm and constant amity and friendship with all the English, and will never confederate or combine with any other nation to their prejudice." Samuel Penhallow, for one, hoped that the Indians would not rise up again, but he sounded the familiar refrain that the British would do well to bring more Indians into their sphere of trade, and to try once again to bring the true gospel to them. "If trading houses, which are now resolved on . . . be well regulated, it may (under God) be a means of our tranquility; especially if the government can also prevail with them to receive the ministry for their instruction in the principles of the true religion."[46]

With Rale dead and hot war stopped again at least for the time being, New Englanders turned their attention to other issues: orderly serial town settlement, expansion of trade and debates over mediums of exchange, contests over power between the governor and assembly, and occasional fights over episodes like natural disasters and epidemics. Surprisingly, the Wabanakis managed to maintain much of their territory and population numbers in Maine despite the historiographical convention that Father Rale's War led them to relocate permanently. New England's silent acceptance of the Wabanakis' continuing presence again suggests the catalytic role played by Rale's image in exciting British hostilities.[47] Whatever the case, in the responses to Rale's War one can see that many New Englanders were deeply concerned with their place in the contests of empire and the worldwide battle for the fate of Christianity. For years, New Englanders had heard with deep concern and fascination about the threatened existence of Protestant groups in France, the Palatinate, and even in England with the 1715 uprising and the continuing Catholic threats from within and without. Now, at the hands of Rale and his legions of sympathetic Indians, world war had, once again, come to New England's provinces. The ministers, officials, and settlers who responded to the war found it terrifying, and yet unsurprising.

Seen from the perspective of an observer troubled by the exploitation of the Wabanakis and their land claims, one might easily and accurately describe this war as the result of unfair acquisitions by British settlers. Likewise, James Axtell has lamented that Rale died because "France and England subordinated religion to politics in their struggle for continental hegemony." But the New Englanders imagined and wrote it differently—they believed that Rale died because of religion, politics, and more. New England's narrators of the war believed that dark forces inspired by the French empire and the Roman Catholic church were gathered in the borderlands, and radical commitment to holiness and the Protestant cause seemed the only hope for New England to fend off its would-be destroyers. Building a noble Christian identity set against the savage Wabanakis and Antichristian French helped these Britons in the borderlands of the North American contest for empire to set clear boundaries; a cultural, political, and, in this case, religious project that some have called the essence of negotiating a frontier life.[48]

CHAPTER FIVE

"The Madness of the Jacobite Party"
Imagining a High-Church Jacobite Threat

Marblehead's George Pigot was concerned for his parishioners. Anglican congregations had enjoyed official toleration in New England since the coming of King's Chapel to Boston in 1686, but many in New England's clerical establishment still viewed Anglicans with a jaundiced eye, and would continue to do so for many years. So it came as no surprise to Pigot in December 1729 that some of his congregants were being harassed in the streets concerning that supposedly popish festival Christmas. "What is become of your Christmas Day now; for Mr. Barnard has proved it to be Nothing else but Heathenish Rioting?" yelled one. Another jeered, "Will you never have done with your Popish Ceremonies, that you must have Four or Five Days running, to observe, what Mr. Barnard has made out to be no such Thing as you pretend?" "Mr. Barnard" was John Barnard, influential Congregational pastor of Marblehead, who on December 25, 1729, preached a sermon both reminding his flock not to celebrate Christmas, and also reminding them of their identity: they stood against the wolves in sheep's clothing, those British Protestants who secretly cherished popery.[1] In this episode and in countless others, New England's Protestant interest demonstrated that its most dangerous imagined adversary was perhaps not even French

Catholicism, but instead Catholicism's secret friends among Church of England men.

These foes were commonly accused of popery, or even worse, Jacobitism, in countless pamphlets, letters, and journal entries in the literature of the post–Glorious Revolution period. "Jacobitism," or the persuasion that the Catholic Stuart line should rightfully return to the throne of Britain, became as slanderous and slippery a term as "Arminian" in provincial New England. Much as New Englanders used the French, natives, Spanish, and other groups as foils against which they could define themselves, opposition to British popery and/or Jacobitism became an essential building block for their cultural identity.[2]

When studying Jacobitism in New England, however, a major conceptual problem immediately presents itself: there seemed through the first half of the eighteenth century to be essentially no Jacobites in New England. Therefore, observers have explained the Jacobite accusations, and more generally the accusations of popery, as smokescreens masking the fear of a high-church Anglican, imperial, and bureaucratic takeover of New England's churches and government. But studies of the idea of Jacobitism in New England have failed to explain adequately the utility of the language of Jacobitism in New English provincial culture, and have not subjected the imagined threat of Jacobitism to systematic analysis. I call the threat of Jacobitism "imagined" not because it was fake or nonexistent, but because the primary reality of the Jacobite threat existed as an image in the minds of New Englanders who used the language of Jacobitism regularly from the invasion of William to the 1745 invasion attempt by Bonnie Prince Charlie, and beyond. It is precisely this "survival of a sense of the Jacobite menace," despite the absence of "real" Jacobites, that makes this subject so interesting. While some might protest that the language of Jacobitism means little historically if there were no Jacobites to be found in New England, and that the accusations of popery and/or Jacobitism were red herrings and the accusers "knew" so, these objections still do not account for the cultural utility of calling someone a Jacobite (or, similarly, a papist). To explain that someone was not "really" a Jacobite does not tell us why the language was used in the first place.[3] Understanding the accusations of popery and Jacobitism helps us understand how friends of the Protestant interest structured their mental worlds, and provides more evidence that their cultural and religious concerns extended across the ocean to the British Isles and beyond.

Likely because there was no "real" Jacobite movement afoot in New England, treatments of Jacobitism have been almost exclusively limited to the historiography of the British Isles, as after the Glorious Revolution England and Scotland faced periodic threats, sometimes more suspected than actual, from friends of the exiled Stuarts who would overthrow the Protestant monarch. Among the Whig synthesis of Anglican low churchmen and dissenting pastors, feared and actual Jacobites became anathema, regularly portrayed in print and sermons as "agents of Antichrist, or as the Assyrian hordes of the Old Testament, savage and warlike aliens threatening God's people Israel." Historians have rarely discussed how the Jacobite threat was used and imagined in New England.[4] This chapter will show how fears of Jacobites played an essential role in constructing the Protestant interest's identity in New England.

The memory of the Dominion of New England weighed heavily on the minds of the New Englanders who worried about Jacobitism. Though some North American and English non-Anglicans, most notably Pennsylvania's Quakers, admired James II for his advocacy of toleration, the New Englanders saw the Stuarts as a threat to their unique clerical establishment.[5] Thus, fears of the Jacobite threat were based on the suspected results of a resumption of Stuart power. First, New Englanders worried that Jacobite victory would end the unusual situation of a dissenting establishment in New England, and proscribe the wide latitude given by the charter of 1692 in religious, political, and economic matters. Second, New Englanders feared that the Jacobites meant ultimately to give the victory in the battle for true religion to Rome and its princes, and the Jacobites' occasional cooperation with France and the Pretender's periodic residencies in Rome and Paris exacerbated these suspicions. And so from the 1688 Revolution onward, leading pastors and political officials demonstrated a remarkable sensitivity to any evidence, especially seen among New England's Anglicans, of sympathy to the Jacobite cause and popery generally, and the print records also reveal an ongoing interest in monitoring the activities of the Pretender and his followers. The nearly hysterical reaction to any Anglican aggression pointed to the way that fear of popery and Jacobitism helped New Englanders construct their feuds with high churchmen as part of the worldwide contest of Protestantism against Catholicism.

The fears of Jacobitism also reflected one of the greatest defining characteristics of the British Protestant interest, the support for the Protestant succession. With the 1660 Restoration of Charles II, the "Puritan" movement had essentially failed in its effort to sustain a program of internal reformation of the Anglican church and to create a godly political establishment outside of the existing monarchical system, and so as a result "Puritanism" as a movement proper ceased to exist. In its place, the growing dissenting movement eventually based its existence on transatlantic ecclesiastical cooperation and winning tolerance from a monarchy more respectful of dissent than popery.[6] This strategy makes more clear why James II and the Dominion of New England were viewed as such abject disasters, and why support for the low-church Anglican "godly revolution" of William III and his successors Anne and the Lutheran Hanoverians became bedrock essentials in the transatlantic dissenting coalition of which New Englanders were such an important part.

Although the Dominion had threatened the dissenting establishments of Massachusetts and Connecticut, the new arrangements that came after 1689 made Anglicans the tolerated dissenters. Any act of aggression on their part to proselytize or subvert the standing order brought accusations of popery and/or Jacobitism quickly to the lips of New England's Protestant interest.[7] Replacing the old Puritan/Anglican dichotomy, New Englanders and their English dissenting brethren now distinguished at least four primary groups in English religious culture: the dissenters, among whom were the Congregationalists and Presbyterians, and increasingly included respectable Baptists;[8] the Whig and low-church Anglicans who supported the Protestant succession; the Tory high churchmen and especially the Nonjurors who felt uncomfortable to some extent with the results of 1688, and who were often suspected, legitimately or not, of plotting against William or his successors; and finally, the small British Catholic interest. Scotland provided another British case of a non-Anglican establishment that the English church had threatened at times, but after 1714 the Massachusetts Congregationalist establishment remained tenuous politically, while the Scottish Presbyterian church became relatively secure.

New England's dissenters considered themselves friends of the friends of the succession, making common cause with the churchmen faithful to William and his successors. Accordingly, New Englanders and other dissenters imagined a "two-church" model of post–Glorious Revolution Anglicanism, aligning themselves with supporters of the succession, and denouncing the Tory high church interest as tainted with Catholicism or Jacobitism. Though some historians sympathetic to eighteenth-century Anglicanism have disparaged this understanding as an "old fiction," New Englanders reflexively painted their conflicts with the high churchmen with the language of Jacobitism and popery.[9] Adding to the Anglicans' problems in New England, many of the dissenting authorities seemed willing to trust in the loyalty only of Anglicans who lived across the ocean, and the local Anglican priests and parishioners often faced accusations of secret sympathy for the Stuarts and/or the pope.

As was typical of the changing culture of New England during the period, the Glorious Revolution marked a watershed moment for treatments of English popery and its sympathizers in the Church of England. Upon the successful accession of William and Mary, British print culture made a swift turn from an uneasy silence concerning the clear Catholic allegiance of James II to open condemnations and ridicule of Catholics, most notably James II himself. The print culture of the American colonies and Boston in particular reflected these changes, beginning with the circulation of such documents as the widely distributed *Animadversions on King James, His Letter to the Pope.* This purported letter from James II to the pope was published to expose the king not only as a loyal Catholic, which everyone already knew, but also to try to establish his disloyalty to England generally and sympathy for both France and Rome. The letter was ostensibly sent by James as a congratulatory note upon the pope's recent accession, and the Williamite annotator savaged James for his fawning devotion to popery and contempt for British and international Protestantism. "This Caress to his New-made Holiness" showed a clear resolve to spread and enforce Catholicism "not only through his three Kingdoms, but likewise through his Territories in the American World too." James's letter called for a truce between Catholic states in Europe in order to face down the real enemy, Protestantism. The commentator noted that "the poor Indulgence of the Reform'd Religion, is an Eye-sore to him all the World over," and that James ultimately meant to root "the pestilent Northern Heresy from the Face of the Earth, as gnawing to his no small Anguish, in the very Bowels of the Church."[10] The foes of Jacobitism in the post–Glorious Revolution era would often make rhetorical recourse to such global claims about the threat of British

Jacobitism to the security of international Protestantism. The stakes in this matter could hardly be higher.

Continuing the synthesis of interests supporting the Protestant succession and likewise mocking and/or excoriating Jacobitism were such publications as *The Jacobites Catechism,* written by Benjamin Bird, rector of Wotton, and reprinted for Benjamin Harris in Boston in 1692. Such documents attempted to paint Jacobites as insidious supporters of popery and arbitrary government. The catechism had the typical "Jacobite" stating that his chief responsibilities were to side with "French Dragoons, and Iresh Cut-throats, against my native Country," to "renounce the English Laws and Liberties," and to despise "the Reformed Religion, and my Protestant Brethren." The Jacobite professed allegiance to the French court of Louis XIV and promised to "foment the Differences amongst all Protestants," "to keep the wounds of the Church open and bleeding," and to "keep up a correspondence with Papists and the French Court" in order to destroy the international Protestant interest. Bird's "Williamite" called on all "Protestants and Protestant Dissenters" to unite behind the new king despite their differences, for their situation called for international Protestant unity, not precisionist squabbling. If the Protestant interest could maintain such unity, he believed, it would result in "a rejoycing to the heart of our good King and Queen and all the Protestants beyond the Seas, and add much to the Infelicities of King Lewis."[11]

Thus, in the post–Glorious Revolution era, perhaps the most important criterion for religious legitimacy in the eyes of New England's dissenting establishment was loyalty to the Protestant succession and the concomitant (or so New Englanders saw it) support for the maintenance of a New England dissenting establishment. In a way, the question of whether one "actually" had Jacobite sympathies or not became moot in New England, and instead anyone could be cast into the category of "Jacobite" should they demonstrate hostility toward the dissenting established order in church authority, or if they demonstrated less than a full commitment to proper "reformed religion." New England's leading pastors and political officials knew what an anomaly their dissenting establishment was, and so they painted themselves as utterly loyal to the Protestant succession and made battle with any aggressive Anglican interests, often by labeling them papist or Jacobite.

New England's print culture served to portray the dissenting interest as faithful by regularly including proclamations from New England pastors and officials, as well as from dissenters in England, concerning the "inviolate" allegiance, fidelity, and loyalty of their interest to the Protestant monarchy, even during Anne's reign, which seemed a bleaker time for the future of the dissenters than either William's or George's. Typical was the *Boston News-Letter*'s account of London's dissenting ministers gathering at Windsor "to congratulate the surprizing Progress of Her Majesty's Arms" on the Continent, and also to remind her of "their inviolable Fidelity; to which not only their Interest and Inclination, but the Sacred tyes of Gratitude and Conscience, oblige them." The *News-Letter* recorded similar addresses at the Hanoverian succession, recording the London dissenters' thankfulness to "Divine Providence" for placing George I at the "Head of the whole Protestant Interest."[12]

The *News-Letter* also followed the Pretender's movements regularly through the paper's early decades, especially at times of threatened Jacobite uprisings or invasions. Beginning in May 1708 the newspaper was full of the most recent reports on the Old Pretender's failed invasion at Dunkirk (foiled in large part because the exiled king came down with measles just before the surprise invasion), including specific details of the invasion plans and how the pope had supplied "a Million of Crowns" to back the expedition. The paper carried Governor Joseph Dudley's (hardly a dissenter himself, yet part of the broad coalition supporting Anne and the Protestant succession) thanksgiving message when it was clear that the invasion had been turned away, thanking God that "they that Serve Graven Images, and boast themselves of Idols, have been Confounded."[13]

Those at the center of New England's dissenting cohort also forged intellectual and social bonds with dissenters in England and Presbyterians in Scotland in order to present a unified front to the threat of hostile interests among the Anglicans. Among the most commonly cited dissenting pastors during the period was England's John Edwards, whom Boston's John Checkley later debated in print. Cotton Mather in particular corresponded with Edwards and regularly cited his opinions on the superiority of the British dissenting interest. In fact, British dissenters like Mather and Edwards sometimes tried to turn high churchmen's arguments against them, saying that really the dissenters were the true primitivists and that they were the ones restoring the pattern of the church fathers instead of the high churchmen who clung to papist innovations. Mather and Edwards for their part went so far as to argue that the "Sober & Moderate" dissenting cohort had effectively saved the high churchmen from full-blown Jacobitism and popery. "If there had been none of that Party, the Church of England had long since been ruin'd; for if the High Churchmen had had no Check, they would have brought in Popery before this Time, by a Side-wind of Arminianisms, and by their over-valuing of Ceremony and Pomp in Divine Worship."[14] Likewise, Mather told Edwards in a personal letter that his works were greatly valued in New England and especially at Yale and Harvard, telling him that he had been loaning Edwards's works out to friends in "many parts of these colonies." Nevertheless, Mather had an ill report for Edwards on the high churchmen: "Our High-Church here, in imitation of their Brethren in *Scotland,* seek all advantage to disturb us."

Mather's highest contempt was reserved for the Society for the

Propagation of the Gospel, who he believed was strategically target-ing leading families in New England towns for corruption. "Their Reputation of it in these parts of the world suffers to the uttermost." Though the aggressiveness of the SPG and the movement to estab-lish an American bishop would wax and wane, sometimes based on the tenor of concerns over Jacobitism, dissenting New Englanders viewed Anglican missions with enormous suspicion, ready at all times to accuse such interlopers of popery or worse. At his most extreme, Mather excoriated the SPG in a letter to Glasgow's Robert Wodrow, calling it "the greatest perversion of an Evangelical Design pretended for, that was ever known in the world," because its agents preposterously acted as if the New Englanders were pagans needing the gospel. Mather painted the Anglican missionaries as the lowest scum, saying they "have generally been such loose lewd profane wretches, and of such horrid moralls, that the very worst of our people could hardly match them for scandal." Quite simply, they were "Emissaries of Antichrist." In *The Stone Cut out of the Moun-tain,* Mather wrote that they "serve the Empire of Satan under the Banner of our Saviour."[15] This resentment of the SPG did not apply to the New England Company, despite the fact that Anglicans often served as its governor, too. The New England Company, as dem-onstrated by Colman's friendly relations with it, was always more friendly to dissenters than the SPG was, and stuck to evangelizing Native Americans instead of dissenters.

Leaders of New England's Protestant interest also received letters from England that indicated the Jacobite threat there was very real. For instance, the New England Company's governor, William Ash-urst, reported to Increase Mather in 1713 that "so many things [are] advanced in favour of the Pretender by our weekly-Scriblers, that if the Protestant Succession be secured, tis wholly owing to a miracu-lous Providence."[16] Whether or not Jacobites could be found among the New Englanders, the threat from a transatlantic and British point of view was very real.

As noted in the case of Benjamin Colman, the momentous events of 1714 and 1715 in the British empire, including the Hanoverian succession and the suppression of the Jacobite revolt, led to a great outpouring of British nationalist sentiment and anti-Jacobite fervor. Beginning in December 1715, the Boston presses were full of news concerning the failed uprising, and the revolt provided fodder for Jacobite accusations for years to come. Colman led the public denunciations of the Jacobites, but his were not the only public comments on the matter. For instance, the December 26 issue of the *Boston News-Letter* reported details of the failed plot, printed the king's address against the rebels, and recorded in precise detail the "Terrible, Hellish Plot and Conspiracy" to have murdered the royal family, to have seized the "Tower, Exchequer, and Bank of England," and to burn the city. But "it pleased GOD," the account reported, to allow the plot to be foiled and to "prevent such Cruel and Monstrous Inhumane Barbarities." William Tailer, lieutenant-governor of Massachusetts during the rebellion, proclaimed a fast for March 22, 1716, asking for prayer that the "Impious Rebellion" might receive a fatal "Blast of Heaven." Likewise, Tailer issued a proclamation of thanksgiving in August for the suppression of the "Vile and Traiterous Rebellion."[17]

With the suppression of the 1715 uprising, one should not imagine that the Jacobite threat or the Pretender himself were forgotten in New England. To the contrary, the newspapers followed the Pretender's movements during these years with sometimes amazingly precise detail, such as in a report of a papal ceremony at the Vatican "where the Anathema's was [sic] thundred out as usual against the Hereticks" and where the Pretender and his consort assisted. Similarly, in a curious reference to the pope's desire to see the Stuart line continue, the *News-Letter* reported an account from Rome that had the pope sending "a piece of Indian Lead to the Pretendress to facilitate the Child-Birth."[18] But for New Englanders, the worst crises that brought the charges of Jacobitism to ministers' lips after the 1715 were domestic, as high-church challenges threatened the tranquility of the dissenting establishment.

Until the late 1710s Jacobitism appeared to New Englanders pleasantly absent from their provinces, but then the twin specters of "Boston's homebred Jacobite" John Checkley and the Yale apostates Timothy Cutler, Samuel Johnson, and others abruptly brought high-church threats directly against New England's establishment.[19] Both the controversy over Checkley and his publications and the so-called Yale apostasy of 1722 are well known, and a narrative of these events is not necessary here, but a brief review of responses to the controversies will demonstrate how New Englanders construed these high-church threats as part of the British Jacobite menace and, more broadly, the contest between Catholicism and Protestantism for control of the world institutional church.[20]

Checkley's work marked a major departure in the controversies over high-church Anglicanism and its relationship to the New England dissenting establishment as he began publishing polemical tracts excoriating both dissent and Calvinism. In 1719 he arranged for Thomas Fleet to print the Jacobite Charles Leslie's *The Religion of Jesus Christ the only True Religion,* an attack on deism but also a defense of Anglican church hierarchies. Checkley's own salvo, *Choice Dialogues between a Godly Minister and an Honest Country Man* (1719), attacked the doctrine of predestination as abhorrent to reason and painted its fatalism as blasphemous. Cotton Mather's nephew Thomas Walter launched a quick response with his own *A Choice Dialogue,* which attacked Checkley as a Tory and a Jacobite. In it, the devil came to "Jack Tory" [Checkley] and thanked him for "maintaining, that the Dutch and Scotch Presbyterians, and all the

Churches of New England, and all their Pastors worship the Devil." The devil remarked that previously he had imagined himself the object of worship from "the Japanese, the Hottentots, and American Salvages. He never imagined that all the Calvinists in the World, which amount to several Millions, and a very distinguished and superior part of Mankind, are also his Worshippers." But in the end the devil revealed Jack Tory's true supporters: "every one knows, that the Jesuites and the worst sects of the Roman Catholics are the most earnest Abettors, and Propagators of the Palagian Principles, which your muddy Dialogues design to infect the Young People of the Country with."[21]

Checkley continued printing his Arminian and high-church writings, however, even being invited by James Franklin to include a satire of Walter in the first issue of the *New-England Courant*. Checkley's most controversial and threatening work would come in 1723, *A Modest Proof of the Order and Government,* which Cotton Mather complained in his diary was a "vile, horrid monstrous Book." This book represented a direct plea for Anglican church government and a sharp attack against the dissenting establishment's polity, both Congregational and Presbyterian. It implicitly challenged the legitimacy of most of the ordinations performed in New England. He called the opponents of the Anglican church hierarchy "Carnal Libertines . . . Who have solemnly combined together to ruin and overthrow that Order, settled by Christ in his Church." Checkley arranged for the pamphlet to be sold widely across Massachusetts, Rhode Island, and Connecticut.[22]

Meanwhile, in New Haven "the heavens opened and consternation rained down" as in September 1722 Yale saw its rector Timothy Cutler along with two tutors and four local ministers convert to Anglicanism. The decision to convert came partly through reading "catholick" Anglican literature available at Yale's library, and partly through the ministry of the aforementioned George Pigot, then an

SPG missionary in Stratford, Connecticut. Again, the quick, outraged responses from New England's dissenting establishment constructed the episode as a threat to international Protestantism from popery. According to the anonymous tract *A Faithful Relation of a Late Occurrence,* endorsed if not authored by Cotton Mather, these despicable "Cudweeds" had essentially renounced "the communion of all the Protestant Churches in the world, except that little party that submits to the English Episcopacy!" This was tantamount to collaboration with the papists who were "trying to weaken and perplex the reformed Churches." Finally, the apostasy was a declaration in favor of Jacobitism, for "such highflyers as these who deserve their ordination from Rome, do generally discover themselves too well affected unto a popish pretender, and enemies to the happy revolution." The pamphlet ultimately blamed Checkley for the apostasy, calling him "a foolish and sorry toy-man, who is a professed Jacobite."[23]

These years were exceedingly difficult for the dissenting establishment of New England, who often seemed concerned for a general loss of cultural authority, perhaps part of their rhetorically useful concern for religious declension. They were forced to deal with not only the threat of Checkley and the Yale apostasy but also the related controversy over the smallpox inoculation (which led to among other things an assassination attempt on Cotton Mather in late 1721) and the outbreak of Father Rale's War, all of which heightened the bunker mentality of the Protestant interest.[24] Many issues needed attention, but in the presses, it was Checkley's threat that demanded the most vigorous response. While the clerical authorities had tried to shuttle responsibilities for responding to *Choice Dialogues* off to the relatively young and inexperienced Walter, perhaps hoping that the controversy would expire with little notice, with the coming of *A Modest Proof* the presses rumbled into action defending the dissenting way and Congregational/Presbyterian polity.

Harvard's Hollis Professor Edward Wigglesworth's *Sober Remarks on a Book* (1724) painted Checkley as a papist trying to steal away the theologically unsophisticated from the true gospel polity and order. "Since . . . the Book is recommended as proper to be put into the hands of the Laity," Wigglesworth proposed a counterargument to keep "unthinking Children or Neighbours" from being led away from "the Order of the Gospel." Wigglesworth's tract countered what he conceived as clumsy biblical interpretation in Checkley's book, and ultimately took the step that so many dissenting critics would take against the high churchmen: accusing them of popery. To put the dissenting interest beyond the pale of ecclesiastical legitimacy, Wigglesworth argued, was to put the "biggest part of the Protestant Churches . . . among Aliens from the Common Wealth of Israel." Demanding apostolic succession, he argued, was nearly the same as advocating allegiance to the popish cardinals and the pope himself. "Now if any thus principled cou'd but gain . . . Ascendant over the Populace . . . and thereby influence them as much in favour of the Romish Papacy, as they have been for the English Prelacy; what shou'd then become of Order in the Church?" To Wigglesworth, this clearly smacked of the "Roman Leaven."[25]

Walter again rose to defend Congregational/Presbyterian churches against Checkley's attacks, and proposed to see if "we can't beat out the little PERT Jacobite, from his fancied secure Retreat and oblige him to make a Surrender of his false Apostolical Episcopacy." Walter constructed the conflict as part of the longtime conflict between the true gospel and popery. It was false to assert, as Checkley did, "That the Dissenters . . . in less than two hundred Years past have arisen like a Wart upon the Face of the Western Church." Walter argued that Presbyterian antiquity could be found in the example of the "Vaudois of Piedmont," the often-celebrated "Protestant" ancestors of southern France.[26]

Walter was also deeply troubled by Checkley's claims that the world Protestant interest, though opposed to popery, was mostly sympathetic to episcopacy. Walter simply asserted that "he is talking of a Point of Geography, which he is very ignorant in." Revealing again how important it was for New Englanders to believe that the balance sheet of world Protestantism was on their side, thus justifying their dissenting status in Britain, Walter argued that the reformed churches of New England, England, Scotland, Holland, Switzerland, and elsewhere well outshone the poor, sickly episcopal interest, among whom Walter numbered "The whole Greek Church, the Armenians, the Georgians, Mingrelians, Jacobites . . . in Africa the Cophties in Egypt, and the great Empire of the Abyssines in Ethiopia. Miserable Christians, upon my Word!" Checkley also accused the dissenters of being fractious and backbiting, to which Walter replied that no one was worse on this point than the high churchmen/Jacobites (Walter made no distinction between the two groups). "What Party on Earth burns more than High Church? . . . theirs is an unquenchable Flame, which tho' King GEORGE has handsomely smother'd, yet was never able to extinguish."[27]

Others, including Thomas Foxcroft and Jonathan Dickinson, also weighed in against the Checkley threat. Dickinson, a Yale graduate pastoring in Elizabethtown, New Jersey, thought that Checkley's piece represented a despicable but predictable move by the high churchman to "depreciate our Ministry" by arguing they had false ordinations performed by ministers out of the divinely instituted line of apostolic succession. Checkley's argument, though a "hundred times baffled," tried to "Unchurch all the Protestant World" except for their small sect, and nullify their ordinances. Dickinson thought that Checkley's "Jacobite Principles" were revealed by his advocacy of passive obedience and nonresistance to unscriptural policies. Dickinson believed that the question of who counted as a faithful Protestant lay at the heart of this debate, and if Checkley's pamphlet was right, it would be "a Triumph to the Papists" because it meant that most Protestant churches employed illegitimate pastors and thus the apostolic world Protestant communion was very small indeed. This obviously raised the question of whether New England dissenters were legitimate Protestants, but Dickinson also noted that it jeopardized the whole church order of Scotland, the "establish'd Presbytery in North Britain." Dickinson countered Checkley's charges with an appeal to the dissenters' status as fully loyal British Protestants.[28]

Perhaps most representative of the popular mood against the imagined Jacobite threat were two pamphlets designed to paint the Checkley and Cutler controversies as a contest between faithful Protestants and disloyal Jacobites, and to show the threat of corruption and slavery should New Englanders dabble in episcopacy. The first, *The Madness of the Jacobite Party* (1724), an anonymous tract arranged to be published by Daniel Henchman, reminded New Englanders of the perils of high-church Anglicanism and the ultimate threat that Checkley and the Yale apostates represented to the Protestant succession. Henchman wrote that this tract was "highly Seasonable" because the Jacobites were still secretly plotting to introduce a "Popish Tyrannical Prince," and because "there are some among Our Selves, who . . . are Labouring by all possible means to corrupt and debauch the minds of Men (and of our own unthinking Youth, especially) by infusing into them the most absurd notions of Government and Loyalty, as well as of Religion."[29] All his readers knew this meant the newly vocal high churchmen.

The tract concluded that the Jacobites "are a pack of Fools and Mad-men, restlessly Conspiring their own, and the Nation's ruin." It outlined the disastrous consequences of Queen Mary and King James II's reigns, and extolled the virtues of the Protestant monarchs, especially William and George. The author finally speculated on the dire results of a Stuart restoration, and how "Inglorious and Ungenerous" it would be for the Jacobite party to "Sacrifice the

Religion of your Countrymen as Protestants, and their Civil Liberties as Brittons? Both which the Pretender is oblig'd by his Religion to destroy." If the Stuart Pretender should return to the throne, it would be nothing less than a triumph for popery: "The whole Land will be over-run with Fryars, Monks, & Jesuits, and such like swarms of Locusts from the Bottomless Pit, carrying the Breaden God thro' the streets in Procession, while the idolatrous Crouds adore." The tract concluded with a rallying cry of loyalty to British Protestants, and especially New Englanders, to support the Hanoverian succession. Against the new high-church threat the author held up the celebrated fidelity of New Englanders, who had "discovered a very peculiar Loyalty & Affection to King GEORGE and His Royal Family." The author made the usual claim that there were no disloyal elements within New England, but this time the claim did have a caveat: "Some there are indeed, who went out from us, tho' they never were of us; but their Hypocrisy begins to be manifest to all Men. And these are but very few in Number."[30]

Similarly, Samuel Gerrish arranged for the anonymous letter *A Brief Account of the Revenues, Pomp, and State of the Bishops*, which made the English church hierarchy out to be swollen with vanity and corruption. The letter warned New Englanders specifically that should they listen to Checkley and the other high churchmen their honest clerics would be replaced by "a Swarm of Ecclesiasticks now unknown to us! Unto whose Maintainance in Ease and Grandeur, Vast Sums will be Requisite." The letter concluded that Jacobitism could not be tolerated because it sought not to obtain a legitimate place within New England society but instead to overthrow the existing dissenting establishment. "If ever the Country fall under a Prelatical Regimen, especially if the Jacobite-High-Church prevails," then would New England find itself under the thumb of "carnal Worldly Clergy; and find occasion to reflect on St. Peter's awful

Prophecy; There shall be Teachers among you, who thro' Covetous-ness shall make Merchandise of you!"[31]

Checkley was eventually fined in 1724 for seditious speech, but in his defense he insisted that he was no Jacobite and that he thought it strange that in a land that so heavily depended on official tolera-tion of dissent, the episcopal interest was persecuted for dissenting against the establishment. Checkley's relatively light punishment marks another important moment in the history of high-church/ dissenting relations in New England, for from this point on through the 1730s the relationship became one of uneasy coexistence. Check-ley was through with his most aggressive and incendiary publish-ing, and Cutler rarely published high-church propaganda in any case. High churchmen from the mid-1720s began to take a less ag-gressive posture and began managing the existing settlement of established dissent in a more irenic and realistic fashion, organiz-ing Presbyterian-looking networks and consociations more regu-larly and giving up most hope for the time being of securing a resident Anglican bishop.[32] Such leaders as Newport's James Honey-man maintained a hostile posture in theory against the dissenting establishment, but direct published attacks on dissent became more isolated and focused on pleas for toleration of high churchmen.[33]

As the 1730s progressed, the most notable debate between high-church interests and the dissenting establishment was carried on between the Yale apostate Samuel Johnson and dissenting opponents including Southbury's John Graham. In a series of pamphlets issued in the mid-1730s, Johnson argued that the dissenting establishment was hypocritical for its reluctance to tolerate the presence of high churchmen despite the fact that the dissenters had depended on tolerance for their favored existence since 1692. Johnson also made clear that the high churchmen were not Jacobites and that they had no seditious intentions toward King George or thoughts of bringing back the Stuart Pretender. Thus, Johnson's defense of hierarchical Anglicanism was fundamentally different from Checkley's publications or Cutler's reputed vitriol. Johnson had come to Anglicanism partly as a result of his fondness for the essentialist religion of the latitudinarian school led by John Tillotson and Edward Stillingfleet, and he avoided blanket condemnations of New England's churches or Presbyterian/Congregational church polity.[34] Despite Johnson's rather irenic pleas for toleration, Graham, Dickinson, and others continued to fight against the more subdued high-church threat. Graham argued that intolerance was necessary in light of the fact that the dissenters were the "Bulwark of the Reformation," not the Church of England, and thus were required to maintain a high standard of gospel purity for the sake of the Protestant interest. Johnson had called for a latitudinarian peace in the church, but Graham dismissed this if it meant laxity in the fight against popery: "Truly this does not stop at London, nor so much as call in at Canterbury, but it has a pleasant Aspect towards his Romish Mother."[35]

So New England's dissenters remained ready to fight against anything that smacked of popery, or aggressive moves on the part of high churchmen. But it also seemed with the passing of the immediate hysteria over Checkley and the Yale apostates, and with the rise of the irenic Johnson as the chief defender of a high-church Anglicanism that in practice looked a lot like Presbyterianism, the imagined threat of Jacobitism also faded somewhat in the minds of leading New Englanders. This reflected a simultaneous weakening of Jacobitism in Britain and on the Continent that lasted from about 1725 to 1739. John Barnard, who earlier had fomented his congregation into harassing Anglicans in the streets over the celebration of Christmas, delivered the election sermon in May 1734 with assurances to the audience that fidelity to the Protestant succession was secure in New England, perhaps in spite of the presence of the high churchmen. "Were I at full liberty, I should choose to be (as, blessed be God, we are,) of the Number of the Happy Subjects of Great Britain, whom God hath blessed above all the People . . . in the Felicity of their Constitution, and I look upon myself happy, that I know not of a single true New England Man, in the whole Province, but what readily subscribes to these Sentiments."[36] While Barnard was hedging with the phrase "true New England Man," his sentiments nevertheless reflected a general sense that resident high churchmen no longer necessarily meant resident Jacobitism.

But the imagined Jacobite threat was not dead, and surged again with the invasion attempt by Bonnie Prince Charlie in 1745, the last serious Jacobite revolt in the British Isles. Jonathan Edwards for one wrote to his Scottish correspondent John MacLaurin of his relief that the Jacobites had not conquered Scotland, and that Britain had "not been totally and finally given up into the possession of papists . . . for which not only you, but we, and all Protestants, have great cause of thankfulness; especially all within the British dominions, which must all have fallen together under the calamity, if the Pretender had gained his purpose."[37] But in the years preceding the awakenings, the imagined Jacobite menace faded, and for a time New England's dissenting interest turned its attention to another facet of the world contest for Christianity, the revival of the true church.

CHAPTER SIX

"The Dawning of that Sabbath of Rest Promised to the People of God"
Eschatology and Identity

It was 1700, and in his course of preaching Cotton Mather had come to Romans 2:16: "In the day when God shall judge the secrets of men by Jesus Christ according to my gospel." Mather knew that this topic would raise the interests of pious congregants at the Old North Church, who would want to know when that "day" might come. "If you ask when," Mather opined, "I answer it will be in the End of the World." But Mather cautioned that some things would have to happen first before the secrets of men would be judged, "that is the downfall of antichrist and the Calling of the Jews." The timing of these was quite uncertain, and Mather noted that divines could not agree as to the methods or dates by which these would happen. But as all New England pastors and their international reformed connections would agree, Mather told his congregation to be watchful for signs of the end. Despite the conclusions of some historians, New Englanders associated with the Protestant interest did watch for the key moments before their hope was revealed.[1]

Historians have long realized that among the most powerful strains of thought in colonial New English culture was the anticipation of the end of the world, or the *eschaton*. If the expectation that key prophecies of the Bible might be fulfilled soon was relegated only to the most obscure writings of theologians, one might be tempted to dismiss these speculations as fascinating but ultimately unimportant. It is difficult to gauge exactly how widespread eschatological speculation was in New England society, but at least in elite seaport circles it was a regular topic for public and private reflection. Consider this rare account from the Reverend Ebenezer Parkman of Westborough, Massachusetts, who came to visit the family of the Reverend Peter Thatcher in Boston in January 1726: "I visited Mr. Thatcher in the Evening. Mr. [John] Webb came in, and the Conversation turned upon the Kingdom of Christ, the calling of the Jews, etc. I observ'd Mrs. Thatcher to discourse with a great deal of pertinence and Solidity as well as Zeal upon the Side of the millenists." The image Parkman presented was of a friendly visit among pastoral friends and families, which turned naturally to discussions of the last days, and even Peter Thatcher's wife cared enough to expound with zeal her opinion of the millennium.[2]

New England's clerical and political leaders associated with the Protestant interest discussed and taught on eschatology regularly, and believed that it was incumbent upon them and the people of New England to insert themselves into the unfolding and accelerating course of historical eschatology, in order to promote the coming of the end. Even the usually skeptical Franklins of the *New-England Courant* offered positive thoughts about a general eschatology, scoffing at those who named names and dates, but reminding their readers that "there will be an End of the World, and a General Judgment," and that "Christ will appear the second Time; that he comes quickly, and his Reward is with him."[3]

This chapter considers eschatology and identity in New England, and in the British Atlantic world, from William of Orange's invasion of England in 1688 to the coming of New England's revivals in the 1730s and '40s. Two developments gave this period's experimentation in eschatological projects strong momentum. First were the circumstances of war and the increasingly ominous French (and sometimes Spanish) threat to Britain generally but especially to New England. Beginning with the Glorious Revolution and the subsequent start of King William's War in 1688–89, war became an ever-present threat in the English colonists' minds. Second was the rise of a thoroughgoing print culture in New England, marked symbolically by the coming of the first newspaper in 1704 but also generally by an explosion of available printed material. Such printed material included many religious tracts but also even more widely popular material like the ubiquitous almanacs, all of which allowed New Englanders to imagine themselves part of a worldwide battle for the fate of true religion, hopefully culminating in "that Sabbath of rest promised to the people of God," as one almanac put it.[4]

The interest in eschatological teleology among New Englanders was varied and nuanced, but there were three primary issues that New England speculators believed would have to be resolved before the second coming of Christ and/or the millennium. Mather suggested the first two: one was the destruction of the "man of sin," or the Roman Catholic church and its princes in Europe. Scholars like Nathan Hatch have clearly demonstrated the anti-Catholic flavor of later episodes such as the siege on Louisbourg, but the deeper roots of these interpretations become evident when one explores eschatological anti-Catholicism and its implications for state policy and cultural identity after the Glorious Revolution.[5] A second issue was the national conversion of the Jews. Many New Englanders were fascinated with the subject, including especially Increase Mather, who played a key role in popularizing expectations of Jewish conversion. Finally, increasingly during the 1720s and '30s, New Englanders expected that the end would be preceded by massive conversions and revivals, sometimes including the Jews. New Englanders wished to insert themselves into this project of worldwide (and local) evangelization, making the coming of the awakenings more historically predictable than is conventionally understood.

There is no doubt that some of the eschatological language used by provincial New Englanders was vague, if not formulaic. We have come to expect that the eschatologically minded will, like twentieth-century American fundamentalists, have a very precise system of theology. Provincial New Englanders, however, typically did not develop anything so reified as the set timetables of the fundamentalists.[6] Many of them did take eschatological beliefs quite seriously, however, especially because of their intimate familiarity with the crises of European Protestantism and celebrated cases of Jewish conversions. This study presumes that when New Englanders expressed beliefs on such subjects as the conversion of the Jews and the second coming, they really believed what they said, and desired to help usher in the final days of the earth, as they might by fighting against the Catholic powers or preaching to lost souls.

The English Protestant movement had long suspected that the papacy was the Antichrist spoken of in John's Revelation, or the "man of sin" in second Thessalonians. The founders of Massachusetts and Connecticut may not have been driven directly by eschatological expectations, but many New England Puritans such as John Cotton and John Eliot kept the tradition of eschatological speculation alive and well. In 1688–89, many New England dissenters who observed the downfall of James II and the relatively peaceful accession of William and Mary believed they were seeing a key moment in eschatological history. With the openly Catholic James II on the throne, the powers of Antichrist seemed to be winning the day. In a letter to Thomas Gouge from 1683, Increase Mather directly associated James II with Antichrist, suggesting that James had the number of the beast. But Mather also expressed hopes that because of Protestant successes in Hungary and elsewhere, the international godly interest could soon hope that the "Whore of Babylon shall fall."[7]

In a great reversal smacking of end-of-the-world drama, the Protestant King William assumed the throne in 1688, once again placing England in the vanguard of the Protestant interest, and perhaps signaling the imminent final victory of God's people in the world. New Englanders now celebrated William's accession in a surprisingly ecumenical spirit. Never before had New Englanders risen to agree so vehemently with the religious agency of the king as they did with Gilbert Burnet's and other English Anglicans' sermons on William's "godly revolution." Burnet, William's chief proponent and propagandist, immediately began interpreting William's arrival as the work of God on behalf of the Protestant interest and as potentially the next step in end-times history. William's coming might signal "the most glorious beginning of a noble change in the whole face of affairs. . . . We may . . . hope to see . . . a new heavens and a new earth," Burnet proclaimed at St. James' Palace on December 23, 1688.[8]

Although Burnet was not a dissenter, New England's leaders heartily agreed with his sentiments and arranged for the publication of Burnet's thanksgiving interpretation of William's accession. The General Court quickly adopted the habit of recommending that Massachusetts residents pray for "the common Interest of the Protestant Religion in the World, which hath so many potent Adversaries; as also the Accomplishment of such Scripture-Prophesies, as seem to be near the birth, and must be ushered in with Prayer." They also prayed that the new king and queen "may have their Throne established" against Jacobite and French enemies.[9]

Cotton Mather and others weighed in with interpretations of William's arrival and the deliverance of the Protestant interest similar to Burnet's. Mather exulted at God's deliverance of England and the establishment of toleration for nonconformists: "we that are a

Countrey of Nonconformists, may not pass it by unmentioned." Given the accession of William and the retreat of James, Mather wondered whether it was not time "for us to Lift up our Heads, with at least some Examination, whether we shall not shortly see the Vintage of the Papal Empire?" He predicted that Italy would likely soon be swallowed up in a great earthquake, and that the "Turkish Power" would soon be decimated, unable to wage war against Europe. He expected that the gospel would soon have "Liberty and Efficacy, not only in Popish Countreys where it is Restrained; but also in Pagan Countreys, in One of which, we hear of near two Hundred Thousand Heathen, Converted unto true Christianity, within these few years." As was typical of the millennial expectations of New Englanders, Mather paired the expectation of the downfall of Rome with the hope for worldwide conversions. Some English Puritans had seen the coming days of Rome's destruction, the Jews' conversion, and Protestant ascendancy as the "Middle Advent," a time well before Christ's second physical appearance when Christ would appear spiritually in a surge of supernatural power to overturn Satan's kingdom on earth. In provincial New England, most speculators believed that these events would precede Christ's second coming, but most seem to have imagined the gap between the two Advents as quite brief. The time of gospel "brightness" would immediately precede Christ's physical arrival.[10]

In perhaps his best-known eschatological treatise, Cotton Mather in 1691 encouraged the artillery company of Massachusetts with *Things to be Look'd For*. One should note that though Mather, his father, and a few other pastors might have been the leading proponents of eschatological theology in provincial New England, often this theology was delivered on such occasions as election days or the militia's training days. Mather again tied the "Late Revolutions in England" to the coming demise of Catholicism. Speaking, as it were, directly to the monarchs, Mather proclaimed that God "has intended your Highnesses to be the Principal Instruments of the Grand Deliverance, which He hath prepared for His Church, when the storm shall be over." In that day, Mather confidently asserted to the listening crowd, "All the Orders of the Romish Clergy shall then be Hissed Out of Humane Conversation; and particularly, the Ignatian Fiery Brood, which . . . shall then be Extinct for ever." To Mather and others, the destruction of the Jesuit order would be one of the happiest results of the destruction of Catholicism. Rome would be destroyed in a storm of fire and brimstone just as was Sodom, "and in the Ashes of the Papacy will be buried most of those Brangles which now set more than all Europe in a flame."[11]

With New England now heavily invested in the British leadership of a worldwide Protestant interest, ideas about the latter-day destruction of the papacy and other eschatological beliefs gained currency in not only sermons but also sources like the ubiquitous almanacs. Samuel Clough regularly speculated on the coming of the end and the destruction of the Roman church. Observing the threats posed by Catholic France and Spain in Queen Anne's War, Clough's 1703 almanac comforted his readers with the thought that the current troubles might signal something better: "there are terrible troubles and calamities hastening upon the World, and now already begun, which may be a means to bring on those Happy Times promised to the People of God, and to the Destruction of their Enemies: The Almighty hasten that time if it be his blessed Will."[12]

In 1706 Clough similarly looked forward to "the dawning of that Sabbath of rest Promised to the People of God," which some suggested had begun with little fanfare in 1703. If so, Clough thought (citing English almanacker John Partridge) "that prophecy in Daniel shall be fulfilled . . . all Superstition, Idolatry and Invention of men in Religion shall be turned out of doors & abolished, and the Gospel truly Preached throughout the World." Clough hopefully noted that many scholars believed "That there will be a great Change in the

World. . . . within this Ten or Twelve Years." Clough maintained a watch on the events of Europe, hoping that the strife there might "make way for the downfall of Popery."[13]

In 1707 the Boston presses were full of anti-Catholic tirades and speculations on the eventual demise of Antichrist. Perhaps the surge in anti-Catholic print reflected continuing fears over war in Europe between the chief Catholic and Protestant countries, now in the form of Queen Anne's War, or the War of Spanish Succession, which drew even clearer lines than the previous war between Catholic and Protestant powers. The year 1707 also saw the outbreak of one of New England's first open political controversies since the Glorious Revolution, in which merchants and political leaders, most notably Governor Joseph Dudley, were accused of mercantile fraternization with French Catholics in Canada, putting material interest above the Protestant interest.[14]

A variety of documents asserted an apocalyptic hostility toward world Catholicism. Samuel Belcher, pastor at Newbury, wrote *An Essay Tending to Promote the Kingdom* as an encouragement to his church and to New England generally to seek and pray for the kingdom of God to come on earth. Before that could happen, however, Belcher cautioned that "All Impediments must be removed." This meant that "God will bring home his ancient People. . . . The Ottoman Monarchy, if not otherwise disposed of, will sink under the weight of its own bulk," and finally, "Our Lord Jesus Christ, will in these last days, shake all Kingdoms, and Nations, till He have shaken out all that Antichristian Mortar . . . And Tottering Rome shall at length fall. . . . The Man of Sin must be Totally destroy'd, Head and Members, Root and Branches." Belcher knew that many of God's people in New England were waiting "for the Accomplishment of these things; Multitudes of Prayers are hastening of them."[15]

Benjamin Colman weighed in with a more activist appeal to the General Court and Governor Dudley to war against the Catholic enemy. Colman argued that it was not only permissible but also incumbent upon true Christians to pray "against the Enemies of God and his Church, for their Destruction and Overthrow." Likewise, when appropriate God's people could also "Seek and Endeavour their ruin and downfall in LAWFUL WAR." His was not a New England mission primarily, but "a Serious and Affectionate Call to Prayer, for our People, and Churches, and for the Interest of Christ in the World. . . . Millions of Prayers are daily going up to God from his Church, in every part of the World, against his Enemies." Colman called on the New England churches, and the Massachusetts government, to join in this effort that would inevitably result in the downfall of the Roman church.[16]

Cotton Mather, ever ready to go to battle with Catholic foes, joined Belcher and Colman in this sizeable flurry of publications with *The Fall of Babylon*. This catechism was specifically directed not at New Englanders but to "the Christians in MARYLAND, who may be in danger of Popish Delusions." Because popery was destined to fall, Mather decided to take the battle to the primary haven for English Catholics in the new world, "to carry on the Triumphs of our Holy Religion over Popery." Mather hoped that true Protestants in Maryland might use the catechism to instruct their children about the dangers of Catholicism, including dialogues like this:

> Q. Is the Church of Rome that Babylon, from which the Churches of the Reformation have done well to make a Separation?
> A. The Church of Rome, has in regard of its Place, and its Idolatry and Cruelty . . . , the Unquestionable Marks of the MYSTICAL BABYLON. And all that would be Saved, ought to Separate from the Communion of it.[17]

Increase Mather was likewise interested in the timing of the papacy's downfall, producing some of New England's most densely theological tracts on the coming of the end. Increase was more bold than most of his contemporaries in suggesting dates for the end, and so in 1708 in an analysis of the kingdoms in the vision of Daniel 8 he speculated that the downfall of the papacy might come in 1716. In a typical New English/British prophetic mode, Increase bolstered this prediction and also his hope for "the Restauration of the Jews" with news reports from Europe. He was encouraged by the movements of the Protestant princes of Europe, especially Frederick I, king of Prussia. Not least among Frederick's beneficent policies toward the Protestant interest was his friendly relationship with the University of Halle and August Hermann Francke, the Prussian Pietist leader who reached near-celebrity status among the New Englanders. Not only was Increase encouraged by the positive signs of Protestant activity, he was also pleased with the troubles of the Roman church. Though the Jesuits continued to "make Proselytes for Anti-Christ" all over the world, "signal Rebukes have lately attended them." Mather believed that their work in America was in disarray, and he heard that many Venetians "are grown sick of Popery." Finally, he noted with some pleasure that the emperor of China had executed "the Popes Legat" in the continuing troubled missions there. "These are Remarkable Providences," Mather concluded.[18]

The Jacobite rising of 1715 spurred a host of writings that suggested a Catholic plot was afoot to subvert British liberties and true Christianity. This sense continued as the Jacobite cause waxed and waned through the 1745 invasion. The coincident death of Louis XIV in 1715 helped New Englanders imagine that some great movements were around the corner with respect to the fate of popery.

Benjamin Colman, and others less inclined toward extensive apocalyptic speculations than father or son Mather, nevertheless made it clear that true British Protestants should hope and pray for the destruction of the Roman church, especially after the news of the Jacobite rising filtered into New England's ports. When the Reverend Thomas Bridge of Boston died that same year, Colman described him glowingly at the funeral as having "The Protestant Religion, the welfare of BRITAIN and of all the Reformed Churches, the Protestant SUCCESSION, the downfall of Popery, and a hearty Detestation of . . . the Betrayers of the Nation and of Europe . . . Engraven deep in his Soul."[19]

Cotton Mather watched the events of 1715 with near ecstasy, as it appeared to him that everywhere "tokens for good" signaled the coming of the kingdom of God. All "attempts to rebuild the Romish Jericho" after the Glorious Revolution had fallen under "the Curse of our Exalted JESUS," so that even in the 1715 uprising King George was preserved and the Pretender failed in his attempt to return to England and "Reign in Blood!" God also cut off the life of "the most Finished Representation of Satan that was to be seen on the Face of the Earth," Louis XIV. If Louis had lived until the Jacobite uprising, Mather believed that he would have sent the French army into Britain to support the revolt, but all the Roman plots were "mightily Damp'd and Cramp'd by the Death of the French Tyrant." Mather also identified the "Union of the Universal Religion of PIETY" as a sign of the approaching end, best exemplified again by the work of the "Frederician University" at Halle.[20] To Mather, one could hardly hope for more positive signs of good.

But Mather's hopes for the downfall of popery were delayed more, a cycle that sometimes revealed hints of weariness in his millennial hope. In a letter to Robert Wodrow, on October 4, 1717, Mather wrote of the impending downfall of popery: "The Strong Tendencies which there are in several Nations, so heavy Millstones about the Neck of popery by the principles of the Reformation appearing . . . to unite good men upon the Basis of True, Real, and Vital Piete; give me hopes that 1716 will yet be found a Term of Ruine unto the Romish Babylon."[21] The inverted relationship between vital piety and the fate of Rome made Mather and his correspondents eager for the spread of true Christianity, perhaps led by the Halle group. But after the exultant tone of Mather's reflections on that wonderful year, 1715, he never again would be so optimistic about the imminent end.

Nevertheless, the Mathers continued until their deaths to promote the most speculative and specific forms of eschatology among New Englanders. For instance, in another letter to Robert Wodrow, from November 11, 1719, Increase Mather speculated on the timing of the end: "I no way doubt, but that Antichrist's 1260 days are well nigh expired, yet that dying Beast may give a cruel Bile. There is great talk of a general peace in Europe, which makes me think of I Thes. 5.3" (I Thessalonians 5:3: "For when they shall say, Peace and safety; then sudden destruction cometh upon them, as travail upon a woman with child; and they shall not escape"). Perhaps the general peace in Europe seemed to contradict the hoped-for destruction of Antichrist, so Mather's thoughts turned to this passage, which suggested that the end might be accompanied by apparent peace between God's enemies and the elect.[22]

Similarly, in a letter to Wodrow from 1725, Cotton Mather commented that "It appears plain to me, That the second coming of our Lord will be at and for the Destruction of the Man of Sin, whose period of Twelve Hundred and Sixty Years is now expiring." Mather expected that at the destruction of the old earth, the elect would be delivered from the judgment and caught up to meet Christ in the air, and then the Lord would establish the new earth. But Mather had few specific ideas as to how this might come about, especially given the relative peace in Europe and the apparently languishing condition of Protestantism across the world.[23]

In the few years before his death, Mather's confidence about the imminent destruction of Antichrist seemed to flag, as did his hope for the Jews' conversion. In fact, Mather became convinced that the destruction of Rome would come not prior to the second coming, but as a result of the second coming of the warrior Christ. In a letter to Robert Wodrow, May 18, 1727, Samuel Mather conveyed his father's opinion "that there will be no settled good Times, til the Son of Man shall come in the Clouds of Heaven, and destroy the Man of Sin with the Breath of his Mouth and with the Brightness of His Personal Coming."[24] As the exciting times of the early eighteenth century gave way to a relative peace and balance of power in the 1720s, those New Englanders waiting for news from Europe of the beginnings of the end had less and less evidence upon which to base their hope.

Closely tied to the hoped-for destruction of Rome were beliefs concerning the eschatological ingathering of the Jewish people "back to God," as reformed Protestants saw it. As with the anticipation of the downfall of Rome, waiting for the conversion of the Jews helped New Englanders fashion an understanding of their cultural identity as part of the godly remnant in the world, and it gave them a much clearer sense of the direction of history. In this vein, in 1699 Cotton Mather produced a typical catechism for Jews arguing that they should convert to Christianity.[25] Works like this helped New Englanders understand their cultural identity by creating a great eschatological other. Because very few Jews ever read pamphlets like this, one must think about the cultural work such a pamphlet might do for New Englanders' identity. In part, such works helped them forge a powerful international reformed cultural identity because they provided such a clear idea of whom they were not.

In *The Faith of the Fathers,* Mather invited the Jews to "persist no longer in your Damnable Rebellion against the CHRIST of God!" Aside from arguing that Christianity was obviously the one true religion, Mather also pleaded with the Jews that their eventual conversion was prophesied by their own scriptures:

> Q. Must the Nation of Israel, in the Latter Days, be brought in, to the Belief of the Messiah, against whom they shall with Incureable Infidelity, Rebel, until those Dayes?

A. Yes. It is written, Hos. 3.5. Afterward shall the Children of Israel Return, & Seek the Lord their God . . . and shall fear the Lord, and His Good One, in the Latter Dayes.

Again, Mather associated the rise of Israel with the downfall of the papacy:

Q. After the Four Monarchies, Exhibited in the Visions of Daniel are Ended, and particularly the Papal Empire, which is the Fourth, in the Last Form of it, comes to its End, shall the Nation of Israel, be Advanced into a Great Condition of Power and Glory?
A. Yes . . .[26]

Surveying the state of the world church in 1702, Cotton Mather began with an analysis of the Jews' situation. He was not particularly optimistic. The Jews were scattered widely, mostly among "the Turks" and in "Popish countries," and those among the Protestants rarely convert. However, Mather did optimistically note one hopeful example that might begin spreading end-time conversions. "Only that brave man, Esdras Edzard, a Divine of Hamburgh, hath lately been an Instrument of Converting more Jews, than have ever been Converted . . . since the Age of Miracles." Mather reported that several hundred Jews had apparently been converted under Edzard, perhaps an indication that the prophesied conversions had begun. Increase and Cotton Mather returned regularly to Edzard's example, appealing again in 1713 to the Jews to look at the "Hundreds of Jews, [who] have in our Days, been brought over to Christianity, by the Blessing of God . . . managed by one Renowned Convert from Judaism, in the City of Hamburgh." In his effort to include more religious news, John Campbell included an excerpt about Edzard from *An Advice to the Churches* in the *Boston News-Letter* in February 1723, demonstrating the continuing interest in Edzard's role in converting Jews.[27]

In 1709 Increase Mather sought an even broader British Atlantic audience as he published *A Dissertation Concerning the Future Conversion* through friends in London as well as in Boston. Mather had a long-term interest in the national conversion of the Jews and for most of his ministerial career was one of the leading authorities on the subject in the British Atlantic world. In his *Dissertation,* Mather took issue with the late Richard Baxter's position that the prophesies about the Jews' mass conversions were fulfilled in the apostolic period. Mather argued that when Paul told the Romans that "all Israel will be saved," (Romans 11:26) he referred to a future conversion. Mather was not absolutely sure of the timing, as usual, but he did believe that their corporate conversions would be "effected as Paul's was, by a miraculous Appearance of Christ to some of them, and be carried on by the Preaching of the Gospel, with a most glorious down pouring of the Holy Spirit therewith."[28]

The Mather family and apparently many of their readers loved to receive news, even if only bits of information, relating to Jewish conversions that might presage the coming of the kingdom. Cotton Mather's chief correspondent from the Halle school, Anthony William Boehm, supplied Mather with all the information he could from his central location in London—Boehm was a Halle chaplain in the English court and a major figure in the international Protestant interest. In a letter to Cotton Mather dated July 23, 1716, Boehm relayed information to Mather about the conversions of Jewish children in Berlin, suggesting that this was more evidence of the approaching end.[29]

In his 1716 pamphlet *Menachem,* Mather made note of these conversions in Berlin as a "Fore-runner of a Great Work, which we are shortly looking for." He excitedly told his readers that there was "in the City of Berlin, a strange Motion from GOD, among the Children of the JEWS. . . . These Children, under Twelve Years of Age, make unaccountable Flights unto the Protestant Ministers, to be Initiated in the Christian Religion." With delight he noted that when the children's parents tried to convince them to return, the children replied "We shall never return to you; 'Tis time for you to come over to us."[30] In *Menachem,* Mather was at the height of optimism, but it would remain increasingly obvious that "Fore-runners" were not enough. Over time this desire to see great evidences of the coming kingdom would lead some, including Mather, to lose confidence in the future conversion of the Jews.

As of 1718, however, Cotton Mather was still promoting printed accounts of Jewish conversions, most notably an extended narrative of the Jewish children in Berlin, likely based on an account received from Boehm. He told his readers they should be encouraged at these reports, for they demonstrated God's promises "for the Converting of whole Nations . . . And more particularly, for the Conversion of the Israelitish Nation." Why had God brought about this remarkable series of conversions? "To let the faithful see, a few Drops, that may Comfort their Hopes of the Mighty Showers, which GOD in His own Time, [when the Three Years and Six Months are Expired!] will cause to fall upon the Children of Men." Boehm agreed, arguing that this instance and similar ones "observed in several Parts of Europe," including in Silesia, represent an "Earnest of a more Glorious Dispensation which shall follow in the Fulness of Time."[31] That Mather finished this pamphlet with yet another appeal to the Jews to convert seems remarkable given the population of Jews among New Englanders was negligible at best as of 1718. Though Mather surely would have explained that he hoped his pamphlet would gain a readership beyond Massachusetts or Connecticut, perhaps among Newport's, Charleston's, or London's Jews, this repeated willingness of Mather's publishers to produce proselytizing literature for Jews where there were almost none speaks of the symbolic fascination the Jews as a group held for many New Englanders. Still considered obstinate and murderous in their corporate unconverted state, many waited for signs of the Jews' return to God as a great redemptive reversal of one of Christendom's primary "others," and ultimately as an essential part of the great eschatological triumph for the millennial church and the kingdom of Christ.

Most of the time New Englanders felt that they played a role in this eschatological drama only through prayer.[32] However, Massachusetts' eschatologically minded evangelicals celebrated what to them seemed an enormous triumph when in 1722 Harvard Hebrew instructor Judah Monis publicly converted to Protestantism. Monis was a remarkable traveler of the Atlantic world, likely born in Venice in 1683, of Spanish or Portuguese parents. Monis was educated in Leghorn and Amsterdam, and spent some time in London before moving on to the British colonies in America. He lived on Long Island, and then moved to New York City around 1715. Monis made a living in those years teaching Hebrew to both Jews and Christians, and the news of a Jew teaching Hebrew in the colonies attracted the attention of many leading New Englanders, both out of academic interest and also because of the simple fascination of meeting a Jew who would teach Christians in Hebrew.

Monis began corresponding with Samuel Johnson, who these years before his conversion to Anglicanism was still a rector at Yale, and he also became acquainted with the Mather family, Cambridge's pastor Nathaniel Appleton, and Harvard's John Leverett. By 1720 Monis had come to live in Boston, and he submitted a Hebrew grammar to the Harvard authorities for use there. Monis at this point obviously hoped to secure a teaching appointment at Harvard, but his efforts would meet some resistance, almost certainly because of concerns the Corporation would have about bringing a Jewish teacher on faculty. Not long after his arrival in Boston, Monis began studying Christianity with local clergymen, and in March 1722 Benjamin Colman and other leading pastors arranged a ceremony at Cambridge's College Hall for Monis's public conversion and baptism. Some observers then and also some later historians have ques-

tioned the sincerity of Monis's conversion, suspecting ulterior motives and financial enticements. Whatever the real motivation of
Monis's public conversion, New Englanders placed his conversion
easily within their expected eschatological framework.[33]

Cambridge's and Boston's residents had never seen the likes of
this before: here in one of the key outposts of the Protestant interest
was a Jew converting to Protestantism, and predictably the occasion
drew an overflow crowd to College Hall. Colman presided over the
conversion and baptism. He welcomed Monis's liberation from the
spiritual blindness of the Jewish people, and said to Monis, "We look
for the happy day of the Conversion of the Jews; and of Israel's
Salvation, we daily and earnestly pray for it with great desire." Colman regretted that the Jews remained under "a vail of Spiritual
Blindness" that kept them from properly understanding the messianic prophecies of the Old Testament. But the time was coming, he
confidently told the assembly, when the "blessed and holy Spirit of
Grace will fall upon 'em, enlighten, convince, and convert 'em; and
free 'em from their present prejudices."[34]

Monis published three treatises himself (though clearly with a
great deal of editorial "assistance" from the Boston and Cambridge
clergy) that Samuel Kneeland and Daniel Henchman arranged to
have published along with Colman's discourse. Monis appealed to
the Jewish people with *The Truth, The Whole Truth,* and *Nothing but
the Truth,* proclaiming that he had found the true Messiah in the
New England Protestants' Jesus. Monis now interpreted the Jewish
scriptures' prophesies about the ingathering of the Jews as one and
the same with the Jews' conversion to Christianity: "this return will
never come to pass, till they acknowledge the Lord Jesus Christ, for
their Messiah and Goell, i.e. Christ and Redeemer." Monis, almost
certainly expressing the wishes of his editors, made his treatises
expressly anti-Catholic as well, making clear that he did not believe
that Jewish conversion to Catholicism amounted to true Christian

conversion: "Indeed, if I had declared my self, to be one of the Church of Rome's Communion, I should not Wonder, in case I was censured by the least of you, because that would be nothing else but practically to deny the Law and the Prophets."[35]

Monis's conversion attracted the attention of correspondents through the British Atlantic network, some with higher confidence in Monis than others. Bishop White Kennett, frequent correspondent with Colman, was glad to hear the news but advised that his friend wait for clear evidence of authenticity from Monis before giving him too much authority at Harvard. The English dissenter Isaac Watts and the London merchant Thomas Hollis both expressed similar concerns. Robert Wodrow, however, was more trusting, and after discussing Monis with Colman, established some correspondence with Monis himself. In a letter to Wodrow, Colman spoke highly of Monis's learning and assured him that Monis would work for the conversion of the Jews. He told Wodrow that "When you pray for the Conversion of that once beloved People, as I believe you daily do, I ask a remembrance for Mr. Monis." Wodrow likewise informed Colman that Monis had "refreshed and comforted us by his coming under the Messias wings," and wondered how he might most effectively communicate with Monis (in English, Hebrew, or Latin?). To Monis, Wodrow expressed the hopes of many in the international Protestant interest, that Monis's conversion and "the conversion of some in Holland we hear of, may be the first fruits of a [great] harvest," the wholesale conversion of the Jewish people.[36]

Monis never gained full acceptance personally or professionally at Harvard or in New England society, and though he was appointed an instructor of Hebrew at Harvard, his classes never went particularly well. Whether this was because the students did not like Hebrew or because of their bigotry against even a converted Jew is not clear. There were allegations that Monis continued to observe a Saturday Sabbath, and the church in Cambridge continued to refer to Monis as the "Christianized Jew." On the other hand, Monis was admitted to full membership at the First Church of Cambridge in 1737, and Monis apparently remained faithful to his public conversion until his death.[37] But Monis's symbolic importance in New England and in the international Protestant community was never questioned. The conversion of this one man among them seemed to add one more piece to the eschatological puzzle, and the clerical leaders of Boston could not have been more pleased that instead of this news coming from Hamburg, Berlin, or Amsterdam, this time they could tell their correspondents what God had wrought in New England. Lacking any modern sense of proportion for what it would take to describe the Jewish people as sufficiently "converted" in order to satisfy the apparent prophetic standards, the immense symbolic value of even one convert such as Monis set off speculation across the Atlantic that the end of the world was coming, and perhaps rapidly.

Likely in response to the great interest spurred by Monis's conversion, Samuel Willard's foundational tract *The Fountain Opened* was printed in a second edition in 1722 (original edition 1700). Willard's sermon on the messianic passage Zechariah 13:1, "In that day there shall be a fountain opened to the house of David and to the inhabitants of Jerusalem for sin and for uncleanness," made yet another appeal to New Englanders to watch and pray for the national conversion of the Jews. Similar to the Mather family, Willard argued that the end of the world and second coming of Christ would be preceded by "the Calling of the Jews, and the fulness of the Gentiles, and the destruction of Anti-Christ." By the "fulness of the Gentiles," Willard and others typically meant the end of Gentile rule in Jerusalem, and/or the full number of conversions among the elect non-Jews. Significantly, Willard prescribed an active role for his listeners and readers in the conversion of the Jews and the hastening of the coming of Christ, by exhorting the people "to Pray much and

earnestly, for the Conversion of the Jews," because "These Happy
Times are to be Ushered in by Prayer."[38]

With the deaths of the Mathers in the 1720s, systematic eschatological treatises on the destruction of Antichrist and the conversion
of the Jews became more rare for the time being, though both were
often mentioned as a common understanding of what things would
precede the second coming of Christ and the end of the world.[39] In
the case of the conversion of the Jews, even Cotton Mather himself
grew weary of waiting in his last years, and though he did not print
his changed opinion before his death, his circulated manuscript
"Triparadisus" and his son Samuel's biography revealed that as of his
death Mather no longer believed that the Jews would convert. Samuel did not make clear why Mather changed his mind: he may have
simply grown tired of waiting and realized that the scanty evidence
of conversions from Europe hardly indicated the beginnings of the
hoped-for massive conversions at the end. If New England truly was
waiting in the shadow of the apocalypse, and the Jews still seemed
resistant to Christ, then perhaps they never would convert at all.
Furthermore, Mather apparently abandoned the position that God
still held a special place for the Jews as the covenanted nation, believing with many reformed thinkers that all the prophesies relating to the future of Israel actually referred to the "spiritual Israel,"
the church.

Mather still believed that the "Fall of Antichrist" would precede
the conflagration and the second coming, but "The New Testament
seems to have done with a carnal Israel; The Eleventh Chapter to the
Romans is greatly misunderstood, where we find all Israel saved."
Mather came to believe that God had no special use for the Jews:
"Of what Advantage to the Kingdom of GOD can the Conversion of
the Jewish Nation be, any more than the Conversion of any other
Nation . . . ?" To believe this would be to suppose that God would
want to build up the wall of separation between Jews and Gentiles

that Christ had torn down (Ephesians 2). Though some might question whether Mather and other New Englanders' eschatology was ever positively inclined toward the Jews at all, now Mather clearly had reverted to a model of historical understanding that saw the Jews as once chosen but now rejected by God in favor of the reformed Christian church. According to Israel Loring, Mather became more concerned with the return of Christ as his death approached. When Loring received word of Mather's death, he noted in his diary that "His preaching and his Conversation of late turned very much Upon the final dissolution of all things, of our Saviour Coming in flames of fire to take vengeance on Such as know not God."[40] Though Mather's ideas changed, his general interest in eschatology seems only to have grown through his career.

By the late 1720s, one can sense weariness among some New England observers who had long waited for the destruction of Rome and the conversion of the Jews. Systematic treatments of eschatology became less common, particularly after the deaths of the Mathers and their generations of leadership, which produced numbers of detailed eschatological treatises by Samuel Willard and Samuel Sewall, among others. But starting in the 1720s one can also see in the broad literature of provincial New England an increasing emphasis on evangelism, missions, and the expected massive conversions preceding the second coming of Christ. Not that these beliefs had been absent before, but if news from Britain and Europe encouraged less speculations about the downfall of Rome and Jewish conversions, New England's religious and cultural leadership seemed more than ready to turn their attention to an internationalist, ecumenical, and evangelical vision of conversions at the end of the world.

As Michael Crawford has ably demonstrated, British writers like the Mathers placed increasing emphasis on "seasons of grace" or periodic upswings in both conversions and the zeal of the already converted. In their various contexts across the Atlantic world, and especially in New England, the revivalist pastors did not simply speculate on premillennial or postmillennial appearances of the kingdom, or even see the millennium as simply the "ultimate product" of revivals. Instead, many New Englanders came to believe that they, their congregations, and the Protestant interest were actively participating in the coming of the kingdom. The eschatological language associated with the promotion of revival expanded earnestly in the 1720s.[41] Not coincidentally, so also did revivals become increasingly common in the British Atlantic world.

One of the key leaders in southern New England's incipient evangelical movement was Eliphalet Adams of New London. As early as 1721, Adams was promoting revival not only in New England but also across the known world. Building on the Connecticut Valley revivals of Solomon Stoddard in the 1710s, Adams and others helped promote more revivals in 1720–22. A revival took place in Windham, Connecticut, in 1721, and Adams published a sermon given there in which he attempted to stoke the millennial flames potentially sparked by this revival, telling the converted to "pray for the Success of the Gospel in other places." He also told the Windham church to "pray for the peace of Jerusalem," a reference to Psalm 122:6 and a phrase often used to suggest hope for an eschatological gathering of the Jews. Finally, Adams pleaded with the people at Windham to "Pray that the Spirit may be poured out from on High upon every part of the Land, that the work of Religion may not die among Us."[42] This kind of language anticipating a latter-day outpouring of the Spirit and a dramatic intervention of God became so common that one might almost mistake it as formulaic. It appeared in sermons, pamphlets, and government mandates for days of prayer, and was usually based not so much on the details of Revelation or Daniel's visions but on the eschatological promises of Joel, Habakkuk, or Isaiah promising a great new work of the Holy Spirit at the end of time.

A selection of references from the period demonstrates how widely this evangelical language was being used in British Atlantic discourses. For instance, the *Boston News-Letter* periodically inserted articles with references to end-time conversions, such as accounts of missionaries from the Halle school. The June 13, 1720, issue's front page was devoted to describing the mission of two Danes associated with Halle in the East Indies. After giving extensive details of the mission work, the missionaries concluded with the assertion that God was stirring "up in Europe many Promoters among Persons of all Ranks, that in these last Times, the Salvation of the Heathens may be fought with Earnestness, and their Conversion promoted by the whole Protestant Church."[43]

Likewise, government pronouncements for days of prayer and fasting often included eschatological revival language. Governor Joseph Dudley usually included some reference to the extension of the Kingdom of God in the world in his proclamations, but increasingly through the 1710s and 1720s references to specific latter-day conversions became more common. For instance, as early as 1716, partly in response to the Jacobite rising, Lieutenant Governor William Tailer asked Massachusetts residents to pray that "not only the Kingdoms of Europe, but of Asia, Africa, and America also, may become the Kingdoms of our LORD and of His CHRIST." Samuel Shute issued a typical prayer in 1721 when he asked that God would "pour on us a Spirit of REFORMATION," "that He would graciously Remember His ancient People the Jews," and that he would "grant Enlargement and Prosperity to the Church of CHRIST throughout the World." Similarly, William Dummer asked that God "would pour out His SPIRIT upon us . . . And that the Kingdom of our LORD JESUS CHRIST may be advanced, & the Earth filled with His Glory." If many of the high government officials were not dissenters, and if the Massachusetts and Connecticut governments increasingly treated politics in a "secular" fashion, this promotion of eschatological prayer and participation in evangelical discourse still belies Perry Miller's image of an increasingly "secular state."[44]

Northampton's Solomon Stoddard, a controversial figure because of his public criticism of the treatment of the Indians, fit his desire for the evangelization and fair treatment of them into a broader eschatological system that included conversion of heathen populations as well as the Jews. Attached to his 1722 *An Answer to Some Cases of Conscience* was a poem, apparently authored by Stoddard in 1701, that sang of the massive conversions expected at the end of the world. When one understands that Stoddard's chief argument against poor treatment of the Indians was that mistreatment and a failure to evangelize them contradicted and perhaps even delayed this prophesied conversion of Christ's enemies, then one can more properly understand Stoddard's public challenge to New England's usual practices of deceit and murder against their Indian neighbors. He prayed that God would "Make haste with thy Impartial Light, And terminate this long dark Night." He hoped that the "English Vine" in America would spread into the native cultures, but through conversions, not murder or deportations.

> Give the poor INDIANS Eyes to see
> The Light of Life: and set them free;
> That they Religion may profess,
> Denying all Ungodliness.

Stoddard then moved from the Indians to the Jews' conversion, perhaps linking them as scattered tribes of Israel:

> From hard'ned JEWS the Vail remove,
> Let them their Martyr'd JESUS love;
> And Homage unto Him afford,
> Because He is their Rightful LORD.

Then Stoddard turned his eyes toward the destruction of idolatry generally, and the ultimate triumph of true religion across the world:

So false Religions shall decay,
And Darkness fly before bright Day:
So Men shall GOD in CHRIST adore;
And worship Idols vain no more.
So ASIA, and AFRICA,
EUROPA, with AMERICA;
All Four, in Consort join'd, shall Sing
New Songs of Praise to CHRIST our KING.[45]

Although many New Englanders shared in Stoddard's hopes for end-time conversions, few saw any hypocrisy in this hope as compared with New England's actual treatment of the native populations. But to Stoddard, and increasingly to others, proper beliefs about the end demanded not just ethereal speculations, but also actions, including prayer, proselytization, and revivals.

Among the chief promoters of evangelism as promoting the end-time interests of God was Benjamin Colman. Colman's more cosmopolitan disposition both lessened his interest in issues such as complex and hostile chiliasm, and increased his interest in an evangelical essentialism colored by a more general, yet still fervent, millennial hope. Colman had truly hit his evangelical stride by 1727 when he preached the ordination sermon for Ebenezer Pemberton, published that year as the pamphlet *Prayer for the Lord*. Colman's text was the call of Christ to "laborers in the harvest," Matthew 9:38 ("Pray ye therefore the Lord of the harvest that he will send forth laborers into his harvest").

Colman's was one of the first activist missionary sermons to appear in New England, with specific suggestions that New England ministers should not restrict themselves simply to finding a church appointment but should consider going out into the world for the sake of the gospel. Colman's message was expectant: "We pray for souls yet to be born, & for churches yet to be formed; that to the end of the world the Lord would provide, & send forth labourers into every part of his church, in all places of the earth." He urged his readers to "pray for the age to come, & for our childrens children; that his spirit may be poured out on our seed," and also for "the perpetuity of the kingdom of Christ on earth." Colman, who as we have seen worked diligently on behalf of Native American missions, noted that within New England, the laborers were plenty, but nearly everywhere else, from New England's borderlands to the distant parts of the earth, the laborers were few. "It is high time this narrow selfish spirit and love of home were broken. . . . The harvest abroad is plenteous." Colman specifically asked that New England ministers consider going on mission to South Carolina.[46] Under the leadership of Colman, Adams, and others in the Protestant interest, an optimistic, conversionist eschatology began to overtake New Englanders in the 1720s.

The "shaking dispensations" of the 1727 earthquake felt in New England led to many conversions and further speculations about great numbers of conversions at the end of time. Erik Seeman has interpreted this "earthquake revival" as a demonstration of the irrelevance of millennialism among the laity, basing his argument upon the lay memoirs extant from converts in this awakening and their failure to mention Judgment Day. A different view of the religious sensibilities prevailing in 1727 reveals that the ministers who led their congregational revivals during this and later years saw the earthquake as a threat from God against the people's sins, and often saw the earthquake and subsequent conversions through eschatological, conversionist lenses. For instance, Joseph Sewall believed that the repentance displayed in response to the earthquake could be a sign of better things to come: "And is not the Day near when the Fountain now mention'd shall be in a signal manner opened [referring to the theme of Samuel Willard's famous treatise] in the extensive Preaching of the Gospel, and the abundant Effusions of the Spirit of Grace, so that many Nations shall be sprinkled, yea washed from their sins." It would be a time, Sewall believed, of massive conversions, even of the Jews: "all Israel shall be saved; and the receiving of them shall be Life from the Dead to the Gentiles!"[47]

Israel Loring of Sudbury was not quite sure what to make of the earthquake, but he did suspect that it heralded a great eschatological moment. "What the import of these things may be God only knows. The Lord prepare me for what may be coming," he wrote in his diary. Loring turned to the seventeenth-century Danish minister Mickel Pederson Escholt for guidance, who penned *Geologia Norvegica* (London ed. 1663) in response to a 1657 Norwegian earthquake. Escholt thought that earthquakes preceded remarkable events in the world, and most especially "in these last times of the World" could presage the final events of providential history. After another minor earthquake in 1730, Loring worried that it might herald both temporal and providential upheavals, including perhaps the "Loss of our invaluable Liberties and priviledges," or the eschatological earthquake of Revelation 16:18. He believed that eventually "Our Lord is Coming to Send a fire on the earth: (but it Shall be visited of the Lord of hosts With earthquakes as Well as fire) and What if it be in the Subterraneous receptacles already kindled?" Loring thought that the signs of the times warranted a readiness for whatever God might have planned next.[48]

Likewise, Thomas Prince Sr. interpreted the earthquake at the particular fast on November 2, 1727, and subsequently at the general thanksgiving on November 9, through internationalist eschatological lenses. Prince saw New England's earthquake as only one in a whole series of earthquakes, likely fulfilling prophesies such as that in Haggai 2:6–7, "I will shake the Heavens, and the Earth, and the Sea, and the Dry Land: and I will shake all Nations: And the Desire of all Nations shall come, and I will fill this House with Glory." It was a fearful time, leading perhaps to worldwide conflagration and destruction. For those who would turn to God it was also a time of hope and fulfilled promises, however, as Prince cited in Joel 3:14–16:

"And the Heavens and the Earth shall shake: BUT THE LORD WILL BE THE HOPE OF HIS PEOPLE, AND THE STRENGTH OF THE CHILDREN OF ISRAEL." Prince believed with many of his fellow pastors that the earthquake was in part a call to New England to reform their many sins. But he outlined how the threat was not unique to New England at all, but was a worldwide dispensation becoming apparently more and more common over the previous sixty years. Prince listed all the notable earthquakes of which he knew, including ones in Persia in 1667, Lima, Peru, in 1687, and Jamaica in 1692. Given these and other judgments Prince pleaded with the people that they do not "have one Minutes time to Repent, Believe in CHRIST, or prepare for the Judgment." Prince insisted that they "remember the GREAT and TERRIBLE DAY of GOD is approaching and how near we know not." In a time of threatening judgments, he was not so optimistic as he would be later concerning massive conversions at the end, "tho' the Jews may have the destinguishing Grace to mourn with Repentance, . . . yet the rest of the Tribes of the Earth shall mourn with utter Despair" when Christ appeared the second time. Nevertheless, he admonished his readers and listeners to "earnestly look and pray for the HOLY SPIRIT to follow and speak in an effectual manner: That He may be Poured out as He was" in the early days of the church at Jerusalem. Prince was thrilled at the "Joy of the Harvest" in the earthquake revival, exulting at this "happy Effusion of the HOLY SPIRIT!"[49]

In the 1730s, the time seemed ripe to many New Englanders and their Scottish and English correspondents for the final revival of religion, and they began encouraging their churches to pray for the great eschatological outpouring of the Holy Spirit. Among the key figures involved on New England's side in preparing people for revival were Colman, Adams, John Webb of the New North Church in Boston, Joseph Sewall of the Old South Church, and Northampton's replacement for the deceased Solomon Stoddard, Jonathan

Edwards. Adams, for his part, told the Connecticut assembly for the May 1733 election sermon at Hartford that because great revivals should be expected "before the consummation of all things and things are hastening to an end, there may be some remote hope & more obscure prospect that things may mend even among a sinful, declining, and Degenerate people; who can say but that these blessed times may come on speedily." No wonder that New Englanders would so eagerly receive the news of Edwards's Northampton revivals a mere two years later. Many hoped along with Adams that "the benign Influences [of the eschatological revival] may reach even to the Ends of the Earth & our Eyes may see it."[50]

Similarly, John Webb begged Bostonians to pray for revival, believing that if "we can once prevail with the Lord, to Revive his Work, in these declining Years; Oh! What an happy Prospect shall we have!" Then would come the fulfillment of one of the most frequently referenced Old Testament prophecies among the rising evangelical cohort, Isaiah 44:3–5, which Webb quoted: "I will pour water upon him that is thirsty, and floods upon the dry ground: I will pour out my spirit upon thy Seed, and my Blessing upon thine Offspring. . . . One shall say, I am the Lord's: and another shall subscribe unto the Lord, and sirname himself by the name of Israel."[51] To Webb, Adams, and the friends of the Protestant interest, the time had come for the reformed Christians of the British Atlantic world to come before God and plead for the great end-time revival, and for a great eschatological turn in which millions would repent and "sirname" themselves as the millennial people of God.

So as the news of Edwards's Northampton awakenings came to New London and Boston, and then under the promotion of Colman and others went across the Atlantic to fascinated correspondents, there was an already developed system of eschatology into which anxious observers could fit the news. Perhaps, they thought, this and the even greater revivals of Whitefield and others were the beginning of the expected end.[52] But New Englanders associated with the Protestant interest, as has been true of the eschatologically minded everywhere, had a hopeful but always fundamentally uncertain tenor about their speculations on the great revivals that came to New England and many other pietistic communities in the British Atlantic and European worlds during the mid-eighteenth century. They believed themselves to be the people of God, as opposed to the Antichristian papists and the long-forsaken Jews, but they also believed that God intended great harvests of souls to expand the kingdom at the end of time, perhaps just before the second coming of Christ. But the call to wait was a difficult one, and one can only wonder how many of these hopeful saints waiting in the shadow of apocalypse entertained secret doubts or frustrations concerning God's interminable delay of the end. In light of eschatological disappointment, the international evangelical movement readily adopted their familiar "almost, but not yet" optimism about what God planned to do for them in history.

Epilogue

The rise of the Protestant interest explains a great deal about how prominent New Englanders responded to the massive political and cultural changes they faced in the decades after 1689. The combined effects of the Protestant succession, British wars with Catholic powers, and increasing concern for the fate of international Protestantism led New Englanders to shed vestiges of their old Puritan identity in favor of a new identification with the Protestant interest. Abandoning their seventeenth-century precisionism and hostility toward the growing Restoration empire, they became intensely devoted to the British nation, empire, and monarchy, especially as Britain fought Catholic enemies within and without. However, the Protestant interest owed its highest allegiance to God's true church in the world, the international Protestant movement.

While there was much initial controversy over the new Massachusetts charter of 1692, leaders in Massachusetts soon became quite willing to shoulder their new role in the British nation. They saw Britain as the leader in the fight against world Catholicism, and thought it foolhardy to undermine the power of the monarchy or the empire in the name of intra-Protestant squabbles. Thus, leading pastors, especially Benjamin Colman, expressed undying fidelity to Britain and the Protestant succession in numerous public proclamations. They also excoriated fellow countrymen who appeared disloyal to British Protestantism, especially the Jacobites. After the death of Anne in 1714, New Englanders had great confidence that they could make common cause with Whig Anglicans in a common British Protestant cohort. Such figures as Colman also hoped that the financial power of Protestant Britain would energize missions to North American natives who had largely been left to the evangelistic efforts of the Britons' inveterate enemies, the French Jesuits.

Print media also helped create the new identification with the Protestant interest. The newspapers, especially the *Boston News-Letter,* maintained a remarkable commitment in their early decades to supplying news of persecuted and warring Protestants in Europe. Many pastors used such available knowledge to call for prayer for the suffering Protestant churches, and to help New Englanders identify vitally with their distant brethren. The popular New England almanacs also helped serve the interests of British Protestantism, especially through the admiration they expressed for the monarchs, and the way they reminded readers of key moments in British providential history.

The threat posed by Catholicism became most immediate to New Englanders in times of war, especially during Father Rale's War of 1722–25. New Englanders had heard for years about the threat of world Catholicism against the international Protestant movement, and in the 1720s they believed that the Wabanakis inspired by Sebastien Rale represented a satanic attempt to destroy their outpost of Protestantism in North America. New Englanders also used the perceived threat of Jacobitism as a way to present themselves as unquestionably loyal British Protestants, and to maintain the power of the Protestant interest in New England against the intrusions of high-church Anglicans.

Finally, leaders of the Protestant interest lived in a mental world filled with eschatological expectations that fueled their intense loyalty to both Britain and the international Protestant community. Many expected that before Christ's return the Catholic church would be destroyed, the Jewish people would be converted to Christianity, and the once-threatened Protestant churches would lead miraculous revivals. New Englanders sought to insert themselves into these apocalyptic dramas by fighting against the Catholic threat, praying for the conversion of the Jews and other non-Christians, and ultimately by promoting their own revivals. To many, the great outpouring of the Holy Spirit for revival seemed finally to come with the arrival of the young Anglican itinerant George Whitefield.

Three years after the great revivals began, Thomas Prince was still waiting for clear evidence of the eschatological expansion of the gospel, and was still optimistic. After all the many prayers offered at fast and thanksgiving days, Prince believed that God was "in a wondrous manner, pouring down all this vast collection of earnest prayers on the present generation, 1st, In a wonderful specimen, a few years ago at Northampton and the neighbouring towns; then in raising up, and sending forth some extraordinary, powerful, and searching ministers of grace." The vision of evangelical empire that Prince and others cast did achieve enormous gains in the post-Whitefield era as the evangelical style of itinerancy bore much fruit in cross-cultural missions. Prince would have to wait longer, though, for the dawning of the millennium, and presumably he went to his grave still expecting that at any moment the end might begin. In Prince's eschatological vision and others', one can see an unfulfilled evangelical hope for what lay on an always-moving horizon, and a confidence that as the people of God they could fit any circumstance into a future that was secure within the divine timetable of history.[1]

Perhaps one of the reasons that historians have debated whether there really was a "Great Awakening" lies with this hopeful uncertainty that evangelicals must maintain. As Whitefield's awakenings swept through New England and the Middle Colonies, evangelical observers knew something "big" was going on, but the very nature of their eschatology made it difficult for them to say how "big" this event really was, or more specifically, whether these revivals would inaugurate the millennium.[2] As Josiah Smith, dissenting pastor of Charleston, South Carolina, put it, "Some great Things seem to be upon the Anvil, some big Prophesy at the Birth; God give it Strength to bring forth!"[3]

In 1743 when the awakenings had begun to die down and the contest for the meaning of the revivals began raging, the revivalist ministers could agree that the remarkable occurrences were "in the main, a genuine Work of God, and the Effect of that Effusion of the Spirit of Grace, which the faithful have been praying, hoping, longing and waiting for."[4] But there was no sense of closure that only the "promis'd Day" would bring. And so the eschatological horizon moved forward.

Though his own Northampton revivals had come and gone, and though Whitefield's spectacular revivals had not ushered in the millennium, Jonathan Edwards still hoped to see an even more massive eschatological revival, and thought he might have happened upon an idea that could draw the international evangelical community a step closer to the evasive goal: a transatlantic concert of prayer. In 1747 Edwards published *An Humble Attempt to Promote Explicit Agreement and Visible Union of God's People, in Extraordinary Prayer, For the Revival of Religion and the Advancement of Christ's Kingdom on Earth,* which supported the concert and considered its possible role in redemptive history.[5]

The 1748 American edition came with the endorsement of some of New England's leading evangelicals, including Joseph Sewall, John

Webb, and Thomas Prince. Their justification for the concert was explicitly historical and prophetic, noting that God had made predictions in his curse on the serpent ("the seed of the woman should bruise his head") and in his promise to Abraham ("in his seed should all the nations of the earth be blessed") that had yet to be fulfilled, but were likely to be accomplished by the prayers of the people of God in all parts of the earth. The promoters envisioned prayers from every nation going up to God as pleasing incense, and argued that the concert would "promote the increase and constancy of these acceptable prayers." They knew that some had a less optimistic view of the future, expecting instead that there would be a "very general slaughter of the witnesses of Christ" before the second coming, but they thought that this possibility should be no "just objection against our joint and earnest prayers for the glorious age succeeding, or for the hastening of it." In fact, if such a terrible time was coming in Europe, "which we in depending America are likely to share in," all the more reason to pray for "suffering graces." And so with ambivalence they offered Edwards's prayer concert to the evangelical community, hoping that it would help usher in the coming kingdom, but knowing that perhaps it might only prepare the people of God to withstand the coming persecutions of Antichrist.[6]

In *An Humble Attempt*, Edwards used Zechariah 8:20–22 as his primary text, which describes a time in which people from many cities and nations would gather and pray before the Lord. This prophecy, Edwards showed, predicted that "a future glorious advancement of the church of God" was yet to come, and that the advancement would be "brought on" or "introduced . . . by great multitudes in different towns and countries taking up a joint resolution, and coming into an express and visible agreement" to join in concerted prayer. Edwards gingerly avoided specifics of the last days' calendar, but he thought that the prophecy and others like it foretold the coming of an "extraordinary spirit of prayer, as preceding and introducing that glorious day of religious revival" when many thousands and even millions, including the Jews, would be awakened and brought into the church. Therefore, Edwards concluded, it was "very suitable" that the saints in England, Scotland, and the colonies should join in the concert of prayer "for those great effusions of the Holy Spirit, which shall bring on that advancement of Christ's church and kingdom." Edwards hoped that the transatlantic union might introduce the last great dispensation of God's Holy Spirit and the spirit of prayer, and interpreted the correspondence for the concert that had gone out from Scotland to Massachusetts and all the mainland colonies as a harbinger of such an eschatological movement.[7]

Edwards likely felt disappointed with the concert's failure to excite a massive outpouring of transatlantic prayer. However, Prince's vision of worldwide conversions and Edwards's hopes for the concert of prayer reflected the highest aspirations of the eschatological hope that colored evangelical piety through the awakenings and beyond. The global vision of the Protestant interest, then, had substantially transferred to the evangelical movement. One can also see in Prince's and Edwards's passages the malleability of their eschatological categories and expectations. Even the enemies often change, from the new emphasis on Spain as the great papist threat with the War of Jenkins' Ear that began in 1739, to the anti-French civil millennialism of the French and Indian War, to the construction of the British as Antichristian by some colonists in the American Revolution.[8]

Though many friends of the Protestant interest did not become evangelicals, there can be no doubt that the Protestant interest helped color what evangelicalism became. We can see the Protestant interest's influence on evangelicalism in several instances. First, evangelicalism is internationalist. Because of the aggressive yet ecumenical nature of gospel essentialism and revivalism, evangelicalism tends toward international networking, and has demonstrated a persistent thirst for international news of missions, persecutions, and revivals. Paradoxically, however, evangelicals have also regularly attached themselves to the national or imperial projects of modern nation-states, in particular those of Britain and America. One might wonder about the fate of such nationalist ties under the conditions of the global economy and postmodernity, but one needs only to look at the evangelical ties of recent American presidents to see that the evangelical synthesis with American nationalism lingers on into the twenty-first century.[9]

Likewise, evangelicalism has always flourished when it had others against whom to define itself. Historically, there seem to have been two options for the great others in the centuries since the Reformation: Roman Catholicism, and later, "secular humanism" (if pressed, evangelicals would always say that Satan himself was their ultimate opponent). These have likely worked because of their aggressiveness and competition for religious and/or intellectual supremacy with orthodox Protestantism in Western culture. Evangelicals thrive when they perceive themselves threatened by cultural crisis and a godless other; that very threat promotes networking, activism, publicity, and the agenda of revival.[10]

One also sees in the Protestant interest, and in the subsequent history of evangelicalism and fundamentalism, an affinity for modernization, and particularly for the use of the latest techniques of mass communications media. The international evangelical movement rose in force through the broad use of print technology and marketing, showing that the strange coincidence of "evangelical faith, mass media, and a finely tuned popular style" turns out to have been not that strange in the history of evangelicalism. It appears that the rising availability of public information and print, which scholars have seen as so central to the creation of nationalism, also helped create and sustain world evangelicalism. Then and now, evangelicals do best when they are "engaged in struggle with the institutions, values, and thought-processes of the pluralistic modern world."[11]

These conclusions concerning the Protestant interest and the early development of evangelicalism should also give us pause to consider the oft-discussed relationship of religion and the modern world.[12] Modernity is clearly not toxic to religion, and in the eighteenth-century context the Protestant interest thrived as a dissenting subculture engaged in the conditions of modernity.[13] The successor of the Protestant interest, evangelicalism, appears to have been born a roughly contemporaneous twin of that great phenomenon of the modern condition, nationalism.

With the Restoration, the Protestant succession, and the condition of dissent, however, the Protestant interest and British evangelicals faced the prospect of being perpetually separated as a sect outside the realms of political power. The condition of dissent swiftly transformed in America's early republic into an evangelical establishment, but with the increasing separation of church and state, secularization of the public sphere, and disintegration of a Protestant moral consensus, in the twentieth century evangelicals became again an embattled sect that imagined it might be swallowed up in a sea of godlessness, this time represented not by Catholicism, but by "secular humanism."[14] Like New England's dissenting establishment before them, American evangelicals have always struggled with whether they want to identify as a sect or the establishment. In recent years, for instance, many evangelicals have cringed at the government's perceived onslaught against "traditional values," even as they helped promote self-professed evangelicals like President George W. Bush to the loftiest heights of American political power. Even if secularization has promoted a more distinct social compartmentalization or even ghettoization of evangelicalism, this ironically has re-placed evangelicalism in precisely the oppositional and revivalist mode in which it performs the best.

Scholars have only begun to note that evangelicalism, and the related movement of Pentecostalism, swept across the globe in the twentieth century in a way that Thomas Prince and the friends of the Protestant interest would have probably found exhilarating. One can only imagine what the Protestant interest's response would have been, though, to the center of Christendom leaving the global north and relocating to the global south of Africa, Latin America, and southeast Asia.[15] From their very beginnings, evangelicalism and one of its chief tributaries, the Protestant interest, were friendly to the trends of globalization. Surprisingly, the blending of internationalism, nationalism, and a crisis mentality has helped sustain a global revival movement that for more than two hundred and fifty years has stood at the edge of the last days.

Notes

Introduction

1. John Erskine, ed., *Six Sermons by the Late Thomas Prince* (Edinburgh, 1785), 27–28; cited in Mark Peterson, *The Price of Redemption: The Spiritual Economy of Puritan New England* (Stanford, 1997), 237.

2. Account based upon Cotton Mather, *Parentator* (Boston, 1724), reprinted in William Scheick, ed., *Two Mather Biographies* (Bethlehem, Penn., 1989), 167; David Lovejoy, *The Glorious Revolution in America* (New York, 1972), 370–71; Francis Bremer, *The Puritan Experiment: New England Society from Bradford to Edwards*, rev. ed. (Hanover, N.H., 1995), 181.

3. This study seeks to further our understanding of the ways in which provincial and "British" history developed in tandem, taking account of both general imperial developments and the particularities of provincial Massachusetts. Alexander Murdoch's *British History, 1660–1832: National Identity and Local Culture* (New York, 1998) has led the call for this sort of British history, arguing that in the eighteenth century, "regions and localities were subject to as much redefinition as the concept of Britain itself," 8. Murdoch self-consciously follows the lead of J. G. A. Pocock's seminal "British History: A Plea for a New Subject," *Journal of Modern History* 47, no. 4 (Dec. 1975): 601–21, which called for further study of what the idea of Britain has meant in the local cultures of the Atlantic archipelago. See also the conflicted local meanings of "Britishness" in Jim Smyth, *Making of the United Kingdom, 1660–1800: State, Religion, and Identity in Britain and Ireland* (New York, 2001), xi–xii. This project attempts to expand our understanding of British history, meaning "the plural history of a group of cultures situated along an Anglo-Celtic frontier and marked by an increasing English political and cultural domination," Pocock, *British History,*

605, by investigating what the idea of Britain meant among the established English dissenters of Massachusetts.

4. Bruce Tucker, "The Reinvention of New England, 1691–1770," *New England Quarterly* 59, no. 3 (Sept. 1986): 315–40. Tucker uses the concept of the Puritan "errand," which is controversial in its form articulated by Perry Miller, "Errand into the Wilderness," in Miller, *Errand into the Wilderness* (Cambridge, Mass., 1956), 1–15, and which likely obscures as much as it helps in understanding eighteenth-century projects.

5. Lovejoy, *Glorious Revolution,* 178–79.

6. Michael Hall, *The Last American Puritan: The Life of Increase Mather* (Middlebury, Conn., 1988), 206–11.

7. On William's invasion and James's departure, see Craig Rose, *England in the 1690s: Revolution, Religion, and War* (Oxford, Eng., 1999), 1–17.

8. Here and elsewhere I use the language of anti-Catholicism, especially "popery" and "papists," in order to explain the categories used by Protestants generally during the period, but I will not burden the text with repeated clarifications that these are their terms, not mine.

9. Tony Claydon, *William III and the Godly Revolution* (New York, 1996), 28–33; Rose, *England in the 1690s,* 19–28; Gilbert Burnet, *A Sermon Preached before the House of Commons, on the 31st of January, 1688* (Boston, 1689), 7–9.

10. Lovejoy, *Glorious Revolution,* 241.

11. Nathaniel Byfield, *An Account of the Late Revolution in New-England. Together with the Declaration of the Gentlemen, Merchants, and Inhabitants of Boston* (London, 1689), 7–8, 17–18. On William's arrival as a key moment in redemptive history and possibly the inauguration of the millennium see Rose, *England in the 1690s,* 262–64. Tim Harris has shown that the Williamite invasion "triggered a British crisis but different Scottish, Irish, and English Revolutions." One might add that the North American revolutions of 1689 also interpreted the crisis differently, and in Massachusetts leading Williamites read the invasion and establishment of a Protestant monarchy as their new hope for the continued establishment of dissent and the defense against French Catholicism in North America. Tim Harris, "The People, the Law, and the Constitution in Scotland and England: A Comparative Approach to the Glorious Revolution," *Journal of British Studies* 38 (Jan. 1999): 31.

12. Gershom Bulkeley, *The People's Right to Election* (Philadelphia, 1689), 6, 10–11; Lovejoy, *Glorious Revolution,* 248–50.

13. Massachusetts Bay Colony, *At a General Court, February 12th, 1689/90* (Boston, 1690), broadside.

14. Jon Butler, *The Huguenots in America: A Refugee People in a New World Society* (Cambridge, Mass., 1983), 26–31, 48; Lovejoy, *Glorious Revolution,* 236–37, 242.

15. Increase Mather, *A Narrative of the Miseries of New-England* (London, 1689), 3, 8.

16. Ian K. Steele, *Warpaths: Invasions of North America* (New York, 1994), 131–33.

17. Quote from George Rawlyk, *Nova Scotia's Massachusetts: A Study of Massachusetts–Nova Scotia Relations, 1630 to 1784* (Montreal, 1973), 71. Howard Peckham, *The Colonial Wars, 1689–1762* (Chicago, 1964), 31, 36–38; Steele, *Warpaths*, 143–45.

18. See, among others, Hall, *Last American Puritan*, 212–55, 264–71; Richard Johnson, *Adjustment to Empire: The New England Colonies, 1675–1715* (Leicester, Eng., 1981), 136–241.

19. Hall, *Last American Puritan*, 238–39.

20. Massachusetts Bay Province, *To His Excellency* [Address of the Ministers, May 31, 1699] (Boston, 1699), broadside, 2.

21. Richard Gildrie sees the impulse for moral reform continuing through the awakenings in *The Profane, the Civil, and the Godly: The Reformation of Manners in Orthodox New England, 1679–1749* (University Park, Penn., 1994). The suspicion of cosmopolitanism has been clearly demonstrated by Louise Breen in *Transgressing the Bounds: Subversive Enterprises among the Puritan Elite in Massachusetts, 1630–1692* (New York, 2001), 98 and passim. See also Janice Knight, *Orthodoxies in Massachusetts: Rereading American Puritanism* (Cambridge, Mass., 1994), 3–4, 152–54, and passim. On the Puritan eschatology of the saints' withdrawal and purification, see among others David Scobey, "Revising the Errand: New England's Ways and the Puritan Sense of the Past," *William and Mary Quarterly*, 3d ser., 41, no. 1 (Jan. 1984): 12–13. But see also the description of the evangelical strain in English Puritanism, Frank Lambert, *Inventing the "Great Awakening"* (Princeton, N.J., 1999), 25–29.

22. Others might describe the move toward gospel essentialism as a means to consolidating clerical power, and/or a reflection of many ministers' latitudinarian sensibilities. This study does not engage these earlier discussions directly but concedes that both factors also contributed to the move. See Patricia Bonomi, *Under the Cope of Heaven: Religion, Society, and Politics in Colonial America* (New York, 1986), 61–71; John Corrigan, *The Prism of Piety: Catholick Congregational Clergy at the Beginning of the Enlightenment* (New York, 1991); J. William T. Youngs, *God's Messengers: Religious Leadership in Colonial New England, 1700–1750* (Baltimore, 1976), 64–91. On international revivalism, see W. R. Ward, *The Protestant Evangelical Awakening* (New York, 1992).

23. Erik Seeman, *Pious Persuasions: Laity and Clergy in Eighteenth-Century New England* (Baltimore, 1999); David Hall, *Worlds of Wonder, Days of Judgment: Popular Religious Belief in Early New England* (Cambridge, Mass., 1990).

24. Derived from Clifford Geertz, "Religion as a Cultural System," in *The Interpretation of Cultures* (New York, 1973), 89–90.

25. My understanding of the problematic nature of binary models of cultural identity has been shaped in part by Timothy Powell, ed., *Beyond the Binary: Reconstructing Cultural Identity in a Multicultural Context* (New

Brunswick, N.J., 1999), and Homi Bhabha, *The Location of Culture* (New York, 1994). See also Benedict Anderson, *Imagined Communities: Reflections on the Origins and Spread of Nationalism,* rev. ed. (New York, 1991).

26. Charles Hambrick-Stowe, "The Spirit of the Old Writers: The Great Awakening and the Persistence of Puritan Piety," in Francis Bremer, ed., *Puritanism: Transatlantic Perspectives on a Seventeenth-Century Anglo-American Faith* (Boston, 1993), 277–91; *Three Letters to the Reverend Mr. George Whitefield* (Philadelphia, 1739), 3. Among the limited but varied uses of the term "evangelical" up to the coming of Whitefield see Eliphalet Adams's description of Isaiah as the "Evangelical prophet" in *A Discourse Shewing* (New London, Conn., 1734), 1; Israel Loring's description of the church age as the "evangelical Dispensation," in *The Duty of an Apostasizing People* (Boston, 1737), 5; Benjamin Colman promoting a turning to Jesus alone as an "Evangelical Phrase," in *Christ Standing* (Boston, 1738), 6; William Cooper calling Peter Thacher an "Evangelicall Reasoner" in *Compendium Evangelicum* (Boston, 1739), 30.

27. David Bebbington, *Evangelicalism in Modern Britain: A History from the 1730s to the 1980s* (London, 1989); Ward, *Protestant Evangelical Awakening;* Mark Noll, David Bebbington, and George Rawlyk, eds., *Evangelicalism: Comparative Studies of Popular Protestantism in North America, the British Isles, and Beyond, 1700–1990* (New York, 1994); Richard Lovelace, *The American Pietism of Cotton Mather* (Grand Rapids, Mich., 1979); Ted Campbell, *The Religion of the Heart: A Study of European Religious Life in the Seventeenth and Eighteenth Centuries* (Columbia, S.C., 1991). On Eliphalet Adams, see David Harlan, *The Clergy and the Great Awakening in New England* (Ann Arbor, Mich., 1980), 59–62. On evangelicalism and media, see Susan [Durden] O'Brien, "A Transatlantic Community of Saints: The Great Awakening and the First Evangelical Networks, 1735–1755," *American Historical Review* 91, no. 4 (Oct. 1986): 811–32; Lambert, *Inventing the "Great Awakening"*; Frank Lambert, *"Pedlar in Divinity": George Whitefield and the Transatlantic Revivals, 1737–1770* (Princeton, N.J., 1994); Michael Crawford, *Seasons of Grace: Colonial New England's Revival Tradition in Its British Context* (New York, 1991).

28. Gerd Baumann, *The Multicultural Riddle: Rethinking National, Ethnic, and Religious Identities* (New York, 1999), 139.

29. See for instance Samuel Hartlib, *The necessity of some nearer conjunction and correspondency amongst evangelicall Protestants, for the advancement of the nationall cause, and bringing to passe the effect of the covenant* (London, 1644). I wish to thank David Scott for providing this reference and for his discussions about internationalist precedents in the Hartlib circle. See his "From Boston to the Baltic: New England, Encyclopedics, and the Hartlib Circle" (Ph.D. dissertation, University of Notre Dame, 2003). An example of this sort of internationalist sensibility among the Scottish Presbyterians is found in Alexander Shields's *A Hind Let Loose, or a Historical Representation of the Testimonies of the Church of Scotland* ([Edinburgh?], 1687), which associated the

Scottish reformed churches' struggles against the Restoration attempt to impose episcopacy with the similar struggles of the reformed churches of France, Hungary, and the Piedmont. See Smyth's analysis in *The Making of the United Kingdom*, 46. See also Francis Bremer, *Congregational Communion: Clerical Friendship in the Anglo-American Puritan Community, 1610–1692* (Boston, 1994).

See the description of John Dury's failed movement for Lutheran and Calvinist unity in Tom Webster, *Godly Clergy in Early Stuart England: The Caroline Puritan Movement c. 1620–1643* (New York, 1997), 255–67; and Richard Lovelace's description of Dury's ecumenism as a predecessor to eighteenth-century evangelicalism's internationalist and ecumenical ethos in *American Pietism of Cotton Mather*, 255–56.

On the interconnectedness of the Atlantic, see Ian K. Steele, *The English Atlantic, 1675–1740: An Exploration of Communication and Community* (New York, 1986), 133, 158–59. On the Seven Years' War as seen through the framework of apocalyptic history, see Nathan Hatch, "The Origins of Civil Millennialism in America: New England Clergymen, War with France, and the Revolution," *William and Mary Quarterly*, 3d ser., 31 (1974): 407–30, and Nathan Hatch, *The Sacred Cause of Liberty: Republican Thought and the Millennium in Revolutionary New England* (New Haven, Conn., 1977). On the ways in which "Atlantic world" history has displaced "colonial British American" history through an appreciation for multicultural exposures and the ways in which the "Atlantic encompassed a world that perpetuated the rivalries and problems" of European states and religious controversies, see Nicholas Canny, "Writing Atlantic History; or, Reconfiguring the History of Colonial British America," *Journal of American History* 86, no. 3 (Dec. 1999): 1105–9. See also Bernard Bailyn, "The Idea of Atlantic History," *Itinerario* 20, no. 1 (1996): 19–44. On the comparative affinities between international "orthodox dissenters," see James E. Bradley and Dale Van Kley, eds., *Religion and Politics in Enlightenment Europe* (Notre Dame, Ind., 2001), 27–37.

30. On the eighteenth-century development of British nationalism, see Linda Colley, *Britons: Forging the Nation, 1707–1837* (New Haven, Conn., 1992). On the use of the term "nation" in provincial New England, see Philip Haffenden, *New England in the English Nation, 1689–1713* (Oxford, Eng., 1974), 60–61. On British and other nationalisms more generally, see among others Ernest Gellner, *Nations and Nationalism* (Ithaca, N.Y., 1983); Anderson, *Imagined Communities*; Bhabha, "DissemiNation: Time, Narrative and the Margins of the Modern Nation," in Bhabha, *Location of Culture*, 139–70; Adrian Hastings, *The Construction of Nationhood* (New York, 1997).

31. On British anti-Catholicism see among others Raymond Tumbleson, *Catholicism in the English Protestant Imagination: Nationalism, Religion, and Literature, 1660–1745* (New York, 1998); John Miller, *Popery and Politics in England, 1660–1688* (New York, 1973); Colley, *Britons*, 11–54. See also Francis

Cogliano, *No King, No Popery: Anti-Catholicism in Revolutionary New England* (Westport, Conn., 1995).

32. Ian K. Steele, "Exploding Colonial American History: Amerindian, Atlantic, and Global Perspectives," *Reviews in American History* 26, no. 1 (March 1998): 82.

33. The literature on the eighteenth-century public sphere began with Jürgen Habermas's enormously influential *The Structural Transformation of the Public Sphere: An Inquiry into a Category of Bourgeois Society* (1962), trans. Thomas Burger (Cambridge, Mass., 1989). Among the most influential works using a version of Habermas's model are Michael Warner, *The Letters of the Republic: Publication and the Public Sphere in Eighteenth-Century America* (Cambridge, Mass., 1990); Charles Clark, *The Public Prints: The Newspaper in Anglo-American Culture, 1665–1740* (New York, 1994); David Shields, *Civil Tongues and Polite Letters in British America* (Chapel Hill, N.C., 1997). For the public sphere in eighteenth-century British history see Kathleen Wilson, *The Sense of the People: Culture and Imperialism in England, 1715–1785* (New York, 1995).

The most significant survey of New England and colonial print culture is Hugh Amory and David Hall, eds., *The Colonial Book in the Atlantic World*, vol. 1 of *A History of the Book in America* (New York, 2000). See also David Hall, *Cultures of Print: Essays in the History of the Book* (Amherst, Mass., 1996). My book utilizes the whole range of available print sources from the period, including sermons, pamphlets, books, almanacs, broadsides, and newspapers, all of which suggest that the developing Protestant interest gained broad acceptance. However, there is no question that a few ministers' voices dominate much of the discourse here. Some might find this limiting, but when looking at public print culture, one hardly expects to find equality of access in this or any period. It is no coincidence that the leading voices of the developing Protestant interest, including Benjamin Colman, Thomas Foxcroft, Thomas Prince, Joseph Sewall, and Cotton Mather, were the most prolific writers of the third, fourth, and fifth generations of New England pastors. See George Selement, "Publication and the Puritan Minister," *William and Mary Quarterly*, 3d ser., 37, no. 2 (April 1980): 226–27.

34. Jeremiah Shepard, *God's Conduct of His Church through the Wilderness* (Boston, 1715), 22; Gauri Viswanathan, "The Naming of Yale College: British Imperialism and American Higher Education," in Amy Kaplan and Donald Pease, eds., *Cultures of United States Imperialism* (Durham, N.C., 1993), 86, 105; Michael Watts, *The Dissenters: From the Reformation to the French Revolution* (Oxford, Eng., 1978), 263–67.

35. Rose, *England in the 1690s*, 203; Colin Kidd, "Protestantism, Constitutionalism and British Identity under the Later Stuarts," in Brendan Bradshaw and Peter Roberts, eds., *The Making of Britain, 1533–1707* (New York, 1998), 336–39.

36. Increase Mather, Letter to Lord Nottingham, 1703, Add. Manuscripts, 29549, f. 111, British Library. See also Cotton Mather, Letter to Lord Nottingham, November 26, 1703, Add. Manuscripts 29549, f. 109.

37. Colley, *Britons,* 46–48; George Trevelyan, *England under Queen Anne: Ramillies and the Union with Scotland* (London, 1932), 91–99; Joseph Dudley, Letter to Jonathan Belcher, February 6, 1705, Stowe Manuscripts 222, f. 352, British Library.

38. *Boston News-Letter,* September 20, 1714, no. 545.

39. Edward Holyoke, *An Almanack* (Boston, 1715).

40. *Boston News-Letter,* October 24, 1715, no. 602.

41. Cotton Mather, *The Glorious Throne* (Boston, 1714), 29, 35.

42. On the 1715 rising see Daniel Szechi, *The Jacobites: Britain and Europe, 1688–1788* (Manchester, Eng., 1994), 73–78.

43. Joseph Sewall, *Rulers must be Just* (Boston, 1724), 29.

44. *Boston News-Letter,* May 18, 1727, no. 21; list of leaders published in *Boston News-Letter,* August 17, 1727, no. 34.

45. *Boston News-Letter,* November 16, 1727, no. 47. On the ongoing threat to Massachusetts' charter see Carl Bridenbaugh, *Mitre and Sceptre: Transatlantic Faiths, Ideas, Personalities, and Politics, 1689–1775* (New York, 1962), 37–38.

46. Thomas Prince, *A Sermon on the Sorrowful Occasion of the Death of King George* (Boston, 1727), 25–27. See also the "Address of the Pastors of the Associated Churches in Boston, New-England" to King George II, printed in *Boston News-Letter,* April 25, 1728, no. 70, Harvard's address, *News-Letter,* May 16, 1728, no. 73, and New Hampshire's address, *News-Letter,* May 23, 1728, no. 74; Thomas Foxcroft, *God the Judge* (Boston, 1727); Joseph Sewall, *Jehovah is the King* (Boston, 1727); Cotton Mather, *Christian Loyalty* (Boston, 1727).

47. Journal of Israel Loring, transcription, Sudbury Archives, www.sudbury.ma.us/archives, 1725–29, 12.

Chapter One: "Fidelity to Christ and to the Protestant Succession"

1. Benjamin Colman, *Souls Flying to Jesus Christ* (Boston, 1740), 6, 9.

2. On Colman and latitudinarianism, see John Corrigan, *The Prism of Piety: Catholick Congregational Clergy at the Beginning of the Enlightenment* (New York, 1991), viii and passim.

3. Howard Adams, "Benjamin Colman: A Critical Biography" (Ph.D. dissertation, Pennsylvania State University, 1976), 106. For information on the wealth of these merchants, see Bernard Bailyn and Lotte Bailyn, *Massachusetts Shipping, 1697–1714: A Statistical Study* (Cambridge, Mass., 1959), 128–31.

4. Ebenezer Turell, *The Life and Character of the Reverend Benjamin Colman* (Boston, 1749), 1–5; Clifford Shipton, *Sibley's Harvard Graduates,* vol. 4 (Cambridge, Mass., 1933), 93, 119–20; Perry Miller, *The New England Mind: From Colony to Province* (Cambridge, Mass., 1953), 241.

5. Turell, *Benjamin Colman*, 6–25, 31.

6. Ibid., 42–44. On the Third or Old South Church during the period see Mark Peterson, *The Price of Redemption: The Spiritual Economy of Puritan New England* (Stanford, 1997), 120–43.

7. Niel Caplan, ed., "Some Unpublished Letters of Benjamin Colman, 1717–1725," *Proceedings of the Massachusetts Historical Society* 77 (1965): 107; see also Paul Lucas, *Valley of Discord: Church and Society along the Connecticut River, 1636–1725* (Hanover, N.H., 1976), 250–51, n. 4, 24.

8. Brattle Square Church, *A Manifesto* (Boston, 1699), 1.

9. Mather quoted in Kenneth Silverman, *The Life and Times of Cotton Mather* (New York, 1984), 140; Phyllis Whitman Hunter, *Purchasing Identity in the Atlantic World: Massachusetts Merchants, 1670–1780* (Ithaca, N.Y., 2001), 94–96.

10. Brattle Square Church, *A Manifesto*, 1–3.

11. For more details on the conflict, see Miller, *From Colony to Province*, 241–56.

12. *A Confession of Faith* (New London, 1710); Williston Walker, *The Creeds and Platforms of Congregationalism* (New York, 1991, orig. pub. 1893), 463–516; Miller, *From Colony to Province*, 266–67; Hunter, *Purchasing Identity*, 94.

13. Benjamin Colman, *A Sermon Preached before the Governor* (Boston, 1708), 6, 15–16.

14. Corrigan, *Prism of Piety*, 18–19; Colman, *A Sermon*, 16, 27, 31.

15. Benjamin Colman, *A Brief Enquiry* (Boston, 1716), 31–32.

16. Benjamin Colman, *A Sermon Preach'd at Boston in New-England* (Boston, 1716), 14–16.

17. Ibid., 18–19, 26, 28.

18. *News-Letter*, no. 681, April 29, 1717. See also London dissenters' address to George on the uprising, no. 684, May 20, 1717. The dissenters throughout the British Atlantic world commonly argued that those loyal to the Protestant succession deserved protection of their political liberties; Jim Smyth, *The Making of the Untied Kingdom: 1660–1800: State, Religion, and Identity in Britain and Ireland* (New York, 2001), 180.

19. Turell, *Benjamin Colman*, 122–33.

20. Benjamin Colman, *The Religious Regards We Owe to Our Country* (Boston, 1718), 28–29, 46.

21. Benjamin Colman, *Fidelity to Christ and to the Protestant Succession* (Boston, 1727), iv, 1–2, 9, 11; J. C. D. Clark, *English Society, 1660–1832: Religion, Ideology, and Politics during the Ancien Régime* 2d ed. (New York, 2000), 112.

22. Benjamin Colman to Isaac Watts, August 17, 1739, Benjamin Colman Papers, Massachusetts Historical Society (MHS).

23. Turell, *Benjamin Colman*, 64.

24. See letters from Sir William Ashurst to Boston, cited in Jonathan Mayhew, *Observations on the Charter and Conduct of the Society for the Propagation*

of the Gospel in Foreign Parts (Boston, 1763), 158–60; William Kellaway, *The New England Company, 1649–1776: Missionary Society to the American Indians* (London, 1961), 169; David Hayton, "Moral Reform and Country Politics in Late Seventeenth-Century House of Commons," *Past and Present* 128 (Aug. 1990): 66–67.

25. Benjamin Colman to Samuel Wiswall, June 1717?, Benjamin Colman papers, MHS. On Wiswall, see Kellaway, *New England Company*, 246.

26. Kellaway, *New England Company*, 241–42.

27. On the missionary attempts in the 1710s and 1720s, see Kellaway, *New England Company*, 258–60; James Axtell, *The Invasion Within: The Contest of Cultures in Colonial North America* (New York, 1985), 250–54.

28. Turell, *Benjamin Colman,* 64–69. Thanks to Beth Barr for translating the Latin.

29. Benjamin Colman to the President of the Scottish Society for Propagating Christian Knowledge, November 11, 1732, December 25, 1732, Benjamin Colman Papers, MHS; Joseph Seccombe to Benjamin Colman, June 27, 1734, Benjamin Colman Papers, MHS.

30. Joseph Sewall, *Christ Victorious over the Powers of Darkness, by the Light of His Preached Gospel* (Boston, 1733), dedication, ii–iii; Peterson, *Price of Redemption,* 187.

31. Sewall, *Christ Victorious,* 30, 35.

32. On Coram, see Verner W. Crane, "Dr. Thomas Bray and the Charitable Colony Project, 1730," *William and Mary Quarterly,* 3d ser., 19, no. 1 (Jan. 1962): 61–63; Linda Colley, *Britons: Forging the Nation, 1707–1837* (New Haven, Conn., 1992), 56–59.

33. Thomas Coram to Benjamin Colman, April 30, 1734, in Worthington Ford, ed., "Letters of Thomas Coram," Massachusetts Historical Society, *Proceedings* 56 (Boston, 1923), 20–22; Turell, *Life of Benjamin Colman,* 144–46.

34. Thomas Coram to Benjamin Colman, July 26, 1735, in Ford, ed., "Letters of Thomas Coram," 26–27. The "sermons against popery" was likely John Billingsley, *Sermons against Popery* (London, 1723).

35. Thomas Coram to Benjamin Colman, September 23, 1735, October 8, 1736, and March 2, 1737, in Ford, ed., "Letters of Thomas Coram," 32, 34; Peterson, *Price of Redemption,* 188.

36. On Colman's promotion of Edwards's *Faithful Narrative,* see Frank Lambert, *Inventing the "Great Awakening"* (Princeton, N.J., 1999), 54–55.

Chapter Two: "Let Hell and Rome Do Their Worst"

1. *Boston News-Letter,* November 26, 1722, no. 983. This sentiment reflects David Armitage's argument that Britons imagined their empire to be "Protestant, commercial, maritime, and free." *The Ideological Origins of the British Empire* (New York, 2000), 8.

2. W. R. Ward, *Christianity under the Ancien Régime, 1648–1789* (New York, 1999), 6; Phyllis Whitman Hunter, *Purchasing Identity in the Atlantic World: Massachusetts Merchants, 1670–1780* (Ithaca, N.Y., 2001), 78–81. It has been conventional in the literature on various "enlightenments" of the seventeenth and eighteenth centuries to note that interest and knowledge about the outside world expanded during the period in the literate republic of letters. P. J. Marshall and Glyndwr Williams, *The Great Map of Mankind: Perceptions of New Worlds in the Age of Enlightenment* (Cambridge, Mass., 1982), 2 and passim. This chapter sees New Englanders' interest in world news as driven by concern over Catholic persecution and a more general eschatological imagination, rather than as a by-product of "Enlightenment" thought.

3. Marshall and Williams, *Great Map of Mankind,* 60, describes similar encounters with travel literature.

4. Benedict Anderson, *Imagined Communities: Reflections on the Origins and Spread of Nationalism,* rev. ed. (New York, 1991), 44. On a similar subject Adrian Hastings has argued that early modern nationalism, particularly English nationalism, was constructed on biblical discourses. I am interested here in understanding how Protestant internationalism may have been constructed and functioned in similar ways to nationalism. Adrian Hastings, *The Construction of Nationhood* (New York, 1997), 12–13, 185–209.

5. Peter Borsay, *The English Urban Renaissance: Culture and Society in the Provincial Town, 1660–1770* (Oxford, Eng., 1989), 128–29. Linda Colley has argued that the expansion of print also had an important role in "unifying Great Britain and shaping [Britain's] inhabitants' view of themselves." Colley, *Britons: Forging the Nation, 1707–1837* (New Haven, Conn., 1992), 40–41.

6. Harris was an associate of Titus Oates, the inventor of the rumored "Popish Plot" in 1685. Wm. David Sloan, "The Origins of the American Newspaper," in Wm. David Sloan, ed., *Media and Religion in American History* (Northport, Ala., 2000), 36–41; Charles Clark, *The Public Prints: The Newspaper in Anglo-American Culture, 1665–1740* (New York, 1994), 71–72.

7. See for instance *The Present State of the New-English Affairs* (Boston, 1689); John Partridge, *Monthly Observations* (Boston, 1692); N.A., Broadside, *London, September 27* (Boston, 1697). See also Clark, *Public Prints,* 70; Richard Brown, *Knowledge Is Power: The Diffusion of Information in Early America, 1700–1865* (New York, 1989), 33.

8. Nicholas Noyes, *New-England's Duty and Interest* (Boston, 1698), 3.

9. Ibid., 64–65, 67–78.

10. Clark's *Public Prints;* W. David Sloan and Julie H. Williams, *The Early American Press, 1690–1783* (Westport, Conn., 1994), 1–50; and David Copeland, *Colonial American Newspapers: Character and Content* (Newark, Del., 1997) are the best histories of colonial newspapers. Though Copeland acknowledges a significant religious content in the colonial newspapers generally, he believes that "there was news about religion, and there was news about important

events," 203. This characterization of religion as separate from important events would have seemed foreign to eighteenth-century New Englanders, and to at least John Campbell, if not all the Boston newspaper publishers. Sheila McIntyre, " 'I Heare it so Variously Reported': News-letters, Newspapers, and the Ministerial Network in New England, 1670–1730," *New England Quarterly* 71, no. 4 (1998): 593–614, downplays the significance of the newspaper, arguing that it merely mimicked and complemented a well-established network of clerical correspondence. Clark, *Public Prints,* 81–83, indicates that the religious aspect of Campbell's work was essentially an "afterthought" and not central to the paper's secular concerns. This seems to anticipate too eagerly secularization and separation of religion as a unique category of news. See also David Paul Nord, "Teleology and News: The Religious Roots of American Journalism, 1630–1730," *Journal of American History* 77, no. 1 (June 1990): 10, 33–35, and passim; Julie Hedgepeth Williams, "Evangelism and the Genesis of Printing in America," Sloan, "The Origins of the American Newspaper," and David Copeland, "Religion and Colonial Newspapers," in Sloan, *Media and Religion,* 1–16, 32–67; Susan O'Brien, "Eighteenth-Century Publishing Networks in the First Years of Transatlantic Evangelicalism," in Mark Noll, David Bebbington, and George Rawlyk, eds., *Evangelicalism: Comparative Studies of Popular Protestantism in North America, the British Isles, and Beyond, 1700–1990* (New York, 1994), 48–51; Hugh Amory and David D. Hall, *A History of the Book in America,* vol. 1: *The Colonial Book in the Atlantic World* (New York, 2000), 2–7; James Muldoon, *Empire and Order: The Concept of Empire, 800–1800* (New York, 1999), 8.

11. Sloan, "The Origins of the American Newspaper," 41–42; "Letter-Book of Samuel Sewall," 2 vols., *Massachusetts Historical Collections* (Boston, 1886–88), vol. 1: 372; vol. 2: 31, 36, 80, 217, 302, 303, 304, 306; Journal of Israel Loring, transcription, Sudbury Archives, www.sudbury.ma.us/archives, 1720–25: 13, 19, 38; 1725–29: 6, 32; 1729–32: 12, 45; Francis G. Walett, ed., *The Diary of Ebenezer Parkman, 1703–1782* (Worcester, Mass., 1974), 20.

12. Jonathan Edwards, *Personal Narrative,* in *Letters and Personal Writings,* ed. George Claghorn, vol. 16 of *The Works of Jonathan Edwards* (New Haven, Conn., 1998), 794–95. Williams funeral quote from John Demos, *The Unredeemed Captive: A Family Story from Early America* (New York, 1994), 172.

13. Samuel Clough, *Kalendarium Nov-Anglicanum* (Boston, 1707).

14. The *Gazette* presents special challenges because the copies available to the *Early American Newspapers* series are for many years in poor condition and often nonexistent.

15. "Popes Gutts" quote from *New-England Courant,* June 10, 1723, no. 98; see also January 25, 1725, no. 183.

16. See Ward, *Christianity under the Ancien Régime,* 81–82; W. R. Ward, *The Protestant Evangelical Awakening* (New York, 1992), 256–57, 304–7; *News-Letter,* January 14, 1723, no. 990.

17. Although gauging reader response remains a difficult problem for most

histories of print, examining what the people who read or heard the newspapers read in public places knew about the world, and analyzing why editors chose the content they did, is quite significant on its own terms. See Clark, *Public Prints*, 252, concerning the problems with requiring evidence of social "influence." David Copeland goes as far as to say that "One cannot determine to what extent religious views affected religious interpretation of news." Copeland, "Religion and Colonial Newspapers," 66.

18. See among others Copeland, *Colonial American Newspapers*, 205–8; Colley, *Britons*, 23–24; Jeremy Black, "The Catholic Threat and the British Press in the 1720s and 1730s," *The Journal of Religious History* 12, no. 4 (Dec. 1983): 364–81.

19. *News-Letter*, July 8, 1706, no. 117; *News-Letter*, December 30, 1725, no. 1145.

20. *News-Letter*, November 6, 1721, no. 928. On the cultural function of satire or comedy see David Waldstreicher, *In the Midst of Perpetual Fetes: The Making of American Nationalism, 1776–1820* (Chapel Hill, N.C., 1997), 207–10, 336–42.

21. *News-Letter*, December 15, 1712, no. 453.

22. *Boston Gazette*, August 17, 1724, no. 248.

23. Noyes, *New-England's Duty*, 67.

24. *News-Letter*, October 9, 1704, no. 10.

25. *News-Letter*, October 15, 1705, no. 79. The *News-Letter* reported on April 15, 1706, no. 105, that the French were suppressing any news about the revolt, and thus they had nothing to report from the Camisards. See also *News-Letter*, September 1, 1707, no. 177, on Huguenots in London, and March 6, 1709, no. 257, on French Protestants in Oxford, Massachusetts. On the Faneuils, see Jonathan Beagle, "Remembering Peter Faneuil: Yankees, Huguenots, and Ethnicity in Boston, 1743–1900," *New England Quarterly* 75, no. 3 (Sept. 2002): 389–93.

26. John Danforth, *Judgment Begun at the House of God* (Boston, 1716), 42–43.

27. Ward, *Christianity under the Ancien Régime*, 29.

28. *News-Letter*, January 7, 1706 (N.S.), no. 91; *News-Letter*, June 28, 1714, no. 533. See report of building controversy in *News-Letter*, August 4, 1712, no. 434.

29. Dale Van Kley, *The Religious Origins of the French Revolution: From Calvin to the Civil Constitution* (New Haven, Conn., 1996), 72–74; *News-Letter*, December 1, 1718, no. 764. On the other side of the Jansenist issue, the *News-Letter* on March 9, 1718, no. 778, reprinted a letter from a French professor that called Clement XI and his followers among the constitutionalists the true "Schismaticks and Hereticks." *News-Letter*, January 19, 1719, no. 771. Similar reports of celebrations of the anniversary of Luther's protest from Protestant countries followed in later weeks. *News-Letter*, November 13, 1721, no. 929.

30. *Boston Weekly Rehearsal,* January 8, 1733; *Boston Weekly Rehearsal,* October 1, 1733.

31. R. Po-Chia Hsia, *The World of Catholic Renewal, 1540–1770* (New York, 1998), 186–93; Arnold Rowbotham, *Missionary and Mandarin: The Jesuits at the Court of China* (Berkeley, Calif., 1942), 119–75 and passim. *News-Letter,* March 1, 1708 [N.S.], no. 203.

32. *News-Letter,* December 20, 1708, no. 245. Kangxi had in fact banished Maigrot and demanded that all Catholics follow the way of the Jesuits or they were no longer welcome in China. Hsia, *World of Catholic Renewal,* 192. *News-Letter,* September 10, 1711, no. 387. See also *News-Letter,* May 28, 1711, no. 372.

33. Increase Mather, *A Dissertation, Wherein the Strange Doctrine* (Boston, 1708), 91–105, quotes 105.

34. *News-Letter,* June 30, 1712, no. 429; *News-Letter,* May 11, 1719, no. 787, see also February 2, 1719, no. 773; *News-Letter,* November 23, 1719, no. 815; *News-Letter,* August 15, 1720, no. 858.

35. Thanks to my colleague Eric Rust for helping me understand the politics and geography of the Palatinate. Ward, *Christianity under the Ancien Régime,* 5; *News-Letter,* August 16, 1714, no. 540. See also August 23, 1714, no. 541.

36. Ward, *Christianity under the Ancien Régime,* 5.

37. *News-Letter,* June 27, 1720, no. 851.

38. *News-Letter,* February 1, 1720, no. 825.

39. Ten were actually executed after two remained uncaught, one received secular pardon, and one received pardon for converting to Catholicism. Stanislaw Salmonowicz, "The Torún Uproar of 1724," *Acta Poloniae Historica* 47 (1983): 63.

40. *News-Letter,* April 8, 1725, no. 1107. See also news of Thorn in Philadelphia's *American Weekly Mercury,* April 1, 1725, and April 22, 1725, cited in David Copeland, "Religion and Colonial Newspapers," 61. The incident is described in Salmonowicz, "Torún Uproar," 55–79; Richard Butterwick, *Poland's Last King and English Culture, Stanislaw August Poniatowski, 1732–1798* (Oxford, Eng., 1998), 33; Ward, *Christianity under the Ancien Régime,* 215–16; Ward, *The Protestant Evangelical Awakening,* 21–23.

41. *News-Letter,* April 15, 1725, no. 1108; *Boston Gazette,* July 26, 1725, no. 296; *News-Letter,* September 2, 1725, no. 1128—see also edition 1128's letter of Frederick William to Louis XV concerning Thorn.

42. *New-England Weekly Journal,* March 27, 1727, no. 1; April 24, 1727, no. 5; Sloan, "The Origins of the American Newspaper," 52–53; Clark, *Public Prints,* 143–44.

43. Mather, *Suspiria Vinctorum,* 1–3, 12–15, 20–21.

44. Benjamin Hoadly, *An Enquiry into the Reasons* (Boston, 1727), 73; *Boston Weekly Rehearsal,* December 24, 1733. On Gordon's *Geographical Grammar,* see Marshall and Williams, *Great Map of Mankind,* 47.

45. John Reynolds, *A Compassionate Address to the Christian World* (Boston, 1730), 88; Paul Dudley, *An Essay on the Merchandize of Slaves & Souls of Men* (Boston, 1731), ii–iii and passim.

46. Israel Loring, *The Duty of an Apostasizing People* (Boston, 1737), 23, 45, 67. Loring supported the awakenings until their perceived enthusiastic excesses turned him against them in 1742.

47. O'Brien, "Eighteenth-Century Publishing Networks;" Harry S. Stout, *The Divine Dramatist: George Whitefield and the Rise of Modern Evangelicalism* (Grand Rapids, Mich., 1991); Frank Lambert, *Inventing the "Great Awakening"* (Princeton, N.J., 1999); Frank Lambert, *"Pedlar in Divinity": George Whitefield and the Transatlantic Revivals, 1737–1770* (Princeton, N.J., 1994).

48. Cotton Mather, *Manuductio as Ministerium* (Boston, 1726), 56–57.

Chapter Three: Protestants, Popery, and Prognostications

1. Samuel Clough, *Kalendarium Nov-Anglicanum* (Boston, 1706–7).

2. Bernard Capp, *English Almanacs, 1500–1800: Astrology and the Popular Press* (Ithaca, N.Y., 1979), 29–30.

3. Marion Stowell, *Early American Almanacs* (New York, 1977), ix–x.

4. Capp, *English Almanacs*, 144–79; Linda Colley, *Britons: Forging the Nation, 1707–1837* (New Haven, Conn., 1992), 20–22.

5. Jon Butler, *Awash in a Sea of Faith: Christianizing the American People* (Cambridge, Mass., 1990), 80–83, 86; David Hall, *Worlds of Wonder, Days of Judgment: Popular Religious Belief in Early New England* (Cambridge, Mass., 1989), 58–61. Though Hall's work in *Worlds of Wonder* is confined largely to the seventeenth century, his description of the sometimes uncomfortable blending of orthodoxy and astrology as well as other kinds of non-Christian belief is a model for my approach.

6. Michael Winship, "Cotton Mather, Astrologer," *New England Quarterly* 63, no. 2 (June 1990): 308–14; Capp, *English Almanacs*, 131–44.

7. "Orthodox Christianity" in this context is a general Protestant term, meaning that on questions of the nature of God, man, and history "the orthodox" held views shaped by the Augustinian tradition. On questions of ecclesiology and liturgy there might be greater variety of belief among the orthodox.

8. Patrick Curry, *Prophecy and Power: Astrology in Early Modern England* (Princeton, N.J., 1990), 80.

9. Although his focus is on published poetry, not almanacs, David Shields analyzes this genre of verse praising the king as a celebration of the "imperial scheme of commerce." The analysis here sees the Protestant succession and war against Catholicism as equally if not more important than the celebration of imperial prosperity and commerce. David Shields, *Oracles of Empire: Poetry, Politics, and Commerce in British North America, 1690–1750* (Chicago, 1990), 21–22 and passim.

10. Samuel Clough, *The New-England Almanack* (Boston, 1703); Nathaniel Whittemore, *The Farmer's Almanack* (Boston, 1714).

11. Nathaniel Whittemore, *An Almanack* (Boston, 1717).

12. Nathaniel Whittemore, *An Almanack* (Boston, 1718).

13. Nathaniel Whittemore, *An Almanack* (Boston, 1720).

14. Quote from Joseph Stafford, *An Almanack* (Boston, 1739). See Colley, *Britons,* 19–20; Francis Cogliano, *No King, No Popery: Anti-Catholicism in Revolutionary New England* (Westport, Conn., 1995), 23–40; David Cressy, *Bonfires and Bells: National Memory and the Protestant Calendar in Elizabethan and Stuart England* (Berkeley, Calif., 1989), 203–5; Simon Newman, *Parades and the Politics of the Street: Festive Culture in the Early American Republic* (Philadelphia, 1997), 20–23.

15. David Hall, "The Uses of Literacy in New England, 1600–1850," in David Hall, *Cultures of Print: Essays in the History of the Book* (Amherst, Mass., 1996), 70.

16. Sewall quoted in David Conroy, *In Public Houses: Drink and the Revolution of Authority in Colonial Massachusetts* (Chapel Hill, N.C., 1995), 32. Edward Holyoke, *An Almanack* (Boston, 1713); *The Diary of Samuel Sewall, 1674–1729,* ed. M. Halsey Thomas, vol. 1 (New York, 1973), 599; referenced in John Corrigan, *The Prism of Piety: Catholick Congregational Clergy at the Beginning of the Enlightenment* (New York, 1991), 24, 142 n.24; George F. Dow, *The Holyoke Diaries, 1709–1856* (Salem, Mass., 1911), viii–ix. On debates over the calendar and public celebrations in transatlantic evangelical communities see Leigh E. Schmidt, "Time, Celebration, and the Christian Year in Eighteenth-Century Evangelicalism," in Mark Noll, David Bebbington, George Rawlyk, eds., *Evangelicalism: Comparative Studies of Popular Protestantism in North America, the British Isles, and Beyond, 1700–1990* (New York, 1994), 90–112.

17. On Stafford, see John Brooke, *The Refiner's Fire: The Making of Mormon Cosmology, 1644–1844* (New York, 1994), 50–53.

18. Hall, "Introduction," in *Cultures of Print,* 5.

19. Clough, *New-England Almanack,* 1703; Peter Eisenstadt, "Almanacs and the Disenchantment of Early America," *Pennsylvania History* 65 (1998): 152–53.

20. John Tulley, *Tulley's Farewell* (Boston, 1702).

21. Eisenstadt, "Almanacs and the Disenchantment," 155.

22. Nathaniel Ames, *An Astronomical Diary* (Boston, 1735). Michael Crowe points out that before 1750 the idea of a plurality of inhabited worlds had gained a respected international audience and had been integrated into English religious thought by such prominent pastors as Richard Bentley and William Derham. Crowe, *The Extraterrestrial Life Debate, 1750–1900: The Idea of a Plurality of Worlds from Kant to Lowell* (New York, 1986), 22–26.

23. Whittemore, *An Almanack,* 1721.

24. Daniel Travis, *An Almanack* (Boston, 1723); Whittemore, *An Almanack,* 1726.

25. Thomas Robie, *A Letter to a Certain Gentleman* (Boston, 1719), 4, 8; Hall, *Worlds of Wonder*, 108; Rick Kennedy, "Thomas Brattle and the Scientific Provincialism of New England, 1680–1713," *New England Quarterly* 63, no. 4 (Dec. 1990): 599–600.

26. Stowell, *Early American Almanacs*, 272; Eisenstadt, "Almanacs and the Disenchantment," 158–60.

27. Nathaniel Ames, *An Astronomical Diary* (Boston, 1731); Nathaniel Ames, *An Astronomical Diary* (Boston, 1736); Samuel Briggs, *The Essays, Humor, and Poems of Nathaniel Ames* (Cleveland, 1891), 79–82, 106–8.

28. See for instance, Poor Robin, *The Rhode-Island Almanack* (Newport, R.I., 1729); Poor Richard, *An Almanack* (Philadelphia, 1736).

29. Nathaniel Ames, *An Astronomical Diary* (Boston, 1738). Clough and Ames both cited John Partridge. Clough, *Kalendarium*, 1706, and Ames, *An Astronomical Diary* (Boston, 1732).

30. Marcel Gauchet, *The Disenchantment of the World: A Political History of Religion*, trans. Oscar Burge (Princeton, N.J., 1997), 162.

31. Richard Bushman, *From Puritan to Yankee: Character and the Social Order in Connecticut, 1690–1765* (Cambridge, Mass., 1967).

Chapter Four: "The Devil and Father Rallee"

1. Cotton Mather to Robert Wodrow, January 1, 1723 (N.S.), Wodrow papers, Quarto 20, ff. 72–73, National Library of Scotland.

2. On Salmon Falls and quote from Mather, Richard Slotkin, *Regeneration through Violence: The Mythology of the American Frontier, 1600–1860* (Middletown, Conn., 1973), 119–20. There is some dispute about whether the rendering "Abenakis" or "Wabanakis" is more accurate. Following Alice Nash and Mary Beth Norton, I have chosen to use "Wabanakis," which is a more general term encompassing several different subgroups in northern New England. See Alice Nash, "The Abiding Frontier: Family, Gender, and Religion in Wabanaki History, 1600–1763" (Ph.D. dissertation, Columbia University, 1997); Mary Beth Norton, *In the Devil's Snare: The Salem Witchcraft Crisis of 1692* (New York, 2002), 85–86, 350 n. 9. Alice Nash graciously explained the distinction between names in e-mail correspondence.

3. Jeremy Black, *Natural and Necessary Enemies: Anglo-French Relations in the Eighteenth Century* (Athens, Ga., 1986), 10–35, 164.

4. Jill Lepore, *The Name of War: King Philip's War and the Origins of American Identity* (New York, 1998), xv; Norton, *In the Devil's Snare*, 4–5; James E. Kences, "Some Unexplored Relationships of Essex County Witchcraft to the Indian Wars of 1675 and 1689," *Essex Institute Historical Collections* 120, no. 3 (1984): 179–212; John McWilliams, "Indian John and the Northern Tawnies," *New England Quarterly* 69, no. 4 (1996): 580–604.

5. Journal of Israel Loring, 1704–1713, transcription, Sudbury Archives,

www.sudbury.ma.us/archives, 21; John Demos, *The Unredeemed Captive: A Family Story from Early America* (New York, 1994); Evan Haefeli and Kevin Sweeney, "Revisiting *The Redeemed Captive:* New Perspectives on the 1704 Attack on Deerfield," *William and Mary Quarterly,* 3d ser., 52, no. 1 (Jan. 1995): 3–46.

6. Robert Thompson to William Stoughton, November 2, 1692; William Ashurst to the Commissioners, March 8, 1698/9; William Ashurst to [Cotton] Mather, March 19, 1703, in Letter Book, 1688–1761, of the Company for Propagation of the Gospel in New England, University of Virginia Library, microfilm.

7. James Axtell, *The Invasion Within: The Contest of Cultures in Colonial North America* (New York, 1985), 248.

8. Massachusetts Bay Province, *George Town on Arrowsick Island Aug. 9th 1717* (Boston, 1717), 1–3.

9. Ibid., 6–7, 9–10. Francis Parkman argued only somewhat convincingly that the correct spelling is Sebastien Rale from an autograph dated November 1712. Rale's last name was alternatively spelled Racle, Rasle, Rasles, Ralle, Rallè, Râle, and Rallee. Francis Parkman, *A Half-Century of Conflict,* vol. 1 (Boston, 1892), 216. The most recent significant work on Rale is a well-researched pietistic biography, Mary Calvert, *Black Robe on the Kennebec* (Monmouth, Me., 1991).

10. Quoted in Colin Calloway, *New Worlds for All: Indians, Europeans, and the Remaking of Early America* (Baltimore, 1997), 89; see also Kenneth M. Morrison, *The Embattled Northeast: The Elusive Ideal of Alliance in Abenaki-Euroamerican Relations* (Berkeley, Calif., 1984), 177–78; Parkman, *Half-Century,* 214–18.

11. Letter contained in James Baxter, *The Pioneers of New France in New England* (Albany, N.Y., 1894), 96–104, quote from 102–3; see also George F. O'Dwyer, "Sebastien Rale and the Puritans," *Catholic World* 112, no. 672 (March 1921): 47.

12. Superior-General quoted in Colin Calloway, *Dawnland Encounters: Indians and Europeans in Northern New England* (Hanover, N.H., 1991), 81; Cotton Mather, *Decennium Luctuosum* (Boston, 1699), 127–28.

13. David Shields, *Oracles of Empire: Poetry, Politics, and Commerce in British America, 1690–1750* (Chicago, 1990), 206.

14. Axtell, *The Invasion Within,* 250–53; William Kellaway, *The New England Company, 1649–1776: Missionary Society to the American Indians* (London, 1961), 258–59.

15. For authorship and date, see Beverly Bond, "Introduction," in *Some Considerations on the Consequences of the French Settling Colonies on the Mississippi,* reprint (Cincinnati, 1928), 8–9.

16. Ibid., 36–38, 41.

17. Robert Ashurst to Samuel Sewall, May 13, 1720, New England Company Letter Book.

18. Robert Ashurst to the Commissioners, March 1, 1720/1, New England

Company Letter Book; Robert Ashurst to Samuel Sewall, September 28, 1722, February 23, 1722/3, New England Company Letter Book.

19. Samuel Sewall, *A Memorial Relating to the Kennebeck Indians* (Boston, 1721), 1–3.

20. *Conference with the Kennebeck Indians,* November 25, 1720, contained in Appendix, Baxter, *Pioneers of New France,* 288.

21. *Boston News-Letter,* August 21, 1721.

22. *Boston News-Letter,* March 12, 1721/22.

23. Shute quoted in Samuel Penhallow, *The History of the Wars of New-England with the Eastern Indians, or a Narrative of their Continued Perfidy and Cruelty* (Boston, 1726, reprint New York, 1969), 90; Parkman, *Half-Century,* 240.

24. Parkman, *Half-Century,* 243–45; Penhallow, *Indian Wars,* 94, 97.

25. See analysis of Indian narrative silence in Lepore, *The Name of War,* 48–68. On Wodrow, A. M. Starkey, "Robert Wodrow and *The History of the Sufferings of the Church of Scotland,*" *Church History* 43, no. 4 (Dec. 1974): 492.

26. Benjamin Colman to Robert Wodrow, June 11, 1723, in Niel Caplan, ed., "Some Unpublished Letters of Benjamin Colman, 1717–1725," *Proceedings of the Massachusetts Historical Society* 77 (1965), 131; Cotton Mather to Isaac Noble, January 14, 1723/24, in Worthington C. Ford, ed., *Diary of Cotton Mather,* 2 vols. (New York, n.d.), 2, 695.

27. Benjamin Wadsworth, *True Piety the Best Policy for Times of War* (Boston, 1722), 2–3, 22–23, 25. For a similar interpretation to mine of the jeremiad's meaning see Sacvan Bercovitch, *The Puritan Origins of the American Self* (New Haven, Conn., 1975), 54.

28. Thomas Foxcroft, *God's Face set against an Incorrigible People* (Boston, 1724), 47.

29. Solomon Stoddard, *Question whether God is not Angry* (Boston, 1723), 6; Ian K. Steele, *Warpaths: Invasions of North America* (New York, 1994), 162; Colin Calloway, *The Western Abenakis of Vermont, 1600–1800: War, Migration, and the Survival of an Indian People* (Norman, Okla., 1990), 113–31.

30. Stoddard, *Question whether God,* 9–10.

31. On Halle and August Hermann Francke, see among others W. R. Ward, *Christianity under the Ancien Régime, 1648–1789* (New York, 1999), 77–82; W. R. Ward, *The Protestant Evangelical Awakening* (New York, 1992), 61–77.

32. Stoddard, *Question whether God,* 10–11.

33. Ibid., 11–12.

34. Penhallow, *Indian Wars,* 98; *Boston Gazette,* June 22, 1724, no. 240; Baxter, *Pioneers of New France,* 173; Francis G. Walett, ed., *The Diary of Ebenezer Parkman, 1703–1782* (Worcester, Mass., 1974), 14.

35. Fannie Eckstorm, "The Attack on Norridgewock, 1724," *The New England Quarterly* 7, no. 3 (1934): 541–78.

36. *Boston News-Letter,* August 20, 1724, no. 1074; *Boston Gazette,* August 17,

1724, no. 248; Parkman, *Half-Century of Conflict,* 245–47; Morrison, *Embattled Northeast,* 186.

37. Walett, ed., *Diary of Ebenezer Parkman,* 6; Hugh Adams, "A Narrative of Remarkable Instances of a Particular Faith," unpublished manuscript, Massachusetts Historical Society, 2–3, quoted in Douglas K. Fidler, "Preparing the Way of the Lord: Three Case Studies of Ministerial Preconditioning in Congregations before the Great Awakening, 1675–1750" (Ph.D. dissertation, University of New Hampshire, 1997), 116–18.

38. Cotton Mather, *Edulcorator* (Boston, 1724), 27. On the symbolic value of hair and the head in English culture see Lepore, *Name of War,* 93; Gordon Wood, *The Radicalism of the American Revolution* (New York, 1992), 40. On the Atterbury plot, see Murray Pittock, *Jacobitism* (New York, 1998), 52–53. See also letter from the government of New Hampshire to King George, *Boston Gazette,* October 14, 1723, no. 204.

39. *Boston Gazette,* August 17, 1724, no. 248.

40. Vaudreuil to Dummer, October 29, 1724, contained in Baxter, *New France,* 341–46.

41. Cotton Mather to Robert Wodrow, June 15, 1725, in Wodrow Papers, Quarto 21, ff.103–4, National Library of Scotland. On scalping and scalp bounties as practiced by the English colonists, see James Axtell and William Sturtevant, "The Unkindest Cut, or Who Invented Scalping?" *William and Mary Quarterly,* 3d ser., 37, no. 3 (1980): 468–72. For secondary accounts of John Lovewell's raids, see among others Parkman, *Half-Century of Conflict,* 259–71; Gail Bickford, "Lovewell's Fight, 1725–1958," *American Quarterly* 10, no. 3 (1958): 358–66; Fannie Eckstorm, "Pigwacket and Parson Symmes," *The New England Quarterly* 9 (1936): 378–402.

42. David Jaffee, *People of the Wachusett: Greater New England in History and Memory, 1630–1860* (Ithaca, N.Y., 1999), 96; Axtell and Sturtevant, "The Unkindest Cut," 471.

43. Penhallow, *Indian Wars,* 114.

44. Thomas Symmes, *Historical Memoirs of the Late Fight at Piggwacket,* 2d ed. (Boston, 1725), 1, 19–20, 24–26.

45. Ibid., 26–27, 32.

46. Penhallow, *Indian Wars,* 120, 124.

47. See David Ghere, "The 'Disappearance' of the Abenaki in Western Maine: Political Organization and Ethnocentric Assumptions," *American Indian Quarterly* 17, no. 2 (1993): 204. See also David Ghere, "Myths and Methods in Abenaki Demography: Abenaki Population Recovery, 1725–1750," *Ethnohistory* 44, no. 3 (1997): 511–34; Gordon M. Day, *The Identity of the Saint Francis Indians* (Ottawa, 1981), 36–37.

48. Axtell, *The Invasion Within,* 254; Jill Lepore's model of understanding the written narrative of war as crucial to the erasure of its inconvenient,

unpleasant, or even barbaric realities helps us understand how New Englanders constructed this as a godly fight by Protestant Britons against aggressive and degraded French Catholics and their Wabanaki allies, despite the historically simpler explanation of the conflict over land claims. See Lepore, *Name of War*, ix–xv. On frontiers and boundary setting, see William Cronon, George Miles, and Jay Gitlin, "Becoming West: Toward a New Meaning for Western History," in *Under an Open Sky: Rethinking America's Western Past*, eds. Cronon, Miles, and Gitlin (New York, 1992), 15; cited in Lepore, *Name of War*, xiii.

Chapter Five: "The Madness of the Jacobite Party"

1. George Pigot, *A Vindication* (Boston, 1731), 6; John Barnard, *The Certainty, Time, and End* (Boston 1731).

2. For a review of the literature on Jacobitism, see Murray G. H. Pittock, *Jacobitism* (New York, 1998), 3–11.

3. Carl Bridenbaugh, *Mitre and Sceptre: Transatlantic Faiths, Ideas, Personalities, and Politics, 1689–1776* (New York, 1962), 70–71; "Jacobite menace" quote from J. C. D. Clark, *The Language of Liberty, 1660–1832: Political Discourse and Social Dynamics in the Anglo-American World* (New York, 1994), 255. On the importance of studying the language and uses of language in early New England see Jane Kamensky, *Governing the Tongue: The Politics of Speech in Early New England* (New York, 1997), 10.

4. Pittock, *Jacobitism*; Daniel Szechi, *The Jacobites: Britain and Europe, 1688–1788* (Manchester, Eng., 1994); Paul Monod, *Jacobitism and the English People, 1688–1788* (New York, 1989). "Agents of Antichrist" quote from Linda Colley, *Britons: Forging the Nation, 1707–1837* (New Haven, Conn., 1992), 76. J. C. D. Clark notes the continuing power of the imagined Jacobite threat in America through the American Revolution, both because of its threat to the Whiggish sense of British "freedom" and because of the threat of "extinction" of the Atlantic/European Protestant interest. J. C. D. Clark, *The Language of Liberty*, 27–29, 254–56. See also Carl Bridenbaugh, *Mitre and Sceptre*, 27–36.

5. Pittock, *Jacobitism*, 15, 19. James sought an alliance between dissenters and Catholics that never seemed to take hold, much to his disadvantage when the crisis came in 1688. Jim Smyth, *The Making of the United Kingdom, 1660–1800: State, Religion and Identity in Britain and Ireland* (New York, 2001), 51.

6. See Michael Watts, *The Dissenters: From the Reformation to the French Revolution* (Oxford, Eng., 1978), 219–20; Bridenbaugh, *Mitre and Sceptre*, 67.

7. Bridenbaugh, *Mitre and Sceptre*, 56.

8. The Baptists increased dramatically in respectability in elite New England and transatlantic culture in large part through the work of such figures as Harvard benefactor and London merchant Thomas Hollis.

9. Robert E. Daggy, "Education, Church, and State: Timothy Cutler and the Yale Apostasy of 1722," *Journal of Church and State* 13, no. 1 (1971): 61.

10. *Animadversions on King James, His Letter to the Pope* (London, 1691), 4–5, 9.

11. Benjamin Bird, *The Jacobites Catechism* (Boston, 1692), 1–4, 14.

12. *Boston News-Letter,* November 25, 1706, no. 137; *News-Letter,* June 27, 1715, no. 585. See also London dissenters' address on the 1707 Act of Union, *News-Letter,* October 20, 1707, no. 184; Church of Scotland General Assembly address to the king, *News-Letter,* December 20, 1714, no. 558.

13. See among others *News-Letter,* May 31, 1708, no. 216, and June 7, 1708, no. 217; Szechi, *Jacobites,* 56–57; *News-Letter,* November 8, 1708, no. 239.

14. Cotton Mather, citing John Edwards, in *The Old Pathes Restored* (Boston, 1711), 24.

15. Cotton Mather, letter to John Edwards, October 10, 1712, Add. Manuscripts, f. 49, British Library. On the SPG, see Bridenbaugh, *Mitre and Sceptre,* 25–32. Cotton Mather, letter to Robert Wodrow, 1725, in Wodrow Papers, Quarto 21, ff. 106–7, National Library of Scotland; [Cotton Mather], *The Stone Cut out of the Mountain* (Boston, 1716), 12.

16. William Ashurst to Increase Mather, March 10, 1712/3, Letter Book, 1688–1761, of the Company for Propagation of the Gospel in New England, University of Virginia Library, microfilm.

17. *News-Letter,* December 26, 1715, no. 611. See also among others February 6, 1716, no. 617; March 12, 1716, no. 622; March 26, 1716, no. 624; August 6, 1716, no. 643.

18. *News-Letter,* July 18, 1720, no. 854; May 15, 1721, no. 898.

19. Checkley quote from John Frederick Woolverton, *Colonial Anglicanism in North America* (Detroit, 1984), 95.

20. For both episodes I am indebted to R. Bryan Bademan for conversations on the subject, and also his "'A Little Sorry, Scandalous Drove': Congregational Reaction to Anglicanism in Boston, 1717–1724" (Paper presented at the American Society of Church History meeting, Chicago, January 2000). On Checkley, see among others Perry Miller, *The New England Mind: From Colony to Province* (Cambridge, Mass., 1953), 334–35; 468–73; Thomas Reeves, "John Checkley and the Emergence of the Episcopal Church in New England," *Historical Magazine of the Protestant Episcopal Church* 34, no. 4 (1965): 349–60; Lawrence Jannuzzi, "'And Let All the People Say Amen': Priests, Presbyters, and the Arminian Uprising in Massachusetts, 1717–1724," *Historical Journal of Massachusetts* 27, no. 1 (1998–99): 19–27. On the Yale apostasy see among others Bridenbaugh, *Mitre and Sceptre,* 68–71; Miller, *From Colony to Province,* 471; Woolverton, *Colonial Anglicanism,* 125–30; Joseph J. Ellis, *The New England Mind in Transition: Samuel Johnson of Connecticut, 1696–1772* (New Haven, Conn., 1973), 55–81; Donald Gerardi, "Samuel Johnson and the Yale 'Apostasy' of 1722: The Challenge of Anglican Sacramentalism to the New England Way," *Historical Magazine of the Protestant Episcopal Church* 47, no. 2 (June 1978): 153–75; Donald Huber, "Timothy Cutler: The Convert as Controversialist,"

Historical Magazine of the Protestant Episcopal Church 44, no. 4 (1975): 489–96; Daggy, "Timothy Cutler," passim.

21. Charles Leslie, *The Religion of Jesus Christ the Only True Religion* (Boston, 1719). Leslie saw moderate Anglican latitudinarians as well as the dissenters as subversive, regicidal, and duplicitous. See William Kolbrener, "*The Charge of Socinianism:* Charles Leslie's High Church Defense of 'True Religion,'" *The Journal of the Historical Society* 3, no. 1 (Winter 2003): 1–24. Thomas Walter, *A Choice Dialogue* (Boston, 1720), 2, 3, 25.

22. Miller, *From Colony to Province*, 334–35; Mather quoted in Reeves, "John Checkley," 352; John Checkley, *A Modest Proof of the Order & Government* (Boston, 1723), 63.

23. Miller, *From Colony to Province*, 471; Ellis, *The New England Mind in Transition*, 75–78; *A Faithful Relation of a Late Occurrence*, printed in Francis Hawks and William Perry, eds., *Documentary History of the Protestant Episcopal Church in Connecticut, 1704–1789*, reprint (Hartford, Conn., 1959), 73–74. On authorship see Kenneth Silverman, *The Life and Times of Cotton Mather* (New York, 1984), 460n.

24. J. William T. Youngs, *God's Messengers: Religious Leadership in Colonial New England, 1700–1750* (Baltimore, 1976), 37 and passim. On the smallpox controversy see Miller, *From Colony to Province*, 345–66; Silverman, *Cotton Mather*, 336–63.

25. Edward Wigglesworth, *Sober Remarks on a Book* (Boston, 1724), 2, 75–76. Miller painted this text as "ostentatious" and rationalist, but Wigglesworth, like his colleagues in Boston and Cambridge, was clearly threatened by high churchmen and turned quickly to the language of popery. Miller, *From Colony to Province*, 472–73.

26. Thomas Walter, *An Essay upon that Paradox* (Boston, 1724), 12, 82–83. On the Vaudois and the supposed antiquity of Protestantism see S. J. Barnett, "'Where was your Church before Luther?': Claims for the Antiquity of Protestantism Examined," *Church History* 68, no. 1 (March 1999): 14–41.

27. Walter, *Paradox*, 84–86, 92.

28. Jonathan Dickinson, *A Defence of Presbyterian Ordination* (Boston, 1724), ii–iii, 43–44; Bryan Le Beau, *Jonathan Dickinson and the Formative Years of American Presbyterianism* (Lexington, Ky., 1997), 68–73. See also Thomas Foxcroft, *The Ruling and Ordaining Power of Congregational Bishops or Presbyters Defended* (Boston, 1724); Samuel Mather, *A Testimony from the Scripture against Idolatry and Superstition*, reprint (Boston, 1725); [James Peirce], *A Caveat against the New Sect of Anabaptists* (Boston, 1724); Charles Owen, *Plain Reasons for Dissenting*, reprint (Boston, 1725).

29. *The Madness of the Jacobite Party* (Boston, 1724), i.

30. Ibid., 1, 6, 9, 12.

31. *A Brief Account of the Revenues, Pomp, and State of the Bishops* (Boston, 1725), 11–12.

32. Miller, *From Colony to Province*, 472; Reeves, "John Checkley," 356–57. On Samuel Johnson's leadership of a more irenic and presbyterian Anglican cohort, see Joseph Ellis, "Anglicans in Connecticut, 1725–1750: The Conversion of the Missionaries," *New England Quarterly* 44, no. 1 (1971): 73–81.

33. See for example James Honeyman, *A Sermon Preached at the King's Chappel* (Boston, 1733), in which he argues both for "catholick" cooperation with the friends of the gospel essentials but also tells his audience, a convention of New England's Anglican priests in 1726, that they should stand against "such who for no reason dissent from that Church" where the gospel is preached in purity, 7, 11.

34. See for example Samuel Johnson, *A Second Letter from a Minister of the Church of England* (Boston, 1734), 25. On Cutler's antagonistic ways see Silverman, *Cotton Mather*, 373–76; Ellis, *New England Mind in Transition*, 94–97. On Tillotson and Stillingfleet's influence in New England, see John Corrigan, *The Prism of Piety: Catholick Congregational Clergy at the Beginning of the Enlightenment* (New York, 1991), 5 and passim. Latitudinarianism no doubt exercised a strong influence over a number of high-church, low-church, and dissenting ministers and professors including Johnson and Benjamin Colman. But for the dissenters, fears of Catholicism and Jacobitism were never soothed by these "catholick" principles.

35. [John Graham], *Some Remarks upon a Second Letter* (Boston, 1736), 14, 36, 75.

36. Pittock, *Jacobitism*, 95–96; John Barnard, *The Throne Established* (Boston, 1734), 13.

37. Szechi, *Jacobites*, 95–104; Colley, *Britons*, 44–46, 72, 77–85; Jonathan Edwards to John MacLaurin, May 12, 1746, in Jonathan Edwards, *Letters and Personal Writings*, ed. George Claghorn, vol. 16 of *The Works of Jonathan Edwards* (New Haven, Conn., 1998), 204.

Chapter Six: "The Dawning of that Sabbath of Rest Promised to the People of God"

1. [Cotton Mather], manuscript notes on Romans 2:16, Newberry Library, Case manuscript C 9911.557. Newberry lists this manuscript as a Mather sermon, and though his authorship is not definitively linked to the manuscript, it appears likely that he was the author. Erik Seeman has made perhaps the strongest argument against pervasive millennial beliefs among rank-and-file New Englanders in the early eighteenth century. Seeman, *Pious Persuasions: Laity and Clergy in Eighteenth-Century New England* (Baltimore, 1999), 8. See also Theodore Dwight Bozeman's arguments about the lack of millennial concerns among the founders of Massachusetts in *To Live Ancient Lives: The Primitivist Dimension in Puritanism* (Chapel Hill, N.C., 1988), 193–236.

2. Francis G. Walett, ed., *The Diary of Ebenezer Parkman, 1703–1782*

(Worcester, Mass., 1974), 8. See also a similar conversation led by Cotton Mather on March 16, 1727, 22, a discussion on "the Signs of the Times" with Robert Breck, likely revolving around recent earthquakes, 29. The best treatment of the particular details of eschatological thought in New England is James West Davidson, *The Logic of Millennial Thought: Eighteenth-Century New England* (New Haven, Conn., 1977).

3. *The New-England Courant,* September 18, 1721, no. 8.

4. Samuel Clough, *Kalendarium Nov-Anglicanum* (Boston, 1706).

5. Nathan Hatch, "The Origins of Civil Millennialism in America: New England Clergymen, War with France, and the Revolution," *William and Mary Quarterly,* 3d ser., 31, no. 3 (July 1974): 407–30; Hatch, *The Sacred Cause of Liberty: Republican Thought and the Millennium in Revolutionary New England* (New Haven, Conn., 1977).

6. See, for example, George Marsden, *Fundamentalism and American Culture: The Shaping of Twentieth-Century Evangelicalism, 1870–1925* (New York, 1980), 43–71.

7. Bozeman, *To Live Ancient Lives,* 237–86; Increase Mather to Thomas Gouge (at Amsterdam), 1683, Add. Manuscripts, 38693, folio 141, British Library.

8. The quote and interpretation of Burnet are based on Tony Claydon, *William III and the Godly Revolution* (New York, 1996), 28–52, quote from 51.

9. Gilbert Burnet, *A Sermon Preached Before the House of Commons, on the 31st of January, 1688/9* (Boston, 1689); Massachusetts Bay Colony. *At a General Court. February 12th, 1689/90* (Boston, 1690), broadside.

10. Cotton Mather, *The Wonderful Works of God Commemorated* (Boston, 1690), 38–41; Bozeman, *To Live Ancient Lives,* 207–8.

11. Cotton Mather, *Things to be Look'd For* (Boston, 1691), 21, 48.

12. Samuel Clough, *The New-England Almanack* (Boston, 1703).

13. Samuel Clough, *Kalendarium Nov-Anglicanum* (Boston, 1706); Clough, *Kalendarium Nov-Anglicanum* (Boston, 1707).

14. This controversy is best represented by the anonymous "Philopolites," *A Memorial of the Present Deplorable State of New England* (Boston, 1707).

15. Samuel Belcher, *An Essay Tending to Promote the Kingdom* (Boston, 1707), 19–20.

16. Benjamin Colman, *Imprecation against the Enemies of God* (Boston, 1707), 24, 26.

17. Cotton Mather, *The Fall of Babylon* (Boston, 1707), 17.

18. Increase Mather, *A Dissertation, wherein the Strange Doctrine* (Boston, 1708), 91–106, quotes from 102 and 104. On Cotton Mather's relations with Halle, see Richard Lovelace, *The American Pietism of Cotton Mather: Origins of American Evangelicalism* (Washington, D.C., 1979), 32–40. On the relationship of Frederick I and Frederick II to Prussian Pietism, see Richard Gawthorp, *Pietism and the Making of Eighteenth-Century Prussia* (New York, 1993).

19. Benjamin Colman, *A Devout and Humble Enquiry* (Boston, 1715), 33–34.

20. Cotton Mather, *Menachem: A Very Brief Essay of Tokens for Good* (Boston, 1716), 28–39.

21. Cotton Mather to Robert Wodrow, October 4, 1717, National Library of Scotland (NLS), Wodrow Papers, Quarto 20.

22. Increase Mather to Robert Wodrow, November 11, 1719, NLS, Wodrow Papers, Quarto 20, ff. 49–50.

23. Cotton Mather to Robert Wodrow, 1725, NLS, Wodrow Papers, Quarto 21, ff. 106–7.

24. Samuel Mather to Robert Wodrow, May 18, 1727, NLS, Adv. Mss. 27.6.7 ff. 39–40.

25. Richard Cogley has described the expectation of the conversion and restoration of the Jews to Israel as part of a "Judeo-centric" strain in Puritan millenarianism. This school of thought was common, though not dominant, in seventeenth-century Anglo-American Puritanism, and believed that the Jews' conversion would be accompanied by the destruction of the Ottoman Empire and Islam generally, as well as the Roman Catholic church. Richard Cogley, "The Fall of the Ottoman Empire and the Restoration of Israel in the 'Judeo-centric' Strand of Puritan Millenarianism," *Church History* 72, no. 2 (June 2003): 304–32. On Mather's views of eschatological Jewish conversions see Reiner Smolenski, ed., *The Threefold Paradise of Cotton Mather: An Edition of "Triparadisus"* (Athens, Ga., 1995), 28–31; Lovelace, *American Pietism*, 64–72.

26. Cotton Mather, *The Faith of the Fathers* (Boston, 1699), A2, 23.

27. Cotton Mather, *An Advice, to the Churches of the Faithful* (Boston, 1702), 3. Lovelace, *American Pietism*, 276–77. See also Mather's comments on the conversion of the Polish Jew Shalome Ben Shalomoh in London, and Shalomoh's conversion narrative, in Mather, *American Tears upon the Ruines of the Greek Churches* (Boston, 1701), 57–80. Cotton Mather, *Things to be More Thought Upon* (Boston, 1713), 20. See also Increase Mather, *A Discourse Concerning Faith and Fervency* (Boston, 1710), xiv–xv. *Boston News-Letter*, February 21, 1723, no. 996, see also 997, 998.

28. See Cotton Mather's comments in *Parentator*, his biography of Increase, on Increase's lecture series on Romans 11:26, "All Israel shall be saved," in 1665, which was subsequently published in London in 1669. Cotton Mather, *Parentator* (Boston, 1724), republished in William J. Scheik, ed., *Two Mather Biographies* (Bethlehem, Penn., 1989), 117. Increase Mather, *A Dissertation Concerning the Future Conversion*, 1–5, quote from 5.

29. Anthony William Boehm to Cotton Mather, July 23, 1716, Curwen Family Papers, American Antiquarian Society.

30. Mather, *Menachem*, 39–40.

31. [Cotton Mather], *Faith Encouraged* (Boston, 1718), 13–15.

32. Arthur Hertzberg points out that a few Jews, including the merchant

Frazon brothers, passed through Boston during the seventeenth century, and that the Frazons attracted attention from Cotton Mather, who tried unsuccessfully to convert them. Arthur Hertzberg, "The New England Puritans and the Jews," in Shalom Goldman, ed., *Hebrew and the Bible in America: The First Two Centuries* (Hanover, N.H., 1993), 106–7.

33. The narrative of Monis's life and conversion is based on Jacob Marcus, *The Colonial American Jew, 1492–1776*, vol. 2 (Detroit, Mich., 1970), 1096–98, Milton Klein, ed., "A Jew at Harvard in the 18th Century," *Proceedings of the Massachusetts Historical Society* 97 (1985): 135–40; and Hertzberg, "Puritans and the Jews," 108–9.

34. Benjamin Colman, *A Discourse had in the College-Hall at Cambridge, March 27, 1722* (Boston, 1722), 26.

35. Monis, *The Truth,* iv, 12.

36. Benjamin Colman to Robert Wodrow (April 1722?), NLS, Wodrow Papers, Quarto 20, ff. 67–68; Robert Wodrow to Benjamin Colman, August 12, 1723, Benjamin Colman Papers, Massachusetts Historical Society. See also Wodrow to Colman, July 29, 1724, in which Wodrow complains that Colman has not updated him on Monis; Robert Wodrow to Judah Monis, July 23, 1724, NLS, Wodrow Papers, Oct. III, ff. 318–20.

37. Klein, "A Jew at Harvard," 142–43.

38. Samuel Willard, *The Fountain Opened,* 2d ed. (Boston, 1722), 17, 26–28.

39. Jonathan Edwards and others picked up similar speculations about the conversions of the Jews in the end times. Edwards, for instance, recalling similar correspondence between the Mathers, Colman, and Robert Wodrow earlier in the century, wrote the Scottish minister John Erskine in 1750 and described a revival among Jews in Europe, news transferred to him by way of Philip Doddridge and Thomas Prince, and also printed in the *Boston News-Letter*. This unnamed German preacher reportedly had great successes among "those miserable people [the Jews] in Germany, Poland, Holland, Lithuania, Hungary, and other parts." Jonathan Edwards to the Reverend John Erskine, July 5, 1750, in Jonathan Edwards, *Letters and Personal Writings,* ed. George Claghorn, vol. 16 of *The Works of Jonathan Edwards* (New Haven, Conn., 1998), 350. On Edwards's views of eschatological Jewish conversions and interest in news of such see also Gerald McDermott, *Jonathan Edwards Confronts the Gods: Christian Theology, Enlightenment Religion, and Non-Christian Faiths* (New York, 2000), 97–98, 164–65. McDermott points out that Edwards had a particular emphasis on the role of an "eminent person" in leading all historical revivals, including the anticipated end-time Jewish revival.

40. Samuel Mather, *The Life of the Very Reverend and Learned Cotton Mather* (Boston, 1729), 144. See also Reiner Smolenski's explanation for Mather's change of mind, and his edition of Mather's never-published "Triparadisus" in which Mather revealed his opinion against last-days Jewish conversions,

Smolenski, *Threefold Paradise*, 34–36, 295–318. Journal of Israel Loring, Sudbury Archives, transcription, www.sudbury.ma.us/archives (1725–29), 21.

41. Michael Crawford, *Seasons of Grace: New England's Revival Tradition in Its British Context* (New York, 1991), 130. Solomon Stoddard was one of the earliest public advocates for evangelical-style revivalism in New England, beginning in the late seventeenth century. Seeman, *Pious Persuasions*, 148.

42. Crawford, *Seasons of Grace*, 107–9; Eliphalet Adams, *A Sermon Preached at Windham* (New London, Conn., 1721), 39–40.

43. *News-Letter*, June 13, 1720, no. 849.

44. *News-Letter*, March 12, 1715/6, no. 622; *News-Letter*, March 7, 1720/1, no. 830; *News-Letter*, March 9, 1727, no. 11; Miller, *From Colony to Province*, ch. 22.

45. Solomon Stoddard, *An Answer to Some Cases of Conscience* (Boston, 1722), 16.

46. Benjamin Colman, *Prayer for the Lord* (Boston, 1727), 10–11, 16–17.

47. Seeman, *Pious Persuasions*, 150–52; Joseph Sewall, *Repentance* (Boston, 1727), 30.

48. Journal of Israel Loring, (1725–29), 17–18; (1729–32), 29.

49. Thomas Prince, *Earthquakes the Works of God* (Boston, 1727), 4, 19, 33–41, 43–44, appendix.

50. Eliphalet Adams, *A Discourse Shewing* (New London, 1734), 17–18.

51. John Webb, *The Duty of a Degenerate People* (Boston, 1734), 41.

52. The eschatological speculations about Edwards's revivals and the Boston-area revivals are treated in Davidson, *Logic of Millennial Thought*, 122–29, and Crawford, *Seasons of Grace*, ch. 6. See also W. R. Ward, *The Protestant Evangelical Awakening* (New York, 1992).

Epilogue

1. John Erskine, ed., *Six Sermons by the Late Thomas Prince* (Edinburgh, 1785), 65; Sandra Gustafson, *Eloquence Is Power: Oratory and Performance in Early America* (Chapel Hill, N.C., 2000), 75. Paul Korshin has called this sort of millennial expectation "queuing and waiting," and has noted that the phenomenon of waiting for something that on one hand may happen very soon but on the other hand may not happen at all makes the categories of millennialism "eternally plastic." Paul Korshin, "Queuing and Waiting: The Apocalypse in England, 1660–1750," in C. A. Patrides and Joseph Wittreich, eds., *The Apocalypse in English Renaissance Thought and Literature* (Ithaca, N.Y., 1984), 241.

2. Jon Butler questioned the significance of the "Great Awakening" in "Enthusiasm Described and Decried: The Great Awakening as Interpretative Fiction," *Journal of American History* 69 (1982–83): 305–25; Jon Butler, *Awash in a Sea of Faith: Christianizing the American People* (Cambridge, Mass., 1990), 164–93. See also Frank Lambert, *Inventing the "Great Awakening"* (Princeton,

N.J., 1999), 69. On eschatological readings of the awakenings see Stephen Stein, "Transatlantic Extensions: Apocalyptic in Early New England," in Patrides and Wittreich, eds., *Apocalypse in English Renaissance Thought*, 282–85.

3. Josiah Smith, *The Character, Preaching &c. of Mr. Whitefield* (Boston, 1740), 20.

4. Jonathan Dickinson, *A Display of God's Special Grace* (Boston, 1742), i–ii, quoted in Lambert, *Inventing the "Great Awakening,"* 222.

5. More information on the Concert's history is provided by Arthur Fawcett, *The Cambuslang Revival* (London, 1971), 223–27; Crawford, *Seasons of Grace*, 229–33; and Stein, "Editor's Introduction," 37–39.

6. Edwards, *An Humble Attempt*, in Edward Hickman, ed., *Works of Jonathan Edwards* (Carlisle, Penn., 1974), 2: 279.

7. Ibid., 280–83.

8. Stein, "Introduction," in Edwards, *Apocalyptic Writings*, 48; Ruth Bloch, *Visionary Republic: Millennial Themes in American Thought* (New York, 1985), 230–31; Paul Boyer, *When Time Shall Be No More: Prophecy Belief in Modern American Culture* (Cambridge, Mass., 1992), 77. Peter Clark, *The Captain* (Boston, 1740) wrote "The Spanish Monarchy, which is deeply stained with the Blood of Multitudes of Innocents, and of the Martyrs of JESUS CHRIST; for which, God will have a Time to reckon with them," 44. Nathan Hatch, *The Sacred Cause of Liberty: Republican Thought and the Millennium in Revolutionary New England* (New Haven, Conn., 1977); Charles Royster, *A Revolutionary People at War: The Continental Army and American Character, 1775–1783* (Chapel Hill, N.C., 1979).

9. Jimmy Carter and George W. Bush have been self-identifying evangelicals. Bill Clinton was reared in evangelicalism though seemed no longer to self-identify as one despite his regular consultation with evangelical pastors. The evangelist Billy Graham maintained a well-known friendship with the presidents since Eisenhower and appears to have been particularly close with Richard Nixon. Ronald Reagan was not an evangelical but had a number of close evangelical contacts and apparently took premillennial prophecies so seriously that they may have influenced his foreign policy decisions. Boyer, *When Time Shall be No More*, 142–46.

10. For similar conclusions about late twentieth-century evangelicalism see Christian Smith, *American Evangelicalism: Embattled and Thriving* (Chicago, 1998), 89 and passim.

11. Joel Carpenter, *Revive Us Again: The Reawakening of American Fundamentalism* (New York, 1997), 125. See also Harry Stout, *The Divine Dramatist: George Whitefield and the Rise of Modern Evangelicalism* (Grand Rapids, Mich., 1991); T. H. Breen and Timothy Hall, "Structuring Provincial Imagination: The Rhetoric and Experience of Social Change in Eighteenth-Century New England," *American Historical Review* 103, no. 5 (Dec. 1998): 1436; Smith, *American Evangelicalism*, 75.

12. See for instance José Casanova, *Public Religions in the Modern World* (Chicago, 1994).

13. "Modernity" is notoriously difficult to define, but mass media and communications, nationalism, and a rising distinction of religion from other cultural categories are commonly seen as some of the salient signs of rising modernity.

14. Casanova, *Public Religions,* 135–57.

15. Philip Jenkins, *The Next Christendom: The Coming of Global Christianity* (New York, 2002); David Martin, *Pentecostalism: The World Their Parish* (London, 2001).

Index

Vaudois, 129
Vaudreuil, Marquis de, 95, 96, 109–10
Viswanathan, Gauri, 19

Wabanakis: and King William's War, 9; and
    missions, 44–45, 50; and Father Rale's War,
    61, 92–97, 99–103, 106–13, 168; maintain
    land and population, 113; name of, 192n2
Wadsworth, Benjamin, 44, 103–04
Walter, Thomas, 126–27, 129–30
War of Jenkins' Ear, 172
Ward, W. R., 15, 67
Watts, Isaac, 42, 87, 154
Webb, John, 137, 164, 165, 170–71
Weber, Max, 89
Westminster Confession, 33
Whitefield, George: and the Great Awaken-
    ing, 1, 15, 29, 165, 169–70; mentioned, 73
Whittemore, Nathaniel, 79–80, 81, 86, 87
Wigglesworth, Edward, 129

Willard, Joseph, 107
Willard, Samuel, 155–56, 157, 162
William III, King: and Glorious Revolution,
    4–5, 6, 139, 140; in almanacs, 79, 81; impor-
    tance for British Protestants, 17, 41, 121, 122,
    131, 141–42; mentioned, 116, 137
Williams, Eunice, 93
Williams, John, 57, 93
Winslow, Josiah, 107
Wiswall, Samuel, 44
Wodrow, Robert, correspondence with: Ben-
    jamin Colman, 32, 102–03, 154; Cotton
    Mather, 35, 91, 110, 124, 146, 147; Increase
    Mather, 147; Samuel Mather, 147–48;
    Judah Monis, 154
Woodside, James, 45

"Yale apostasy," 43, 126, 127–28, 134

Ziegenbalg, Bartholomew, 35